Variations
on a Garden

Variations on a Garden

Robin Lane Fox

R&L

Robin Lane Fox

Publisher · Oxford

Published by R. and L., Oxford 1986.

Copyright © Robin Lane Fox, 1986

A revised newly illustrated and enlarged edition of Variations On a Garden,
published by Macmillan, U.K. (1974).

Typeset by Leaper & Gard Limited, Bristol.
Made and printed in Hong Kong by South China Printing Company.

ISBN: 0 9511392-0-7

Cover photos: front, the garden of Mrs Heathcoat-Amory at Chevithorne Barton, Devon.
       back, the garden of Mrs Margery Fish at East Lambrook Manor, Somerset.
Photographs by Valerie Scott.

Contents

To my parents, whose garden is full of my mistakes.

Preface

When choosing plants or trying to visualize a flower-garden at different seasons, I never know where to begin. Like a motor-mower, I need to be sparked into action and I find that a simple list or gardening-dictionary is not enough of an ignition. They cannot do a plant justice in a small, factual entry nor can they express a taste. I like to be ignited by others' preferences, rebelling against them, seeing beyond them, adapting or imitating them or standing in awe of what I can only struggle to achieve.

This book derives from my own love of gardening which time, and the business of writing about it weekly, have done nothing to diminish. Rather, they have extended it. Many people have told me they wished Variations in its first English edition was still in print, but it has taken me eleven years to return to a text which was spoilt by the lurid, over-blown colours and heavy type of its first publishers. In that time, I have learned much more, while gardening itself has developed and gained new emphases. What I first wrote on wild gardening in 1973 looks very different to a practised eye in 1986. New magnolias, pinks and annuals have come on sale and I have come to realize that we can, in fact, buy more things now than fifteen years ago. The most important allies of my gardening have always been the nurserymen. While rewriting and adding to the text, I have tried to show throughout it where the plants in question can be obtained. My bedside reading has included nursery-catalogues for thirty years and I owe so much to their combination of enticement, honesty and sudden flights of fancy. I have also learnt most about how to grow plants from their advice, tested in the front line of battle. If I have omitted some favourites from my list of suppliers, it is because they dislike postal business, or refuse it altogether.

The invitation to extend this book to American gardeners too has posed some new questions. English gardeners believe that their own gardens and growers are the best available, but I have repeatedly been forced to question the truth of these views by conversations with American gardeners and by study of the mail-order nurseries which they recommend. Their concentration of botanical and breeders' knowledge has taught me much, while there are things I envy in their lists too. Britain has an unsurpassed range of gardens and a climate in which so much is possible, but its gardening has never been best when it has closed in on itself and some narrow, 'English' tradition. I have been gratified that so much I like myself is also available and enjoyed in one or other American growers' list. If you want plants, you can almost always find them: in the index, I have given the relative hardiness of most plants I name, rating them in terms of America's many zones of climate.

I am very grateful to the various botanists, publishers and gardeners who have helped me on either side of the Atlantic. Linda Brownrigg, herself a West Coast gardener, gave me particular assistance with several of the nurseries I recommend. Valerie Scott has provided new illustrations for the cover and the colour plates with great skill and speed. Anne Robinson turned a disorderly manuscript into a typescript with similar skill and rapidity: Jane Tanner kindly made visual sense of my ideas for the jacket. My own gardening centres on Oxfordshire and its alkaline soil and it is that fact, not prejudice, which causes me to write less about lime-hating plants. Above all, I must thank the Financial Times newspaper for continuing to print the weekly columns on gardening from which these ideas continue to take shape.

WINTER

Winter

Good gardening is not the same as good growing: to garden well is to appreciate plants and their possibilities, not only to cultivate them in a satisfactory way. Gardeners work with an ever-receding ideal of perfection: no sooner is something growing well than they see how to place it better or give it a better neighbour. To others' eyes, all may look as well as could be expected, but a good gardener's eye sees more to be improved. Change is the constant companion of a gardener's life and in the past thirty years, I have found myself making most changes in the search for scent and architectural form, flowers for the less usual seasons and the ideal of a garden which is close to informal wildness while not lacking planned design. Other changes are forced on me by the abundance of weeds, the travels of plants and that supreme right of everything I grow: a hunger-strike, and rapid death. This book is an exploration of these constant reasons for change. It may help you to plan changes of your own or provoke you to react against changes I have made or proposed. Either way, it will have led you down the gardener's path, more aware of what you want to grow and where you want to grow it.

While writing and choosing, I have been brought up against a deeper question: what is so English about our widely-praised English gardening and what, indeed, is a garden, not a natural wilderness? Throughout, I have tried to consider those other English-speaking gardeners, the many gardeners of America, as disparate a group as the many zones of climate in which they go about their business. By checking their nurserymen's lists and discussing the problems of those I know best, I have come to feel that English gardening is not an enclosed, superior world. Some of our

1

best ideas and plants have travelled to and fro across the Atlantic and it is helpful to read of others' reactions to plants which we sometimes take for granted. My feeling is that 'English' gardening has seldom been narrowly English where we most admire it and that it will stagnate if it ever becomes self-contained. So, too, will gardens, for like nature itself, they are an idea which we have invented and whose boundaries are never hard and fast.

These feelings have grown in the years while I have been writing on gardening, but other feelings have been more constant. From season to season, I have found myself writing on plants and methods which have worked well with me for many years. I have also found myself enlarging on their own identities and histories, features we humans have given them but which change the way in which I come to think of them now. Gardening needs its moments of romance after the cold winds of early spring and those long hours spent heaving water in the height of summer. I will begin with an example, brought to my notice in the Oxford where my gardens lie.

Winter Jasmine

Much is made nowadays of the merits of a garden for all seasons and this is a fashion which should be taken seriously. One flower in winter is worth ten in summer and we should all find a place for the winter irises, snowdrops and hellebores which keep the garden alive in the dead of the year.

The result is never a blaze of colour: a winter garden does not compete with a bright fire. Its pleasures are quiet, and none the worse for that. But they have to rise above their setting, and in January and February they are hampered by a mood in the garden which I describe as winter drip. Even a witch-hazel cannot shake it off.

This winter drip was very evident as I walked among the old stone walls of a college garden, praised by many for its summer display. Beads of rain hung on the bare stems of the shrub roses, while the earth beneath looked like a sodden brown carpet, not improved by groups of despondent ever-grey leaves. I know I like these plants, I told myself, but I do not want to live with them for the winter half of the year. As for evergreens, even they look wretched in cold weather. Being leafy, they drip more sadly than twigs and thorns.

I was wondering whether the whole garden would not look prettier as a grass meadow, not a rose bed, when, tucked away in a southerly join of a library's wall, I saw a green-stemmed shrub with butter-yellow flowers. Doubts were dispelled like clouds in a brisk west wind. I knew no meadow would ever offer the common winter jasmine and at once I was away in a world of fancy, far from weeds and yellow turf.

The bare-flowered jasmine, or Jasminum nudiflorum, is an unbelievably obliging shrub, at home in distant China. I like to see it sprawling in a tangle, not making its well-ordered way up a wall. If you try to grow it vertically and clip it into a shape round windows, like an obedient pyracantha, you will have to shorten the long summer growths which otherwise cover their length in yellow flower. You will also end up with a thick barrage of twigs and branches pinned against your wall. Let the winter jasmine spill forwards and please consider its use on banks or awkward slopes where, mindlessly, we tend to opt for periwinkle or the mean little leaves of the heather. Winter jasmine is available in almost every garden-centre in Britain: in America, Wayside Gardens of South Carolina will satisfy mail-orders and I note that it is just as well behaved across the Atlantic. It "flowers during the dullest days of late winter in the mid-Atlantic states and southwards": it "succeeds even in the Boston area with minimum protection". Winter jasmine is true to itself, wherever it is planted.

In mid winter, its yellow flowers are welcome in themselves and I would never garden without them, a first priority among plants for awkward corners. In times of winter drip, I especially like it because of its family connections. It is a relation of the sweet, white summer jasmine which has never flowered very freely for me but has made up for its sparseness with a story which does the name of jasmine credit. The sight of its yellow-flowered relation turned my mind from dripping roses to a duke who once lived in Pisa.

Four hundred years ago, the jasmine grew in the Pisa garden of the Duke of Tuscany. A cutting had reached Hampton Court but, for the purposes of the story, it had soon been lost by British incompetence: the Duke was left with a monopoly of jasmine in Europe. Being as yet unacquainted with the doctrine of restrictive practice, he decided to keep his assets strictly to himself. Orders went out to the gardeners that not one sprig or flower of jasmine was ever to be given to a stranger: the punishment was five years' service in the sculleries. Most of the gardeners preferred their life with the plants to the disgrace of a life with dishes and obeyed their master's instructions. Not so the superintendent of the ducal glasshouse. He might have been faithful if he had not loved.

Beyond the garden wall lived the penniless daughter of the Duchess's femme de chambre. She was adored by the glasshouse gardener who would give her a bouquet on her birthday, each year's more special than the last. As time went by, each treasure of the greenhouse had been picked for her benefit and the gardener began to fear that next year he would be reduced to repetition, which might imply that his love was going stale. Only the jasmine remained to be given and, on the eve of the birthday bouquet, it burst into flower. The gardener could not resist it. Early in the morning, before the routine watering, he picked a sprig for the lady he loved.

Never had his bouquet been more popular. She smelt it, and puzzled at the source of its curious scent; she wore it in her bodice and marvelled at its unfamiliar whiteness. Wishing to save its ingredients, she planted the pieces in a pot and six months later she found that only the jasmine was growing. When her next birthday came, the jasmine was in bud; quietly, she took more cuttings and two years later she had enough of a stock to start a stall of her own. The people of Pisa were entranced and such was the price they paid for her treasure that soon she could give her lover the present he deserved. Twenty ducats from jasmine was enough in those days to start off a couple in a home of their own.

At this point, the story goes, fate and the Duchess intervened. She had never cared much for gardening, but she had cared slightly for the Mayor of Pisa and one day, he gave her a pot of white jasmine with his love and best regards. Innocently, she wore it to dinner, unaware that it came from pirated stock. From the far end of the table, the Duke recognized it and ordered an inquiry to discover its source. Threats revealed the manner of its origin, but the Duke could not stand by his word. If he relegated his most skilled gardener to the scullery, the greenhouse would suffer, let alone the plates and dishes; meanwhile, his wife's favourite maid would hand in her notice and nobody would ever understand the problems of her dressing so well again. He gave in to the servants, and the gardener and the chambermaid's daughter were married, as they wished.

The moral of this story is not that monopolies are mean or that even in Tuscany workers could break their employers' demands. It is only a story which adds to the jasmine's charm. There are flowers which have brought men together, just as they still take them out of themselves and their various preoccupations. They need attention and they also need knowing. But once known, they can roll away the gloom of the garden and by the faintest show of flowers, start a train of fancy which leads far from melancholy winter drip.

Winter Borders

Gardening dictionaries and handbooks appear every year, aimed at new gardeners, but I remember how I began and suspect that other beginners do not always start from the newest title. In my family's book-case were older books dating back to the age of Edwardian gardening when my great-aunt had pencilled in her marks of approval in the section on "bedding schemes and dot-plants". Dot-plants gave a contrast to a surrounding surface of blue lobelia or orange wallflowers: good dotting began with white water-lily tulips in dark red wallflowers or yellow snapdragons in a bed of cherry-red petunias.

I chose the heaviest and thickest volume, believing it would know the most. The section on seasonal flower gardening had a prominent chapter on how to lay pipes for a moraine: moraines were much valued by Edwardian alpine gardeners because they seemed to simulate the conditions of a mountain-hillside and copy the sharp drainage and under-ground water which alpine plants enjoyed at home. Nowadays, nobody thinks they are necessary: they belong in an age of knickerbockers and stiff collars for young children, an over-formal adjunct to things which will grow without them.

After sectional drawings of moraines, my guide-book listed plans and plants for the 'winter terrace'. Moraines were basins of underground concrete and have disappeared without loss, but there is more to be said about winter terraces. The idea has hardly been more persistent, but if we scale it down, it still has its attractions. So many of the best winter flowers are scented, especially those from Far Eastern homes: there must be some connection with Oriental insect-life and pollination. I will be returning to many of them as the year advances: here, I wish to dwell on my favourite flowers for winter, the witch-hazel and the one winter plant which everybody can accommodate: the highly sinister hellebore.

It is sinister because of its ancient properties. In the classical world, like the aconite, it was believed to be most poisonous. The Romans were agreed that it induced madness. In Roman comedies, when a slave might be about to discover that he was really his master's long lost brother, fathered from a matron now disguised as a music mistress (who was in fact his new girlfriend's identical twin) he would ignorantly threaten his next-of-kin with a dose of hellebore to heighten the drama further. Complicated plots did not first enter Italy with the rise of opera, but the hellebore, companion of stage intrigue, is the least complicated of garden plants.

We can all grow it because every garden has a shaded corner, beneath a tree, perhaps, or against the back wall of the house. It is a problem to know which sort to choose, especially as hellebores' names are an intricate tangle. The Christmas Rose is the best-known, but I will save it to the end, as it is rather particular. I will begin with the Lenten Roses, Helleborus orientalis, and touch on a Greek one before the Corsican ones which are the easiest of all.

Lenten Roses begin to flower in February and are superb plants to mass under lightly-shaded trees or between tall shrubs. I admire two distinctive groups of them, one, beneath a little corner filled with hazel-trees, another, between the spring-flowering viburnums and the Mock Orange Blossom, or Philadelphus, of high summer. In early spring, these companions have no leaves and cast a slight shade: beneath, the many tones of oriental Hellebores can be seen quite clearly, ranging from a sullen, mysterious purple through greenish-pink to white. In Britain, Elizabeth Strangman of Washfield Nurseries, Hawkhurst, Kent sells some especially good crosses based on the Lenten Rose, but the plant is current in many lists; in America, Wayside Gardens, South Carolina will despatch selected plants of Helleborus orientalis atrorubens, a great beauty with flowers of plum-purple and green, a sombre, intriguing colour which repays a close inspection. They also sell the ordinary orientalis forms and I note from that bible of gardeners on the other side of the continent, Sunset's New Western Garden Book (from Lane Publishing, Menlo Park, California 94025), that the Lenten Rose is agreed to be easier than the Christmas Rose in southern California and elsewhere on the west coast. It is less famous, and therefore less sought, but my impression of its easier nature is confirmed world-wide. One way to distinguish it from the Christmas one is colour (the Christmas Rose is white) and season (Lenten Roses flower later, in February to March).

6

INFORMAL PLANTING BY PATH AND STEPS

HELLEBORUS CORSICUS AND EARLY SPRING FLOWERS

Another way, when both are out of flower, is to watch their leaves: Lenten Roses have many little teeth on the young leaflets, whereas Christmas Roses have a few bigger fangs. The Lenten hellebore grows happily in semi-shade and any soil which is deep and not disturbed too often by busy gardeners.

My second hellebore is rarer and apparently new to American nurseries, though you can import seed easily enough: perhaps you can make them stock it, because Helleborus olympicus, the black hellebore, was once believed to rejuvenate the aged. This extravagant claim has yet to be proved true in my university, but whether you are old or young it does not object to heavy shade if its soil is deep and rich. A very dry place beneath a tall tree would not suit it, but few plants grow there anyway.

The black hellebore flowers from January to March on stems about 18 inches high, though in the milder West I have seen it open by November. Its flowers are rounded and hang their heads downwards, facing shyly into their broad evergreen leaves: their greenish white fades to a true green near their base. Plants grow slowly from home-saved seed which ripens, if at all, in March. Though you have to be patient with your seedlings, it is well worth building up a colony.

My third hellebore is better known, but insufficiently understood and appreciated: I would never garden without it, but I first understood its point on a holiday in June in its native Corsica. Travelling through the rough mountains by a local 'bus, I had been tantalized by the local flora, flashing irretrievably past the window, until a tyre obligingly burst. While the wheel was changed, I made friends with Helleborus corsicus on a nearby hillside. I bless the iron spike that caused this delay: corsicus is an essential plant for any garden, not insistent on shade, whatever the books say, and long-lived if given a stony soil. Its leaves are as good as any in the garden when they are at their best; they have an off season in March and April when the old growth collapses and the stems fall heavily forwards under their weight. This period gives the Corsican Hellebore a bad name, but the dying leaves can be cut off without distress and the plant promptly looks bearable again. In early spring, its clusters of flower are a superb shade of apple-green, gathered in huge heads, and burst most abundantly from their fattened buds. Disregard the black fly which they sometimes attract after flowering. They are well able to resist it.

Plants, however, are not immortal and corsicus may die when only five years old. It will almost certainly flop forwards and straggle before then.

7

Enthusiasts are willing to stake it to keep it upright but this habit can look artificial. My plants are planted along the edge of a gravel path and although they fall forwards they look appropriate because they break what would otherwise be a hard line. They also seed themselves happily into the gravel, which is now a nest of their seedlings. That, I feel, is the best way to grow corsicus, in a gritty soil as on a Corsican hill. My feeling is now confirmed by tracking this Corsican across the Atlantic. True, the one mail-order catalogue to offer plants is Wayside who describe it as "rare"; it will not be rare for very long, as my plants beside the gravel have seeded themselves by the score into the path and I have to discard young Corsicans by the handful. It really is a very easy, common plant. On the West Coast, the Sunset guide acutely observes that Corsicus is the "best hellebore for southern California and is drought-tolerant when established". Plainly, it does not change its spots at different latitudes, although I cannot accept that it prefers a neutral soil: my plants grow in a highly alkaline bed, while elsewhere I see it on acid soil among azaleas.

Early in the year, you are sure to want to cut flowers from your Christmas, Lenten, Corsican or Olympic Roses: this brings me to the hellebore's one little secret. The only way to make their flowers last is to slit the stems open for half their length and put them in warm water, renewing it each day. Do not use scalding water and do not slit the stems too high. Corsicus, however, is easier to keep, as you can pick each individal flower with a short stem and float it in a shallow bowl. It is pointless to pick the main stem as it is too thick to allow water to pass up to the flowers. Its apple-green cups wilt within a day unless picked individually, but by floating them in a bowl you can enjoy them by the hundred, such is the crop of one plant of corsicus. Maybe we shy away from the luxury of the Edwardians' winter terrace, but with the help of the hellebore we can still move a mass of winter flowers indoors.

Christmas Roses

I now feel able to do justice to Helleborus niger, the Christmas Rose. At its best, it is unforgettable, a clump of broad white flowers in January which have called forth all manner of poetry and hazy approval. None I know is more poetic and hazy than the German lyrics of the Romantic poet, Mörike, set to music by Hugo Wolf. "Daughter of the wood, cousin to the lily … Your pure body, full of hoar frost, is nourished by the heavenly cold and balsam-scented air … Childlike, at Christmas time, you adorn your white robe with a trace of palest green …". Mörike detected a scent from the golden centre of Helleborus niger "so subtle one scarcely perceives it": my nose has not been sufficiently poetic to discern it yet.

Christmas Roses have their particular foibles: "to you", the poet added, "would be fatal what to other flowers is bliss". Horticulturally, I would put it differently. This hellebore requires the 'bliss' which others can do without: deep, rich soil, a dressing of rotted manure and a proper feeding as the flowers begin to fade. The leaves, I always feel, are the problem, because they look drab and lifeless just as the flowers begin to open. Here, I would endorse a tip from that great gardener, Vita Sackville-West. She used to dig up pieces of her clumps of Christmas Rose in late November, pot them up with a large lump of their original earth, give them a deep pot and cover them over for two weeks with another pot, like a hat over their heads. Take off the hat, and you will find that the stems have greatly lengthened and that the white of the emergent flowers is pure enough to inspire a poem.

Every book, guide and handbook, from Kew to California, continues to repeat that Christmas Roses "resent disturbance". As a result, it is years since anyone disturbed them and checked the result. Vita Sackville-West used to dig them up annually with a big ball of earth and then replant them, finding that they only shuddered for one subsequent season. I have copied her and found the same effect. It is worthwhile to uproot them, for the sake of clean flowers and long stems.

In America, White Flower Farm, Connecticut sell Christmas Roses whose vigour has been commended to me; in England, you sometimes find the special Potters Wheel form which originated in a simple Staffordshire garden. The rounded flowers are remarkably large, but you will have to travel around to find it as the nurseries who sometimes stock it do not like mail-orders. Finally, remember that Lenten and Christmas Roses will germinate quite well from seed if you freeze the seed for twenty four hours in the refrigerator's ice-box before sowing. Park's of Greenwood, South Carolina offer a 'Giant Flowered Mixture' which can lead to any number of spotted or stained flowers, the prettiest Hellebore-variations. Alternatively, Thompson and Morgan of London Road, Ipswich offer a specially-chosen mixture of orientalis in which spotted varieties (guttatus) should predominate, nine other hellebore-mixtures and best of all, seed of the Olympic Hellebore, all of which can be exported. So, gardeners everywhere can rejuvenate themselves with the best white hellebore, after a few years' patience while it matures.

Bewitching Witch-Hazel

Gardening-writers like to harp on the beauty of winter-flowering shrubs because they have to find something to write about in the four dark months of the year. You may, then, suspect their judgement, but if you shut your eyes to all their suggestions, you are joining the herd who ignore not just the hellebore but the Witch Hazel too. Honestly, I know of no prettier shrub, at its best if your soil is neutral or acid and well-mulched so as to stop it from drying out.

In gardens, too, there has been a familiar pattern: a discovery in America, then a secondary discovery transferring the market and consumer-interest to the Far East. The hamamelis, or witch hazel, is a primary example. The gardeners' first plant was Hamamelis virginiana, discovered in a grove in Virginia some seventy years after the Mayflower landed. Enterprising suppliers spread it around Britain, yet one of its earliest reviewers curtly remarked that 'nothing more need be said to our people respecting this shrub, which Nature seems to have designed for the stricter eye of the botanist'. However, much has happened to the witch-hazel since 1742.

The last century was the great age of plant collecting in the Far East, and among the hazards of these expeditions, one important find was Hamamelis japonica arborea, the tall Japanese tree witch-hazel. It is not so tree-like in our climate, usually growing only 8 or 9 feet high, but it bears its dark matt-yellow flowers from January onwards on the top half of the bush against the leafless, grey-green branches. The clusters of flowers are very simple. The four ruffled yellow petals, about half an inch long, look like thin ribbons crinkled by water, but they are able to stand a sharp night's frost. The leaves are like those of an ordinary nut tree and appear after the flowers in spring. In October they turn the clearest yellow, especially in the variety zuccariniana, whose citron-yellow flowers are an improvement on the more usual type. Too often we forget the autumn leaf-colour when we choose our plants.

10

Twenty years later came China's retort, Hamamelis mollis, collected by the great Charles Maries but left unrecognized for another twenty years in English nurseries. It may surprise you that we were so blind for so long, but collected material has a way of lying unpublicized in busy institutions and myopia is a recurrent complaint in the story of the "Englishman's garden". Finally, the sharp eyes of Mr Nicholson, Curator of Kew, spotted the beauty of its larger, unruffled, reflexed petals of clear yellow (the colour of forsythia) against the bare dark brown stems. Every twig was increased by grafting as soon as it had won high prizes in gardening shows.

It was inevitable that the Chinese and Japanese plants should be forced into marriage by the hybridists. The best known results are the intermedia hybrids, especially the dirty red and copper-flowered Jelena and Ruby Glow. These reddened colours are not to my taste, as the flowers do not show up well except when struck by winter sun with a dark green background behind them. This effect is not easy to contrive. Much the best of these hybrids is 'Arnold Promise', bred at the Arnold Arboretum in America and the best variety, now, for American gardens. Wayside supply it, as do Weston Nurseries of Hopkinton, Mass. and British garden-centres could usefully take the hint: I have seen Arnold Promise in full flower in the Bronx during a crazily mild January in New York. It is a strong primrose yellow, noticeably scented and a good grower, "vase-shaped", the magazines say, to a height of twelve feet. It is totally hardy and in the right soil, damp and neutral, it will grow into an outstanding small tree, conspicuous for its bright yellow leaves in autumn.

English gardeners, meanwhile, do best to order the pale lemon-yellow Hamamelis mollis pallida, probably the finest witch-hazel for our gardens. It has the cowslip scent of its fellows but its petals are more delicate, a pale contrast to the characteristic red-brown neck of the flower. With patience you will grow a small tree 15 feet high. Even the impatient will get a generous show of flowers from a 2-foot-high young sapling. They stand out clearly against its leafless outline. Often, I notice this contrast between nursery lists on either side of the Atlantic: enlightened suppliers in Britain emphasize the paler, subtler colours in a variety, whereas American ones tend to stress clarity and the strength of a particular tone. On a generous view, the differing light of the two climates may account for the difference: strong colours look better in brighter sunlight. But I also suspect there is a layer of subtlety which even the most adventurous

American gardeners can still explore, the possibilities of pale-flowered planting, which come into their own in the evening and do not force themselves on the eye or try to show off.

Not that the best witch-hazel suppliers are all English: if you are reading my plant-names and feeling that they are all very well for a cosy Englishman in the south-east of the island, send off to Gossler Farms Nursery, 1200 Weaver Road, Springfield, Oregon 97478. Their hamamelis, let alone their sixty current forms of Magnolia, put anything in English lists in the shade. They are also very well-grown. Personally, I have a sneaking fondness for the original American, virginiana. This flowers in October before the leaves fall and is thus thought inconspicuous and only regarded as an American stock on which to graft the Chinese. I like peering closely at a plant and do not mind a concealment of leaves over its green-yellow flowers. Its scent is good, and October is not an easy month for scent. Its autumn colour is the best of all. It is the source of witch-hazel for the bumps and bruises of childhood. It bears fruits and flowers together, hence Hamamelis. Hama is Greek for 'at the same time', melon for 'a fruit'. Even the ugliest names have a reason.

No witch-hazel needs pruning, but you can shape them into a tree if you wish by selecting one stem as a 'trunk'. They are hardy and only blackened at the tips in the very foulest winters. Their scent is excellent indoors. They need a deep and rich soil in a dampish place if possible. In some eighteenth-century informal gardens, the old virginiana is still grouped on a mound or against an evergreen hedge where the flowers show up well. If you can give it a sunny site, you will enjoy it much more. I see no reason why plants of it should not flourish in the shelter of a city garden. They do not mind lime in moderation, but grow more freely without it.

If you have room for one big shrub and your soil is not too shallow and limey, try them out, continuing their history in your garden. There is no need to fear the witches that their name suggests. The Anglo-Saxon *wich* means 'supple' and explains the name for their bendy stems. Though their near namesake, the hazel, will indeed divine water, witch-hazels, I am afraid, are unlike to divine black magic in your garden.

Winter Stems

The winter jasmine, hellebores and witch hazel give enough of a framework for flowers for the winter: a winter garden remains a gamble, because the weather can spoil it and deter you from visiting plants outdoors. To support their effort, I prefer coloured stems and berries which are less of a risk in bad weather. Even in the snow, sun on stems of a willow or dogwood throws as bright a light as many flowers in summer.

To see the possibilities, I have to admit I left Oxford, with a good witch-hazel in its Botanic Garden, and spent time in Cambridge instead. Here, the rival Botanical Garden has set aside a special area for beds of plants which are fun in winter. They range far beyond flowers and after my first visit, sent me back to planning and designing with new ideals in mind. Perhaps I can pass them on, even if you cannot reach Cambridge in January.

It is a recurrent theme of this book that quite ordinary plants have particular varieties or uses which lift them out of the rut and fit unexpectedly with gardeners' wishes. The common snowberry is a case in point. On wet winter walks in a wood, I have always admired it, as it stands on the edge of a grass ride, showing a few of its white berries, like mothballs on its twiggy branches. But I would never trust it. In the garden it would sucker rapidly and barge its way out of confinement: its berries are too few for the space it would seize. It is described in dictionaries as suitable cover for pheasants. As a gardener, not a game-keeper, that does not endear me to it. It is a bush like hawthorn, I thought, to be enjoyed in hedgerows only: I once grew a cutting of a small variegated relation but threw it away, perhaps overhastily, when it started sprouting an ordinary green.

Nowadays, snowberries have been brought out of the woods. They are now called Symphoricarpos and the breeders have been busy. At Cambridge, I was happily ticking off the old winter friends in flower: viburnums, winter honeysuckle, witch-hazel, but what were those 2-foot-high bushes smothered in round white buds? Inspection showed them to be not flowers but snowberries of a recent form called Hancocks. They are an improvement. Their berries are tinged with pink and borne in profusion. They will tolerate shade under trees but they give an even brighter show in dry sunny places. They have obviously crossed the Atlantic, as Sunset's New Western Garden Book emphasizes Hancocks' dwarf habit and value in any climatic zone, especially in dry places or on slopes where erosion has to be controlled. I could not pin-point it in a mailing list, but Westons of Mass. offer its parent, the Chenault Coralberry' which is different only in being taller. They will also sell you the next best thing in Cambridge, the Mother of Pearl Snowberry which has brilliant berries and grows six feet tall.

It is rare among winter shrubs to find one whose features stand out distinctively, despite the absence of leaves. These snowberries catch the eye at a distance, as if in full flower. They should not spread more than 4 feet wide, though I do not know fully matured specimens. They throw up suckers from the root but these are not uncontrollable and have their uses as smotherers of weeds. A group of three would cheer up a dingy corner under tall and sparse trees. They grow anywhere, and a cold winter does not spoil the effect.

Prompted, again, by the Cambridge display, I have fallen heavily for the winter charm of willows. Gardeners are seldom fair to this family: there is much more to the family than weeping and tree-like stature. Subtle gardeners and flower-arrangers find many rewards in the stems and furry buds of the many varieties which can be pruned like shrubs. Last winter, I spent a freezing afternoon with a keen willow-grower whose wood was alive with young buds and potential catkins in shades of black, purple, grey, pink, rose and orange-yellow. We picked them avidly, so avidly that I persuaded myself I had lost my car-keys in the lower reaches of her willow-grove and was thus unable to leave her in peace after an hour's thawing and botanical identification over tea. We returned to hunt the keys as the last sunlight was catching the upper buds and branches of her lovely wild plantation. The keys, of course, were in the lock of my car's back door, where we found them, freezing, half an hour later.

The experience did wonders for my goodwill to willows. This family is still full of surprises which lazy-minded gardeners would enjoy. The best of them need no cultivation: you plant them into turf or your wilderness of weeds and keep a clear circle of ground round their roots by applying one of the recent glyphosate-based weedkillers (Tumbleweed, or Roundup, pioneered for farmers by Monsanto Chemicals). These poisons kill only through the leaf, not the soil, so they are quite safe if applied to ground and weeds beneath young shrubs, so long as you do not spray them on the shrub itself. After two or three years, the willow will be so strongly established that a collar of grass or weeds will not bother it.

Every other spring, you can cut your willows back hard (except for Salix daphnoides, which likes to be left alone). The cutting encourages younger shoots and a freer display of coloured stems and catkins. Conventionally,

14

you are told to line out these cuttings, burying them up to half their length in a shaded flowerbed where they will root and become young plants. My willow-teacher stresses that she finds that willow cuttings root much more readily in late autumn when the branches still have some impetus and she advises us all to ignore the books and line out cuttings from September till early December.

Willows have just the right atmosphere for a garden's informal boundaries, wilder prospects, curving approach-ways and entries into orchards or areas of rough grass. I learned to appreciate the purple-black catkins on Salix melanostachys, the powdery-white stems of the quick growing Salix nigricans and the silver-grey young buds on Salix caprea whose catkins are tinged with pink: in Britain, Sherrards of Wantage Road, Donnington, Newbury, Berks are good finders of tall willows, while Hopleys of Much Hadham, Herts offer a fine range of pink, yellow and grey-budded low-growing forms. In America, you have to hunt around, but the three I mention are all sold by Weston Nurseries in Hopkinton: I will go on to others which seem to be ignored, though one is an American native.

All these willows are superb material for flower-arrangements where their buds glisten for weeks on end and their branches stand at such elegant angles. I particularly value the fat buds and greyish colouring of Salix gracilistyla, one of the easiest in a wild garden: the Sunset Western garden-book recommends it for all zones in America, so it must be available in good local garden-centres. This adaptability is a reminder that many willows do not insist on wet conditions and that they are almost all unstoppably hardy, extending into the higher reaches of the Arctic where the purple-stemmed osier is such a feature of the river-banks: American gardens make good use of Salix purpurea nana as a clipped little hedge about two feet high, a use which ought to be copied widely.

I am particularly fond of two unusual willows which will tolerate dry conditions and which I came to know through the Cambridge display. The first, called Salix daphnoides, has a silvery bloom on its young stems and eventually grows into a little tree about twelve feet high. It does not like to be cut, but its buds and catkins are splendid and show to their best advantage in February. All the while, its stems have this frosted bloom on them which shows up so well against a dark hedge. At Cambridge, its neighbour is smaller and bushier and therefore more obliging. Its name is Salix irrorata, which means the dewy willow, a languid title. Most surprisingly, it is a native of Arizona, the least dewy-eyed of landscapes. In a dry soil in the garden, it soon makes a tidy shrub, equally notable for this silvered effect of the stems. Its catkins have a touch of pink which is very appealing. If cut back hard, it would fit into a space about six feet wide, preferably in an isolated clump where the line of its stems would not have competition. Its fellow-Americans do not seem to have woken up to it: Sunset's guide does not even notice it for western gardeners, but it ought to be brought into captivity by the thousand and used in gardens, wet or dry.

There are willows with bright scarlet stems (Britzensis) and a very easy willow with yellow twigs (vitellina), both of which respond well to hard pruning and mass planting. I would like to plant thickets of them at the furthest point of the view from a country garden, preferably on a sunny slope facing the house. There, I would combine brightly-stemmed and silver-budded willows with the stems of the Westonbirt dogwood, well described as sealing-wax red, and its yellow relations, Cornus flaviramea, each in their separate plantations. Apart from a pruning each spring, they would need no attention. Every winter, looking across to the hillside, I would see them as the spears of an advancing barbarian army, first, the silvered twigs of the willow, then, the red and yellow stems of the dogwood in squadrons behind them, bare and pointed in the winter's sun. This is not mere fancy as the long spears of Alexander the Great's army were indeed cut from cornelwood, cousin of the dogwood whose stem is reddened, as if dipped in an enemy's blood. There are no more appropriate shrubs for a field or large bank which needs gardening without trouble. Somehow such landscapes can take the ornament of winter twigs and stems more easily than the unnatural garb of many summer shrubs.

General Principles

Perhaps you are catching the feel of my garden-variations, strong on individual plants and particular varieties and looking for boldness and beauty on the borders of informal, wild planting. Before we multiply suggestions, it may help if I sketch in the framework within which I work when presented with the challenge of a new area of flowerbed or better still, a new garden.

My first principle is to take a hint from the site's surrounds and the materials already on it. I do not want garish, unweathered brick in a setting of old stone, nor expensive stone in a setting of modern glass and concrete. Usually, there is a tree, a line to the neighbour's planting or some particularly awful feature in the view which has to be excluded. The site decides whether you are to open outwards, as if to my army of willows on a hillside, or turn resolutely inwards, to block out the crimes of garages and modern architects. It also guides you to particular types of flower: do not insist on azaleas in a surrounding area of limestone and alkaline soil or pursue some absurd vendetta against the rhododendron if you are in a belt of light woodland, mild winters and acid soil. Develop the direction in which a site points you: if you recoil from it, create your own private garden by edging it with a thick green curtain of creepers. As on a stage, so in the garden, the most effective backdrop is a single dark colour, most naturally green. Books will often tell you to whitewash walls in order to 'reflect light' and 'create a sense of space'. It can be just as effective to mask them and gain depth, not brightness.

Moving into the open, you would do well to site your borders against a background, a fence or hedge or perhaps a favoured wall. For flower gardening near houses, I always prefer informal planting within a formal design. But first, there are problems of arranging the general types of plant.

When you begin, how do you plan height? The standard advice is that the tallest plants should be half the width of a border but that some of the taller groups should be allowed to sweep forwards into the border's front row. The more basic problem, I think, is a bed's width. The wider a bed, the easier I find it to fill. If you are planning to cut a new border out of a lawn or to lay one on an uncultivated site, I bet you tend to make it too narrow. Certainly, I do. After one attempt, I find myself widening it so as to give myself room for at least three generous variations in height: anything under three metres wide is difficult to plant as a mixed border, and you can usefully go wider than that. When you stand back and view it head on, depth always narrows and the front row's planting can easily look cramped.

Once you have the width, I think it is less important to allow taller plants to sweep forwards than to contrive some bold contrasts of height and form within the planting as a whole. I find the contrast is more effective if a low-growing plant runs back into a border: tall plants flop near the front and obscure their neighbours. Height in the row is more effective, if you organize it well: it is one of the particular strengths of a mixed border, using shrubs at intervals with low-growing plants.

Form, too, affects the perception of height. In a border, a tall group of leafy Galega or Artemisia has much less impact than the finely-cut leaves and spiky flowers of the acanthus or the bold leaves and plumes of flower on the tall Plume Poppy, or Macleaya, one of my favoured allies in the background of a planting. I never tire of the huge grey-blue leaves of the biggest glaucous Hosta, Sieboldiana elegans in most nursery-lists, whereas the narrow-leaved varieties lack the impact of this form whose leaves grow a foot wide. I like it as a sequel to flowers on the damp-loving Spurge, Euphorbia palustris (from Hopleys, Much Hadham, Herts) which then returns with orange leaves in autumn. Alternatively, it can set off tall shrubs, classically the older roses, perhaps the pale pink Rose Fantin Latour and the delicate white-flowered Gillenia, an airy plant with the feel of a wild woodland. These contrasts are more effective than any old tall michaelmas daisy, sweeping obediently to the border's edge.

Having planned contrasts, I like to have enough length to repeat a prominent feature once, perhaps twice or more. Repetition, at intervals, leads the eye reassuringly down a long bed and helps it to perceive continuity, where the changing sequences of flowers might otherwise lack coherence. Liking this repetition, I dislike "island" beds in open spaces, cut to irregular shapes. Invariably, they are planted in awkward lumps and unless you have time or labour, you will not maintain a neat balance between the plants in the front of the curves and the competing grass of the lawn. Their owners find themselves obliged to leave gaps in the front in order to maintain the edges. I find the shapes unmanageable, narrowing into pinched little triangles and extremities without the width for height or contrast. Keep beds more or less straight and let the plants play on the contrast between formality and informality.

Within this shape, I accept the classic advice of the great border-planners that it is easier to plant in elongated drifts than in blocks or square clumps. Colours run into each other more softly and when the drift, say, of iris is finished for the season, it is less noticeable if it runs between similar drifts than if it occupies a block, straddling the heights of a chunk of the flower-bed.

What about colour? Here, too, I like coherence and prefer a majority of paler colours with fewer, sometimes no, stronger shades. This preference does not lead to a garden of washed-out pinks and lavender-mauves. I like strong scarlet, orange or crimson, but find it much more effective in a greater company of pale lemon-yellow, sky-blue or white than in a violent mixture of hot 'sunshine' shades. Strong colours deepen a border and lead the eye into it if they stand in the middle to back section: strong clumps of bright colour in the foreground detain the eye and foreshorten the bed, costing it depth and mystery.

What do you do when the plan becomes stuck? This problem confronts every gardener, but the answer is not to thumb to and fro through a catalogue, picking any unknown investment because the description sounds quite plausible. When in an impasse, I think first of all of grey or silver leaves, either to prolong the season or separate neighbouring colours of too great a strength. I then start to think of plants for related uses, a climber, perhaps, which can always be grown up a bundle of canes or pea-sticks, a shrub like the long-lasting small Lilac, Syringa microphylla, or the neat Viburnum opulus compactum with its flowers, fine berries and autumn leaves. The answer might even be a vegetable, let alone a good group of sweet peas. Or you might like a tree or tall shrub, pruned hard to keep it within limits, while promising you a firm presence in the awkward back row. Try to think sideways round a problem, rather than sticking a pin in at random and trusting to luck in the same old rut.

It is here that some of my suggestions may help you already: border-planners forget the leaf and form of silver willows, the contrasting shape of the Corsican Hellebore's leaves (a good match for hostas) or the possibilities in groups of yellow-flowered Winter Jasmine, inserted as weeping plants in their own right, which will spill forwards and prolong the border's interest into winter. As a general rule, do not plant one of this or that in a jumbled collection if you wish to design a coherent whole. Coherence is much more restful to the eye. Remember, too, that the eye is not everything; gardens should also appeal to the nose, a sense which is topical even in mid-winter and to which I now turn, as often throughout this book.

Scents in the Early Season

The topic of scent is a constant education. To appreciate it, you often have to live closely with plants. If you know them intimately, handle them, look after them and even feel them you will discover their distinctions. The Moroccan broom, Cytisus battandieri, produces a short flower as yellow as a daffodil which smells of pineapple when it opens, ageing to boiled sweets as it fades. The small-flowered yellow Clematis rehderiana smells of cowslips. That unfamiliar winter evergreen called Sarcococca makes the January sunshine heavy with the smell of heather honey, if planted in groups of six or more. It flourishes in heavy shade: Wayside in South Carolina sell a good low-growing variety (hardy in zones seven to nine) and in Britain, Sherrards of Newbury also have well-grown plants available in containers. It is not a spectacular flower, but this "Scented Box" is neat, shiny-leaved and very sweet scented on the first warm day of the year.

Underneath a house window facing south, it is comforting to plant these evergreens, especially in a small garden so as not to be confronted by bare decaying branches in midwinter. But winter green is better for a touch of grey and no grey-leaved plant is easier to tuck into a border than Helichrysum angustifolium. Damp, not frost, is a grey plant's enemy but I have grown this with great success on heavy clay; some sand round the roots when planting is always advisable. It grows a little over a foot tall, and at this time of year sends up 6-inch stems tipped by flat clusters of silver and yellow buds. Unlike some of its relations, it does not look better with the buds removed. These open to a rather dirty yellow but the attraction lies not so much in its flowers as in its very strong smell of curry, most noticeable when the plant is brushed by a passer-by or rubbed in a disbeliever's hand. It combines most pleasingly with rosemary and gives an exotic uplift to less aromatic neighbours: in Britain, a good supplier is Graham Trevor, Sandwich Nurseries, Dover Road, Sandwich whose list is full of aromatic ideas and whose nursery will export to any country if the order is over a value of $60. They tell me that this Curry Plant was swamped by sea-water during last winter in several gardens on the sea-front and despite the very cold February, it was one of the few plants which survived.

Leaves are aromatic as soon as spring begins to hint at its presence and it is a pity to neglect them in a planting near the house. The hardiness of aromatics varies so greatly from region to region that I would simply like to refer favoured gardeners to two good sources, proven by two of the most fastidious planters I know: in south west England, the recently merged Burncoose and Southdown Nurseries at Gwennap, Redruth, Cornwall are a sound cheap source of plants you might put in your conservatory or against your house's heated walls, depending on the climate. In America, I should mention Logie's Greenhouses, 55 North Street, Danielson, Connecticut 06239 which specializes in the many scented-leaved geraniums for growing and stroking indoors and also in a wide range of half-hardy aromatics for favoured gardens and terraces.

One scent, however, is within reach of us all. It is the famous Winter Honeysuckle, Lonicera fragrantissima, whose creamy flowers actually appear on the borderline of early spring. Its sweet scent is almost sickly, but I would like to endorse an American use of this plant which I know from photographs of a great garden in Virginia. The Winter Honeysuckle can be clipped into a splendid hedge, about six feet high, which will be semi-evergreen in mild areas. Like the low purple willow, this honeysuckle is a hedge-plant, ignored by English gardening: I have just planted a group as the background to a small area for sitting and for through-traffic in academic life where the scent may tempt passers-by to become temporary sitters among a high proportion of evergreen shrubs. Admittedly, this Winter Honeysuckle is not the toughest or the prettiest form when in flower: for those virtues, you need Lonicera tatarica, a spring-flowering shrub whose selected American forms (Arnold's Red, from Wayside) could helpfully cross the Atlantic. This Tatarian Honeysuckle was ruled out for my purpose because its flowers are slightly later, but it is a superb plant, largely ignored by English gardeners.

In Britain, John Scott, The Royal Nurseries, Merriott, Somerset sell the ordinary scented winter Lonicera, and much else besides: in America, Wayside's catalogue offers to despatch it anywhere. Admittedly, it is a dull plant in summer or late autumn, but I find it an admirable host for a late autumn-flowering Clematis, either a viticella variety or especially the yellow flowered, fluffy-headed tangutica which I will discuss in early autumn, together with their suppliers, Treasures of Tenbury Wells and Blackthorne Gardens, 48 Quincy Street, Holbrook, Massachusetts 02343. These autumn clematis can be pruned back in February to give the Lonicera a clear run: they then grow up through it later in the season and transform it from August onwards. Whenever I recommend this use of climbers through shrubs, please note that the climber should be planted about a metre, at least, from the host-plant so that it can gain momentum before ascending its support. Otherwise, the host's roots will deprive it of any strength.

Potted Fruit Trees

In these dark months there are always times for reading as well as smelling and I usually come across some new idea from an old gardening book or a new seed-catalogue. Ideas do not all go out of date, so I would like to pass on a charming suggestion, pursued across nearly a hundred years to a time when it was widely practised.

Nowadays, the great days of private fruit are over and only a few private orchard-houses still survive from the past where fruit was forced to suit its owner's out-of-season whims. Fruit trees would be brought whole in pots to the dining-room table so that the guests could select their dessert as it grew. This elaborate ritual of the movable orchard has little to recommend it to gardeners today. But it contains a hint which I feel we might follow up to our advantage.

It is the growing of fruit in pots which attracted my attention. Doubtless commercial fruit-growers practise it whole heartedly, but in the small private garden I rarely see it tried. If you do not believe that your garden begins and ends with its flowers, a few potted fruit trees would make a striking impression outdoors.

Suppose you have a small front garden, paved or gravelled, or even a space on a balcony or roof; whether at office or at home, this space would always be the better for a large potted plant and none is more enticing than a generous bush of fruit. First comes the blossom, then, the very elegant leaves, then fruit which is decorative as well as edible: unless your hunger gets the better of you, a well-fruited apple tree is as attractive to the eye as any autumn flower. The polished green and red skins of its apples are more subtle than a Michaelmas daisy.

Determined to pot up a fruit tree and try for myself, I cast around for what gardening dictionaries call 'cultural hints'. Working on the theory that the Edwardians brought private fruit growing to its peak, I turned to an Edwardian book for advice. Much the most helpful was written by a Mr Thomas and a Mr Bunyard in 1904. Their method of work was most amusing. Mr Thomas would describe the tarring and spraying, the back-breaking digging and the hazards of the ladder. Mr Bunyard would provide the epilogue, running through dozens of different varieties in a few masterly pages, describing their fruits and commenting crisply on their flavours with the expertise of a man who had personally savoured them all.

THISTLY ERYNGIUM GIGANTEUM

MAGNOLIA   GRANDIFLORA
DAPHNE   'SOMERSET'

I could picture them in their orchard: Thomas in his braces, bustling from fig to early apple, tracking down the codlin moth and grumbling at the peach leafcurl; Bunyard in his deckchair munching his way through a Vicar of Winkfield pear and calling abruptly to Thomas for a Duchess of Oldenberg apple to take the taste away.

My picture, however, is a little unfair. Both were experts in their own right and Mr Bunyard was as industrious a grower as taster: he was a director of Laxton and Bunyard, that fine nursery which long continued his name. On potted fruit trees, their book is most informative: 'It is often said, and with much truth, that it takes years to convert a Britisher to anything novel or distinct, and fruit trees in pots are a case in point'. With the help of a Mr Hudson, they set out a powerful plan for its wider practice, explaining it in detail.

Trees are best potted-up in autumn, needing nothing more than a 10-inch-diameter pot. Modern plastic kinds tend to split, so if you can, choose a thick clay instead. Add rotted manure and a dressing of lime, preferably from old mortar rubble, to a good loam soil. If a dry spell follows, the trees must be syringed to stop their wood shrivelling. By November watering and syringing can be dropped to a minimum. During the following spring, and increasingly as the fruit forms, the roots must never be allowed to dry out. When a potted tree is bearing fruit, it may need two waterings a day. Liquid or artificial manure should be applied in summer in moderation.

Fruits must be thinned progressively as they form and ripen: a tree in a 10-inch pot should be left with seven or eight ripe fruits and a tree which has borne fruit for two years should be given a rest in the third. Remember, however, that many fruits may be lost naturally between their first formation and their final stages.

Pruning is a matter of common sense; once the fruits are forming, the shoots can be trimmed back to the wood-bud next above the fruit. They can be similarly shortened throughout the summer. The vital point is that each tree should be repotted annually and that very seldom indeed do they need a larger size of pot. If a plant looks weak, put it in a smaller container. The old roots should be pruned hard with a knife in order to encourage young fibrous replacements. The ball of soil should be reduced so that you can fit your hand between it and the edge of the pot. Soak the roots, repot and top-dress with rich soil.

Fruit trees in pots will not be too quickly exhausted. They may last for twenty years, outliving contemporaries in open ground. They are much less prone to canker and insects. In a cold frame or greenhouse, peaches and nectarines (especially an old variety called Cardinal) can be satisfactorily fruited. Outdoors, plums and apples and even pears are very successful if you attend to them and do not let them dry out. I will mention a few of Bunyard and Thomas's selections which are still current in gardens I know, but please do not be bound by them: they valued the plums called Ontario, Cullin's Gage or Marjorie's Seedling; the apples called Charles Ross or Egremont Russet, George Cave or Cox's Orange Pippin are especially worth trying. Of the pears, Fondante D'Automne is recommended by the potting experts. If you find others and cannot find these ones, do not worry: it is more important to go to a good nursery and ask their opinion, where people are used to selling specially-trained and confined fruiting trees. In Britain, I recommend Highfield Nurseries, Whitminster, Gloucester; in America, Henry Lewthardt, Box 666, East Moriches, N.Y. 11940.

The great advantage of these potted trees is that they do not need enormous pots. It is this convenience which makes them an unusual addition to a conventional paved or courtyard garden. Good results take a little time, but if they bring apples to hand from the drawing-room window or balcony, they are worth our patience. We may no longer be able to haul them into the dining room for guests, but it is still worth walking a few extra paces to taste and admire them for ourselves.

Simple Seeds

Late winter is not only a time for these scented shrubs and accompanying hellebores, turning a brave white face to the elements. It is also a time for gardens of the imagination, planned with the help of lists of seeds.

When gardeners complain that they cannot find this or that locally and cannot afford it when they do, they are forgetting the cheap convenience of seeds. Through seed-lists, gardening is made international, for it is through their packets that we all keep in touch, bringing better penstemons to Britain, sending better campanulas across the Atlantic and into Europe. People are alarmed by seed-sowing, but I will only say here that I find it useful to top up a four or five inch-wide pot with the finest grade of chopped bark (in Britain, I use Cambark) and then to sow particularly fine seed directly onto it, covering the pot with black polythene or any lightproof substance until the seed germinates. I never fill a pot anywhere near its rim, as I find the seedlings on the outer edges make more lasting roots if they begin rather low down a pot, enjoying better drainage.

In what follows, I will assume two seed-lists, Thompson and Morgan of London Road, Ipswich, and Park's of Greenwood, South Carolina 29647: T. and M. also export and have an American list, through P.O. Box 100 Farmingdale, New Jersey 07727. To make matters easy, I will confine myself to the more hardy annuals only, the seeds which you can sow directly into the ground as it warms up, usually in mid-April in Britain. Most of them can also be sown in pots and boxes and transplanted outdoors either when they are making their second pair of leaves or when you have pricked them out, one by one, into a separate flat box, growing about thirty plants to an average box's area: this method is preferable for some of them in areas with frost in May. The main exceptions are the poppies and their relations which develop a central tap root and hate to be transplanted, as the root breaks.

Not all the news from modern hardy annuals is bad news. On the whole, colours are tending to come in mixtures, not separate shades, although separate blues, whites, reds and yellows are much prettier for most gardens' plans and colour-harmonies. Heights are also tending downwards as the growers hare after dwarfs, miniatures and Thumbelina Assortments. Tall hardy annuals are a godsend wherever we have gaps after a cold winter, but soon, even the sunflowers will be two feet high and we will be left to grow nasturtiums up canes in order to fill in a background.

Among recent hardy annuals, height is one reason why I prize the splendid Helianthus Italian White. It was slow to reach Britain from America, but its pale lemon-white to white discs of flower are the happiest addition to borders of gentle colours and the entire plant rapidly branches to a height of four feet. In a dry summer, these sunflowers are at their best, but I have succeeded with them in all weathers. You can sow them directly into the ground in late May, but I like to give them a quicker start in a box indoors. For this method, a mid-April sowing is quite early enough, as they hate to be checked once they are growing.

Lower down the scale, I prize the new brightly-coloured Dianthus. They are all-American prizewinners but have yet to make their mark on many gardeners who prefer to pay a fortune for boxes of half-hardy petunias, grown under glass. Dianthus Queen of Hearts is a magnificent scarlet, upright, neat and about nine inches high. If you want a vivid edging or front grouping, this plant is unimaginably easy and persists in flower throughout the summer. Telstar is a mixture of red and white, a bicoloured dianthus in the family tradition of the familiar Sweet William and Carnation. In Britain, we also have Snowfire, a clear white with a lovely red centre, a variety which I find to be particularly tough in wet or dry summers. In areas of late frost, which means the whole of Britain, really, these dianthus are best started off in a box indoors: I use the convenient plastic boxes of Flora margarine which hold the contents of a Thompson and Morgan packet and can be turned into miniature propagators by a covering of transparent kitchen cling-film until the seedlings show through the soil.

I also recommend two recent mallows, the bushy Lavatera Silver Cup which has open mallow-flowers of a silver-pink in good clumps throughout the summer and the memorable Mont Blanc, a startlingly white variety which reminds you what a strong colour a white can be. Mont Blanc is best started off indoors, but Silver Cup can be sown directly: I like to keep them in separate borders and enjoy them in their different ways whatever the weather.

In cooler beds, I am a keen supporter of the sky blue Nemophila. Last summer, it was in its element during the rainy weather and it would be a brave person who ever omitted it from a British bedding-scheme. Nemophila menziesii is the familiar form, six inches high and covered in rounded flowers of sky-blue with white middles and black stamens. It is a rotten plant in full sun or dry gardens, but it thrives as an edging or grouping in any bed which is slightly damp and shaded: a foggy autumn day brins the best out of it. This year, I expect to be an equally keen supporter of Nemophila maculata, brought on sale by Thompson and Morgan. It spreads like its sky-blue cousin, but its flowers are a variable shade of lavender marked with five black spots, as if from fingers dipped in ink. It is extraordinarily easy to grow and the good gardeners who have already latched onto it are very enthusiastic about its behaviour.

There are some simple old friends, too, which most people know and few people sow: a pinch or two of Night Scented Stock for scent in the evening among solid plantings: Love-in-a-Mist, a Nigella which I much prefer in its pale blue Miss Jekyll form, not its white, rose and blue mixture; obliging nasturtiums, which I grow only in the tall scented forms and use as climbers and trailers for the gaps in late summer borders; bright double poppies and the scarlet Flanders Poppy, Papaver commutatum with a black spot, now restored to commerce by T. and M.; scarlet annual Flax, the lovely white form (from Dobies of Clwyd) and the various quick-blooming blues, recently offered by T. and M. and all of which flourish in sunny places. These plants are all hardy and very easy to grow, but unless you send off for them early in the year, you find that you have forgotten or that the exact variety is sold out. While you are at it, add Echium Blue Bedder, the coarse Mediterranean cousin of the Echium of Madeira, Echium fastuosum, whose great spikes of blue flower are familiar in the few great gardens of the south of France and the more imaginative planting of dry slopes in Californian gardens: Blue Bedder is utterly hardy, weather-resistant and bushy and floriferous to a height of eighteen inches. It never lets me down, but its stems twist and become coarse when the petals have dropped. Cut them back hard and the plant will flower a second time, six weeks later.

Lastly, three words of advice on some very well-known plants. The low-growing Sweet Peas are a shining exception to my comments about dwarf varieties but the best, as yet, is Thompson and Morgan's own Snoopea, about a foot high, scented and free of those annoying tendrils which tangle into everything. It can be sown directly outdoors and is better than the taller Super Snoop or Jet Set Mixed: it really has turned the Sweet Pea into a manageable bedding plant, without losing all scent.

What about Zinnias? Some people shudder at them because they are so artificial: I agree that they are obvious bedding plants, stiff, formal and heavily petalled, but I still like them in the right place and will only pass on my own experience, that zinnias grow away more readily if you sow them directly into a bed like hardy annuals, in mid-May, and spare them the bother of moving from box to box and box to bed.

Verbenas provoke similar reactions: too formal, too "hot-house", too strongly coloured. Again, I disagree and I must commend the blue-ish Verbena called Amethyst because it is much the most robust and the best able to withstand dry or wet weather. Resistance to extremes of climate is the quality I most value in my annual flowers: you may have your doubts about the general look of verbenas and zinnias, but they are as nothing to the look of weak verbenas and zinnias in our inevitable summer of extremes.

SPRING

Spring

By the time I have ordered my seeds, I feel that spring ought to be in the air: it never is, but on one or two days I am tempted to explore the debris of winter, checking for weeds beneath the dead top-growth of borders I never clear until March and hunting for the first signs of my sworn enemies, the purple-red snouts of growth on the Bindweed, or Convolvulus.

During these explorations, I continue to enlarge my knowledge of scents. Collision with that useful in-filling, Geranium macrorrhizum, first taught me to appreciate the musty, minty scent of its leaves. Testing recently for hardiness, I twiddled a few leaves of the Choisya, the so-called Mexican Orange, between my fingers and discovered that they left an acrid flavour, as pungent as cheap gin. This year, I added a new scent to my repertoire. I blush to admit my ignorance: for the first time, I discovered how sweetly so many crocuses smell. There is a reason for my unawareness of this elementary fact. I have always planted crocuses outdoors and have never tried crawling through them. I have also favoured what the great alpine gardener, Reginald Farrer, used to call the fatties, detesting them so much, he said, that the ink would clot on his typewriter whenever he came to mention them.

Farrer was referring to the large-flowered Dutch hybrids which we all plant for a good show in the garden. When the sun shines, the whites and yellows are pleasingly flamboyant, though the so-called King of the Blues is a blown-up purple-mauve which is not so congenial. In drifts, as I will explain later, they are pretty enough, but crawl through them though you may, they will delight the eye, not the nose. Like many hybrids, the Dutch crocus have sacrificed scent for size, causing us to overlook the family's natural virtues.

The species crocus are another matter: you would do well to grow them in broad pots or pans where you can admire the flowers away from the rain, and so I will simply state that Potterton and Martin, Moortown Road, Nettleton, Caistor, North Lincolnshire and P.J. and J.W. Christian, Pentre Cottages, Minera, Wrexham, Clwyd, N. Wales sell the rarer varieties I mention and the former, especially, are willing exporters to the U.S.A.: there, Breck's Bulbs, Peoria, Illinois are one of the best sources, but if you have difficulties of supply, I strongly recommend the ten-dollar subscription to the famous Herbertia, an International Journal of Bulbous Plants, at Box 150, La Jolla, California 92038. It is over fifty years old and runs a seed exchange scheme and four newsletters a year which have taught me much since I discovered them in our Oxford library ten years ago.

Last autumn, I was growing my species crocus in pots, for comparison, and after their success, I will try not to miss planting them ever again. It was Crocus medius which first surprised me, breathing a noticeable sweetness from its scarlet stigmata and lilac-blue petals which open wide in mid-October. Hopefully, I then buried my nose in a nearby pot of speciosus albus. Though its flowers are a glistening white, they do not give off the same scent of honey.

Clearly, the sweet-smelling crocuses have to be hunted out with care. Since that October, I have hunted with varying success. December is the climax, a time when Crocus longiflorus is scenting my desk, while laevigatus is doing the same for the mantlepiece. Both these forms are lilac-coloured and very delicate: longiflorus is also attractively marked with bronze. They both smell of heather-honey mixed with a hint of primroses, an extraordinarily fresh scent for midwinter.

The scent is carried on into the new year by Crocus imperati, another lilac-coloured flower whose outside petals are buff-brown marked with purple. It is particularly bright and it is no surprise to discover that it comes from Italy, being named in honour of an Italian botanist: its scent is more pungent and more subtle than any of its fellows. As the year turned I expected much of the bright yellow varieties which were also opening, but their scent is a disappointment. Their colour is marvellous, especially in the susianus variety, whose long, pointed flowers are backed with dark stripes, but none of them has the scent of their lilac relations.

Spring

I began to fear that Crocus imperati might prove to be the last sweet crocus of the crocus-year. Happily, the whites came to the rescue in February, led by the lovely Snow Bunting. Again, their scents vary: Crocus biflorus weldeni is also white and lovely, but it does not seem to smell. Some of the chrysanthus varieties do have a scent, though rather faint: Cream Beauty and Warley White seem to be the most noticeable: they suggest the scent of hay when they begin to fade.

There is only one variety to be kept away from the nose. A few years ago, I raised the unusual Crocus graveolens from seed offered in a botanic garden's list. Three years later, its straw-coloured flowers opened out into a flat star and I hurried to smell them. They gave off a fearful scent, like a bush of elder or a yellow-flowered broom. On looking them up, I learn that dried flowers of this crocus can defile a room for several years "in much the same way as a petrel's eggs scent the drawer in which they are kept". Keepers of petrel's eggs will need no further warning, but the rest of you are advised to give this curious crocus a wide berth.

Satisfying Snowdrops

The season of these crocuses is a time of false starts, and perhaps you need a pledge, like a rainbow, that the cold weather will eventually disappear. Historically, this has been the role of the snowdrop. One glimpse of its snow-white flowers and even the better poets lose their sense of proportion. Tennyson talked of the "fair white maid of February" and then went on to praise the "harbinger of spring". I like snowdrops, preferably when they are not harbinging. They are not bulbs for grand driveways and parks only, but before I discuss their individuality, I must give you the romantic legend which accounts for their existence.

When Adam and Eve left the Garden of Eden with thorns and thistles before them and a flaming sword on guard behind, the book of Genesis forgot to tell us that it was the depths of winter and the snow was falling thickly. The farther Adam walked, the more Eve dropped behind, resigned to a life of perpetual cold weather. Finally, she fell down exhausted, whereupon an angel appeared before her; winter, he promised, would swiftly be followed by the spring and snowstorms were only a passing phase in the weather. Stretching out a hand for the snowflakes, he fashioned them into a snowdrop's petals as a pledge that

31

spring would soon be coming. Heartened by her new flower, Eve trudged on through the snow once more.

This pretty story makes the snowdrop the emblem of every housewife, marooned in the winter countryside. In many people's experience, it is not such an angelic gift as the legend suggests. There is an element of unpredictability, as snowdrops take to some soils, not to others, and choose to flourish on particular slopes or beneath forgotten woods. They dislike a dry soil and the great connoisseurs do not give them rich manure: instead, they mulch them with leaf-mould, applying this cover in the late autumn. Snowdrops' commoner forms also like association with other plants, growing well in the company of grass or the weeds of a woodland's floor. I observe two bits of advice. First, I top-dress the bulbs with bone-meal as they go out of flower. Second, I try only to buy bulbs which are growing in green leaf in early spring: snowdrops bought as dry bulbs are much more erratic and although they are cheaper, they do not come up in such numbers as to be a good buy. On a favourable soil, a few snowdrops will spread very quickly. On a poor site, they will die anyway. Better, then, to begin with a few growing plants, if you can, mulch them and see if they spread: E. Parker-Jervis, Martens Hall Farm, Longworth, Oxon is a particularly good source of some of the rarer snowdrops, grown in pots. Otherwise, you should find a friend with a clump and tell him the convenient truth: snowdrops benefit from the division of their clumps, carried out as soon as they have flowered. Their persistence in neglected gardens makes people unaware that they like to be split up and spread around. Do the job in mid-March: autumn is no time to be thinking about most of this family.

Otherwise, they thrive happily on gardeners' most abundant commodity: neglect. I like the plain Galanthus nivalis mixed with a few patches of yellow aconites which repeat their flowers miraculously if caught in a second round of frost: I also like the doubles with their varying markings of yellow and crystalline green. It is here the snowdrop-connoisseurs come into their own.

Flowers with particularly long petals, clear green markings on their inner skirts or, glory of glories, a yellow centre change hands for very high prices. Almost everybody argues about these forms' identity, but if you have seen the bigger and taller flowers of Galanthus elwesii, Sam Arnott or the rare and supremely lovely John Gray, you will realize how a few chosen snowdrops can stand out in any flowerbed and make a great impact before the leaves are on the surrounding shrubs. These three varieties are all worth their price, especially if you are taking the right course and ordering bulbs individually in green leaf. I also favour Galanthus Straffan, an Irish variety which bears two flowers on each stem.

The latest of the spring snowdrops is the charming Galanthus ikariae which I always keep in the garden because it only grows on one Greek island, the one to which Icarus is said to have fallen when his wax-wings melted from flying too close to the sun. It is very small with bright green broad leaves and a dark green blotch on its outer petals. Its flowers come later than most in April, and are distinctive.

These varieties are particularly rewarding in a cold greenhouse: it is a fallacy that greenhouses are only useful if heated. Plant the bulbs 3 inches deep and as much apart in September, and keep them damp and shaded till they flower. You can best enjoy the detail of the flowers this way, unspoilt by mud and rain. Many would not bring them inside the house without a qualm, but in the Middle Ages, monasteries believed their flowers would purify a room. The legend that snowdrops bring bad luck if brought indoors does not do justice to a flower which is said to have been made by angels.

Architectural Planting

While we are still poking hopefully about among the snowdrops and aconites, it is worth standing back and looking at the relation of a garden's more permanent planning to its other sister-arts. If you have a clear idea of the ideal you aspire to realize and the tone you wish to convey, you will not become bogged down in the search for a perfect green marking on a snowdrop, but you may design something original around these isolated features of particular beauty.

Gardening has often aspired to the ideals of painting, science or even sculpture. Nowadays, the word 'architectural' keeps cropping up, not only in the small talk of garden designers but even in nursery catalogues: what, if anything, does it mean, and is it useful? Comparisons between living plants and architecture can be made neatly, and enrichingly. If you try to see the bare branches of an avenue of elms in winter as the pillars and tracery of a Gothic cathedral, you will see them, despite the high-flown simile, in a new and congenial way. The comparison is a very old one, first used by Italians of the fifteenth century to decry the rival Gothic architecture of Germany. Its pillars, they said, were rude and tree-like, reflecting on the barbaric way of life in a German forest.

The analogy is not quite what we mean by calling a plant or shrub architectural. We mean it has a firm and bold outline, stiff and pointed leaves, perhaps, and flowers of only secondary importance. It is a feature which is there, like a brick, all the year round, on which the gardener can build for the future. The spiky leaves of yuccas, so effective in London gardens, the outline of a dwarf willow, the leaves of the giant rhubarb or the titan of all water plants, Gunnera manicata: these are plants for the architect-gardener and all the better for it. Most of them are evergreen and worth examining throughout the year.

There is an apt, chance remark by the great landscape gardener, Russell Page, who worked and lived for the most part in France. He described herbaceous and annual plants affectionately, but called them only so much gaily coloured hay. They are usually weedy in shape and leaf, dead for half the year and alive with colour for three weeks or less. The annual cutting-down of the herbaceous border is like the mower's scything of the grass and wild cow-parsley along our country lanes, that wonderful display which 'today is, but tomorrow is cut down and cast into the furnace'. A flower-border is luxuriant but has no firm shape: it is here that architectural plants come into their own.

And yet they have seldom been popular. In the first flush of herbaceous plantings early this century, discriminating gardeners compared their aims with those of the painter. They wanted to distribute their flowers' colours in drifts and original mixtures to form impressionist effects, like Monet, friend of the gardening Miss Jekyll. Miss Jekyll herself studied Turner and was influenced by her close friend Hercules Brabazon, whose watercolours were painted in careful tones to a special theory of colour. Architecture was seen, if at all, through a haze. The distinctive subject of English garden-books in the early twentieth century was "colour planning": they gave "colour schemes for the border", while shape and form were discussed in separate books by architects, writing on garden ornaments and urns.

The greatest makers of gardens did see beyond this single topic, largely because they were aware of a tradition of gardening which was not English at all. They absorbed the values of architectural evergreen planting from their visits to the Mediterranean or books on historic gardens. Lesser gardeners were mesmerized by the ideal of 'cottage' gardening in which flowers of all colours were jumbled together in what used to be called "gay profusion". Where a site had no other graces and was anyway very small, such profusion could be charming, but the cottage-gardeners made it conform to a framework of their needs and practical uses: it was broken up by vegetable-plots, bean-poles, glass-cloches and sheds for the inevitable chickens. In other sites, without a backbone, this type of planting could look like Russell Page's "hay".

Naturally, the great Miss Jekyll saw beyond the sole claims of painting and colour-planning: her years of work with the architect, Edwin Lutyens, made her specially aware of architectural qualities in a garden's planting. I think especially of her courtyards and entranceways where she used the dark green leaves of ivies, hostas and hellebores to give a mood of permanency, calm and repose. The planting was tied to the architectural features of the adjoining house and colour was carefully controlled. Here and elsewhere, she had a sharp eye for contrasting leaves, the spikes of a yucca or a phormium or the leaves, like the ace of clubs, on the tall Macleaya cordata, or Plume Poppy.

Before we are plunged into the flowers of late spring and summer, I wish to emphasize the value of looking to architecture, not painting, as our model when planning. The change may make you more wary of the ideal of English cottage gardening which has often specialized in an excess of gaily coloured hay. It suggests a greater value for body and bones, prickles, spikes and stems: it means introducing buttresses of yew (or box, where space is limited) into herbaceous plantings and using them to hold the hay together out of season. Long borders look well if divided into separate bays by evergreens: up to half of their plants should be chosen for firm and lasting leaves. As architects, we will drop our current taste for mini-irises and knee-hi roses and will welcome back the giants, beanstalk and all. The taller varieties make the greatest architectural impact.

The garden architect approaches the gardener's families of plants with a new and eager eye. The painter-gardener may like his delphiniums: the garden architect will bring back the despised thistles, the eryngiums, especially those with sword-shaped leaves and 5-foot flower-stems such as serra, the huge-leaved globe artichoke and the waving stems of fennel. Because architecture does not depend on colour, the architectural garden will be longer-lasting and, by the very nature of its plants, more firmly planned.

35

It will be full of evergreen rosemaries and evergrey helichrysum, especially the marvellous fontainesii form where the soil is dry enough to suit it. Its roses will be grown for their hips, like the wild rugosa varieties, and their thorns (like the tall Rosa omiensis pteracantha) as much as for their flowers. Plants will be set off individually as well as being massed in borders; they will be happier, less in need of staking, less in need of cutting down and tidying up. There will be evergreen fatsias, the sword-sharp leaves of phormiums, the huge leaves of rodgersias in damp places, a special place for grey-leaved sea kale and the red-leaved large Rheum palmatum, or ornamental Rhubarb. Architectural style is particularly well suited to gardens at nature's extremes, the very wet or the very dry when plants poke up from arid slopes and run dramatically to seed. Here, the possibilities vary, but the principle is the same. Before haring after the latest flowering rose-bush, stop and wonder if it fits your site and the architectural tone of the plan it has suggested to you. In winter, after all, a normal rose is only a dreary cluster of twigs.

Thoughts on Thistles

As an illustration of architectural planting, I would like to develop a scheme round one bold and despised class of plant. Thistles, Dr Johnson might have said, are a symbol for Scotsmen and a food for donkeys. To gardeners, they mean sore fingers and tufts of down blowing into the strawberry bed, a prickly problem for the next year's croppers. But when I last walked across a stubble field, I looked at them closely and felt we had been unfair. Their prickly leaves spread outwards like a star which has fallen from heaven and been left lying face up on the ground. They have a bold shape and their prickles glisten in the rain. In a word, they have distinction. Something of this distinction may have rubbed off, at times too literally, on travellers to the Mediterranean in high summer and autumn. If you have never seen one of the thistly plateaux of Spain, Greece or Turkey, I recommend the descriptions of a thistle-landscape in the greatest contemporary Turkish novel, Memed, My Hawk by Yashar Kemal. There has never been a finer connoisseur of thistles in their element.

"The tallest thistles grow about a yard high, with many twigs decked with spiny flowers, five-pointed like stars, set among tough prickly thorns.

There are hundreds of these flowers on each thistle ... In spring the thistles are an anaemic pale green. A light breeze can bend them to the earth. By midsummer, the first blue veins appear on the stems. Then the branches and the whole stem slowly turn a pale blue. Later, this blue grows steadily deeper till the whole boundless plain becomes a sea of the finest blue. If a wind blows towards sunset, the blue thistles ripple like the sea and rustle. As autumn approaches, the thistles dry up. The blue turns white and crackling sounds rise from them. Small milk-white snails, as big as buttons, cling to them in thousands, covering them like milk-white beads. The village is surrounded by a plain of thistles. There are no fields, no vineyards, no gardens. Only thistles."

Have I begun to persuade you or, like Kemal's characters, will you cut thistles down on sight, not even waiting for the drama of the second volume of the story? My favour for thistles is not, I trust, where we part company. I value daisies certainly, elder bushes possibly, but common thistles never, not even in a weed-ridden garden which we try to pass off as natural. Thistles are too prolific to be given a chance. But they have many more respectable relations. Catalogues conceal the similarities for fear of scaring customers away, but there are some rare and original plants, not difficult to grow, which have the same prickly habit and downy flowers as thistles themselves.

They come in all shapes and sizes, some as small as Carduncellus rhaponticoides, which sends out a flat rosette of stiff leaves as a setting for its lavender-mauve flowers like a tiny globe artichoke's. Others are as tall as the onopordon, that invaluable biennial with silver thistle-leaves which is 6 feet tall, like a huge pewter candlestick when given room to stand in isolation. Onopordons seed themselves from year to year, and can be bought in seed packets from firms as respectable as Burpees, Parks and Thompson and Morgan. Needless to say, they germinate very readily.

So does the annual Mary's Thistle, or Silybum, a superb hardy annual whose thistly dark green leaves are spotted with white, like drops of that ubiquitous liquid, the Virgin Mary's milk: Thompson and Morgan list and export these seeds which are almost fool-proof and admirable value in any garden-planting. They also sell the hooked and spiny Morina longifolia whose leaves are as nothing to its whorls of flowers, first white, then pink, then a blushing red when they have been fertilized. Like so many thistly plants, these flowers hold up nobly when dead and can be used very strikingly in a bowl of dried stems and flowers. The thistly globe artichoke is another friend of architectural planters: you can eat the buds, especially in the named Vert de Laon variety, and you can also enjoy the huge clumps of jagged grey-green leaves. At a lower level, you can pick the heads of the alpine thistle Carlina acaulis, which are disc-shaped and only a foot tall. They can be matched prettily with Eryngium alpinum, fluffiest and smartest of the smaller sea hollies, easily raised in dozens from seed. In Britain, Thompson and Morgan sell all these thistles and many eryngiums, including the superb grey-white biennial, Eryngium giganteum, named popularly after Miss Wilmott, a prickly Edwardian gardener who sowed it secretly in gardens she visited. In America, Park's sell seed, conveniently, of both the eryngiums I have named.

So much for the outlines of the idea. Their angular shapes and prickles belong with the concrete yards and plate-glass windows of much modern building: their irregularity can enliven surroundings which are often left too flat. It is fashionable for gardeners to think of planting profusely and mixing their flowers in the abandon of the old cottage style. But it can be as subtle to plant too little as to plant too much. Style depends on the site and there are places where nostalgic, cottage profusion looks untidy. Gardens can be sharp and spiky as well as rose-embowered and honeysuckle-twined: there are corners and settings where thistles are not such an asinine taste after all.

Magnolias in March

By March, we are beginning to enter a time of strong colour, brilliant blue scillas, yellow daffodils, red Ribes and yellow Forsythia and the yellow-green and plum-red growth on young day lilies, paeonies and other border plants. But there are still several weeks of anticipation, a lull before the sudden rush of growth. During these familiar interludes, I find myself kept on the move by the cold March wind, symbol of a month which is never so pleasant as we expect. I also find myself with time to pay visits, the last such moment before the grass starts to grow and mowing ties us all to our homes.

It was in just such a mood that I made a visit to London's Hampton Court in a recent March. I had come to inspect the remains of Cardinal Wolsey's 280 guest-bedrooms, his arched kitchens and great court, rather than to take in the details of the surrounding gardens. But even that

MULTICOLOURED HARMONY OF A SPRING TERRACE

ERYNGIUM ALPINUM AND LADIES' MANTLE

worldly intriguing Cardinal had time for his garden amidst his cares of state: wheelbarrows, watering cans, 'pots for the 'erbs and twine to fix the arbours' feature among the earliest accounts for his grand buildings. The palace gardens are very much later than the intimate style of Wolsey's own day; visiting them, I was amazed out of season by a towering specimen tree.

In the winter sunlight, against the twirled and twisted Tudor chimneys, a gigantic Magnolia grandiflora had spread itself to the full. It must have been 20 feet tall and every inch as wide. Early March is not the accepted season for magnolias, largely because we concentrate our eyes and attention on flowers.

In early March, Magnolia grandiflora's charms are subdued, like the redcurrant's. It has no flowers, only leaves, but the leaves are quite magnificent; they are as stiff and as long as a rhododendron's but without the ribbing or the dankness of most varieties' green. When Magnolia grandiflora is struck by the sun, it lives two different lives. On the leaf's upper surface, the light dances, less reflected by a shining green: the under-surface gleams in a shade of ginger-brown, absorbing the light in its layer of natural fur. If you turn over this magnolia's leaves, you will find them lined with pale suède, like a country colonel's shoes on a day at the races.

As for flowers, you have to wait a while, in every sense of the phrase. In March, flowering magnolias have to be sought elsewhere, especially in the recent crosses between Far Eastern varieties which flower so exquisitely before the leaves. Most of the best have been bred and marketed in America where they suit gardens in milder, moister climates: my favourite is the pinkish white Magnolia loebneri Leonard Messel which likes to be mulched heavily in its first three autumns. In America, it often does not flower till May, but in Britain you can verify my fondness for it as early as the first week in April in the splendid woodland planting of Hillier's arboretum in Hampshire. The petals are like thin ribbons, ten or more in a flower, and stand out superbly against the bare branches. In America, White Flower Farm, Connecticut and Gossler Farms Nursery, Oregon sell Leonard Messel, eventually a free-standing tree about twenty feet high. In Britain, try Sherrards of Donnington, Newbury, Berkshire.

As for Magnolia grandiflora, it is a tree which British gardeners struggle to please against a wall. This deficiency in the 'Englishman's garden' will amuse any American from the south or west where this plant, as one list puts it, is an "indestructible and most attractive feature of virtually every cultivated landscape". It will also amuse anyone who knows Italy: this magnolia soars twenty or thirty feet high in almost every urban park or green space from the plains of the Veneto to the straits opposite Sicily. The finest old Magnolia trees I know line the esplanade in Reggio, on the very southern tip of Italy, a walk which D'Annunzio described as the most beautiful in any Italian city. Italians were quick to heed his nineteenth century judgement: they laid a major railway below the promenade, festooned it with overhead wires and added a road for hooting Vespa motorcycles and a concrete dock for freighters on either side of the prospect. But the magnolias are mature, huge trees with trunks and bony roots and canopies of suède-backed leaves.

In a warm English summer, Magnolia grandiflora begins to show signs of opening in July and does not finish until late October. The buds are like long white candles, hidden amongst the thick green leaves. Though you often have to search to find them, the more they unfold, the more unmistakable they become. The flowers grow huge, as much as a foot wide, and the petals are like very smooth white wax held together by a central cluster of stamens. They look too exotic to be true; even so, their final glory is untold. Grandiflora's leaves may be fascinating, its flowers incomparable among whites, but it is for their scent that they are enjoyed most of all. On a late summer's evening, they overpower you with spices and lemons and an ingredient of their own, like the smell of a stone-pillared church, so cold that it makes you shiver, even in August. The flowers are frequented by beetles, groping blindly, who have come to look for the pollen. Be tolerant to their presence, for it is far older than gardeners: beetles were among the world's oldest pollinators, before bees visited flowers.

In America, its home, this magnolia is free-flowering and free-growing but in England it is so shy that it needs the shelter of a good south wall. In the south, with other shrubs around it, it will form into a rounded tree in an open position, but young plants are expensive and I do not suggest you risk it in this way.

If you have a house wall with a chimney behind it, it is the perfect place: the chimney's warmth can bring a young plant through a cold winter. But it will never hasten grandiflora into flower. For that happy event, you must often wait ten years, allowing it to spread and thicken while you enjoy it as evergreen cover. You can sometimes encourage it by careful 'barking' in the spring, by stripping off a semi-circle of bark near the base of the trunk, while leaving a piece in the front untouched. Do not allow both ends of the circle to meet: if they do, they prevent the flow of sap up the trunk. The aim is to restrict it, not prevent it: you thus encourage flowers, not leaves.

If you do not fancy this risk, you have two alternatives. You can plant the Exmouth or Goliath varieties which are available through Sherrards and which make smaller shrubs, flowering at an early age. They are excellent buys, and I recommend them to all grandiflora-growers. Or you can agitate for the new Magnolia Maryland which is the best of all. In Britain, odd plants turn up and ought to appear more often when we wake up our nurserymen to this American plant's quality. It flowers in its third year, bearing the true white candles of a great grandiflora. In America, apply to Gossler Farms Nursery, Oregon who have excellent stock of sixty varieties of Magnolia, putting English gardening smartly in its place.

Early Spring Scents

By mid-March, we have some excellent little daffodils, those which wrongly contain the word 'February', February Gold and February Silver, and the memorable pale yellow and white Jack Snipe. The February forms open in that month in mild West Country gardens, but the weather hits them more often than not. I value them because they are not tall; they are fairly cheap and they make superb fillers for awkward edgings where lawns meet paths or walls or driveways skirt banks or mown grass. They are not at their strongest if you naturalize them under turf; try to keep them for these awkward places where nothing much will be growing later in the year. They can be followed by a lovely white Thalia, another small form which opens just as February Gold has turned to a dead-head. Do not make my mistake and mix the two: segregate them, so that Thalia's season does not coincide with the other's death.

Scent, meanwhile, is more elusive, unless you are still willing to crawl among my small crocus. Assuming you have a bad back or a tendency to arthritis, I will confine myself to shrubs, four of which are constant themes in any variation I play on a garden and one of which is a rose with curious leaves.

The best scent in March comes from the small shrub which I most value and would always plant near a south or west facing door, window or pathway. It belongs to that temperamental family, the daphne: it is Daphne odora aureomarginata, a 2-foot-high bush which eventually spreads to about a yard in width. In America, Wayside sell good plants of it: in Britain, try Scotts of Somerset.

I first tried the ordinary odora, not caring for variegation and not realizing that it is often not so hardy. Two months later, it was killed by frost. Since then, I have grown to like its gold-variegated relation. Its gold is not so strident as that of a variegated elaeagnus nor so prominent as that of the admirable Privet. It runs round the edges of the pale green leaf and keeps the whole bush as interesting as any flower. It is evergreen, of course, but March, undoubtedly, is its season of glory; the off-white flowers finally open among the tips of the branches, though their buds have been swelling in a shade of magenta-pink for weeks before. They are small and rather tubular; their outsides retain the bud's bright magenta.

This daphne, as befits an odora, is the sweetest-smelling of its family. It smells supremely of spring and it is not a difficult customer to please. It must be in a sheltered corner, preferably beneath a south wall, and must have a light soil, well laced with leaf mould and manure: then, it grows apace, making a three foot mound in three to five years' time. Drainage, as with most daphnes, is important, and when young, a plant should not be allowed to beg for water. Young plants move most easily. If you can afford to wait a few years, do try it in a bed against the warm wall of the house, one of those narrow strips which we all have and which can be so difficult to fill. When you fling open the windows to begin spring cleaning, this daphne will charm you into inactivity. Alternatively, it can be grown as a charming plant for a seven-inch pot indoors. You can bring it into a heated room in February and encourage the buds to fatten quickly. Watch, however, for white fly which like this daphne's leaves.

If the daphne is my first true sensation of spring, I regard my second scented shrub as the last post-script to winter. Abeliophyllum distichum is an awkward bundle, both to pronounce and to place. It is a Korean shrub, up to five feet high and very twiggy in habit, like a denuded Spiraea. I like it on the end of the sort of bed which you make beneath a south-facing wooden boundary fence or greenhouse. The point about this Korean bundle is the dusting of white flowers, like almond-blossom, along its branches and the exquisite scent when they open from their pink buds in March. It is a superb cut-flower, because you can pick it when just in bud, like Ribes, and bring it along until a vase scents a whole room. In America, White Flower Farm first publicized it and still sell it, calling it White Forsythia and advising it for "zone four and southwards". In Britain, too, it needs a south wall, but it is worth chasing it up from Notcutts, Scotts or Hilliers.

I find my next scent more difficult, but only because I do not garden on acid soil where azaleas would run happily in light woodland. Corylopsis is an enchanting plant, nicely nicknamed by Wayside Gardens as the "Buttercup Winterhazel". In fact, its flower is not a butter-yellow, but a pale primrose yellow in the easiest form, Corylopsis pauciflora which will tolerate a slight trace of lime. Above all, this family likes to be damp in summer in a bed of leaf-mould, well mulched to any depth you care to create. The branches spread outwards into a pleasant shape and masses of bell-shaped flowers appear before the rounded hazel-leaves, breathing a scent of cowslips on the warmer intervals of a sunny March day. Azalea-growers often forget this superb shrub which does not look its best at shows or suit its season to the great exhibitions. Yet it is as lovely as any pale azalea, although it is less hardy in bud than branch and needs careful placing away from spring frosts. Best of all, I like to see it on a slight slope, underplanted with the woodland anemones which remain in flower as it fades. Like lilies, whose soil it prefers, it is the sort of shrub which I associate with damp soil in Oregon. Sure enough Gossler Farms Nursery specialize in good varieties of Corylopsis, not all to be found in Britain. On the East Coast, Wayside sell pauciflora (fit for zones five to nine) and in Britain, John Scott of Merriott have strong well-grown plants. In frosty Britain, Corylopsis spicata is slightly hardier, but the flowers are not such a pretty pale yellow.

Neither this 'Winterhazel' nor the Korean bundle of twigs and syllables is evergreen. As a solid companion for them, I recommend the robust Osmarea. My plants have faced north across a horribly cold vista, extending for twelve uninterrupted miles, yet the most they have suffered is a slight browning of their buds in the past twelve years. They are totally evergreen, about seven feet high and set with narrow toothed leaves of a dark matt green which has a hint of olive green to enliven it. I am convinced that this shrub is much hardier than books admit; it is known in America, but I cannot yet find it in a good mail-order list; it ought to be planted by every perplexed gardener who lives on lime and wants an evergreen architectural plant which can be lightly clipped or allowed to spread into a loosely-branched feature. I like to see it as the frame for a seat, blocking off each end and running behind it as a dark scented background. In twelve years, I have never spent any time or effort on my plants: the tubular white flowers are sweetly scented without being overpowering and open with the last of the willow-buds by mid-April.

Finally, the scent of an emergent rose-leaf. I much enjoy the incense rose, Rose Primula, which turns out to be known in America as the Tien Shan Rose. It is an eastern species rose whose stems are reddish brown, about five feet tall, and thinly thorned. Its leaves, like those of many species roses, resemble a small acacia leaf drawn to scale. Its flowers are welcome without being very noticeable; pale yellow and an inch wide, they decorate the ends of the shoots in late May. But it is when rubbed or wetted that this humble rose comes into its own, far outclassing its blowsier brothers. Soaked by the rain, a tea Rose looks sorry and battered, shedding the petals which have earned its name, but under the trees in the shade of a shrubbery Rose Primula is spreading the smell of incense far around it, as its long-lasting leaves are brought to their best by a heavy stormy afternoon. I have never found it difficult, but bits of it do die back and leave you to prune them away. The Incense Rose is best, then, among a surrounding planting where you can lose its uninspiring shape and puzzle yourself and visitors with the scent of incense wafting off its insignificant leaves. In spring, Rose Primula is just coming into leaf and its hours of incense-breathing lie ahead: my plant stands beside some happy osmareas so I have placed it so early in the book, as if by association. Anticipation is very much the mood of March.

In Praise of Daisies

On lawns and grass paths, anticipation now shades into action. The mower's blades have been oiled and sharpened; the winter service will have ensured that the damn thing refuses to start without several dozen tugs at your guts and its easy-spin starter-string. War is about to begin to maintain the grass sward for the season. Before you launch out of the toolshed, spare a thought for one of your undeserving victims.

'Call no flower happy until it's dead'. Even in the garden reputations rise and fall and perhaps even the magnolia will be rejected by posterity.

Yesterday's favourite is tomorrow's abomination; bedding nowadays is out and the ferns of our forefathers are no longer visited upon us children. Tastes, of necessity, change and change is often cruel. To none has fashion been crueller than to Bellis perennis, the common English daisy.

The daisy's disgrace is complete. Her reward is a fortnightly dose of poison, her death a growth industry for chemicals and machines. Like all tragic heroines she has been brought to ruin by her own qualities. Imprudently, she began to grow too easily in grass. Obtrusively, she flowered from February to October. The Furies gathered, the shears snipped but the daisy refused to surrender. Where cutting and poisoning had failed, only hormones could humble and reform. Bellis must grow till she burst, victim of her own pride. Daisytox was born to kill her.

There are, however, two sides to a tragic story. For centuries, the daisy was admired, prized for the very qualities we now revile. Lovers would appeal to her wisdom, children would turn her into chains and poets would praise the artlessness of her charms. She was even believed to exude a juice which would stunt the growth of dogs.

A dossier of daisy lovers still reads impressively, a list of sensibilities which are not to be despised. At its head stands Chaucer, Bellis's best friend, who called her the 'Emperice and flour of floures alle'. He would lie in the field to watch her open in the morning: he would return to see her close again at night, a peculiarity which earned her popular name: daisy is a corruption of day's eye. In the Legend of Fair Women, Chaucer's Queen Alceste is turned into a daisy and retains as many virtues as the florets in a daisy-flower. The compliment is not to be despised, as the yellow centre of the daisy is a mass of these tight-packed florets, and what we would loosely call the white outer-petals are only a fraction of the total. Queen Alceste is a woman too good to be true.

Chaucer's example was not neglected. Ophelia in her madness, Burns in his coyness, Keats near his grave and Milton in his blindness, all showed favour for the day's eye's beauty. Thomas Hardy's wife loved it; Tennyson addressed it in four separate poems and Shelley considered it the pearled Arcturus of the earth. Wordsworth made two attempts to praise it, one of which was better than the other: 'A little Cyclops with one eye Staring to threaten and defy ...'. That was the secret of the daisy's success. From the tombs of the Egyptians to the floors of medieval monasteries, from the decoration of the Petit Trianon to Lady Beaufort's emblem in the Henry VII chapel in Westminster, Bellis perennis flowered its way into many responsive hearts.

But hearts began to harden. 'Oh, daisy, daisy cease thy varied song, A plant may chant too often and too long'. In 1831, Mr Budding's first lawnmower lumbered into attack. Wearied by the poet's praises, we were persuaded that henceforward, our daisies were better numbered. Flowers were to be stamped out from the largest single area of an English garden and paradoxically, the most boring perennial plant in the gardener's dictionary, bent, creeping or browntop fescue, became the symbol of horticultural excellence. The English took it exclusively to heart, for all must be for the greenest in the greenest of all possible lands.

Daisies, I suggest, are due for a revival. They need no mowing, manuring, spiking, worming, sanding or liming. They flower for seven months of the year, smelling sweetly and shining whitely, and they wear as well as those fine bowling green grasses which are named Emerald Velvet, as if velvet or emeralds were two materials upon which sensible gardeners would wish to walk.

Of course, a gardener is tied to the soil and to the need to cut his lawn, living with only an illusion of his freedom. But by coming to terms with the daisy and learning to love what advertisements ask him to abuse, he can cut through some of his labours, decking his hours in the grass with daisy-chains. Even the poisoners and grumblers admit, with a grudge, that Bellis Perennis will have the last word. All go in the end to push up the daisies, however much they love and spray their lawn.

Spring Colours

Smoking and roaring, the mower is out of its shed; April is under way and for the next three and a half months, gardeners have little time to stop and think. In April itself, I do not think this unreflecting hurry matters. Almost any spring flower goes well with another because the colours are so fresh, the leaves are lush but not yet dominant and above all, the light is still quite gentle, casting odd patches of sunlight at intervals between the clouds and showers. I like a miscellany of flowers in spring: auriculas, yellow jonquils and the first of the purple violas; golden daffodils with the catkins of small willows, especially Salix wehrhahnii; sky blue hyacinths with emergent pale-variegated leaves; several bushes of white-flowered Viburnum, especially carlesii and juddii, the supreme scents among spring-flowering shrubs (Weston and Wayside have them both); Blue-eyed Mary and primroses; polyanthus in profusion (try the Barnhaven strains from seed: I give the addresses for the U.K. and U.S.A. in my List of Suppliers); my beloved dark red Flowering Currant, or Ribes, and the white flowers of the glorious Magnolia soulangeana. Among the smaller alpine and meadow plants, there is also a tapestry of colours, with no clashes. In April, they enliven a garden with a planned architectural frame of evergreen shrubs and firm lines (mine come from Box and scented Osmarea). Their brightness and informality are not so pervasive that they detract from a garden's backbone; in spring, if you go steady on the harsh yellow forsythia, your planning cannot go far wrong.

To make it go even more right, I would like to explore two types of corner, both suited to spring planting. One is awkward, the other sentimental: while you continue to hunt for osmarea, I will take the awkwardness first.

Awkward Corners

In spring, gardeners think of bulbs and bedding-plants. April in the garden brings daffodils and hyacinths, the first wallflowers, the last camellias, many a primrose, more polyanthus and a 20 per cent increase over last year's national quantity of forsythia, that infallible growth stock which was first launched in honour of William Forsyth, Regency England's expert in apple tree diseases.

Each spring I am also struck by the forgotten herbaceous plants of April, when paeonies are only showing their clumps of thrusting red shoots and the poppies have a very long way to grow. My favourites are not exotic. They would be appropriate in the wild and woodland garden, were there any woods and wildernesses still being gardened in these days of cramped space. Copses filled with meconopsis, woodland ponds profuse with primulas: except for enthusiasts, these are gardening dreams of the past. Hence, I suspect, the disregard for early spring herbaceous plants rather than bulbs. Lack of space should not deter us from applying a convenient idea on a smaller scale. These spring plants still have a place in a small modern garden in a wild, untended corner.

Their great advantage is that they will all grow in shade. It is in spring that we can make something of awkward shaded corners because the competing leaves and branches are not yet at full stretch and there is still some damp in the ground from the winter. They are not suitable for bulbs because they are not well-drained, but they do suit early-flowering herbaceous plants which become coarse or go into a decline after May. Take the doronicum, for instance, the Leopard's Bane of herbal legend; its cheerful daisy-flowers of yellow are common in continental Europe and America but few gardeners bother with them in Britain. However they are the most dazzling plant for the foot of a north wall. The caucasicum variety is the pick of the family, partly because it is only one foot high, partly because its yellow is clear and its petals are free from any taint of orange. The joy of the plant is the colour of its accompanying leaves, a fresh lime-green which sets off the flowers in a bright and spring-like way. There is a range of all or double forms, but the plain caucasicum has a freshness and a contrast of flower and leaf which they lack. In America, White Flower Farm sell it, as do Weston Nurseries (more expensive) and Wayside: in Britain, try Scotts in Somerset. After flowering, this splendid plant tends to shrivel its leaves in dry weather and look as if it is dying. In fact, it is taking a rest, a habit which suits it admirably for dry shade or dry American summers. When the conditions are most adverse, the doronicum wisely goes to sleep. Anyone can divide the mats of one plant into dozens of new divisions: I like to run them as a carpet between later flowering shrubs, the evergreen ceanothus, the scented Philadelphus and the later Buddleias.

If yellow Leopard's Bane sounds too flamboyant, there are blues and whites in other spring families to tone it down. Blue-Eyed Mary, or Omphalodes verna, has long been a standby for heavily shaded corners. It is some 3 inches high, quick to spread, fresh-leaved and innocent. It might well be mistaken for an early sky-blue forget-me-not. There is, however, a new variety which is even better: Anthea Bloom, a name indicative of its quality, as it was first spotted in the Bressingham Nurseries of Diss, Norfolk, source of many fine plants. It flowers freely and accompanies its pale-blue show with leaves of grey-green. It would fit into any garden whatever its size: I have it as a happy underplanting beneath roses. In America, you will have to order from Bressingham direct, but they are willing and experienced exporters and stock almost every border-plant I will name from now on in the herbaceous months of the garden's year.

Every gardening country knows a blue-flowered companion, the Pulmonaria, known for its white-spotted leaves as Spotted Dog. On the evening of its spring display, I would plant it in any problem corner and know that every April it would reward me. Its flowers are a shade of pink or blue and it forms a spreading mat of leaves from March onwards, holding its flowers 6 to 9 inches high. It is so easy, generous and infallible that it would win every horticultural prize but for one dreadful failing: after flowering, its leaves grow larger and coarser until you long to tear them off in desperation. But gardeners in difficult corners cannot be too choosey and by the time the Spotted Dog looks most shaggy, the attention has shifted to other flowers. In America, Wayside offer a good pink flower and white-spotted leaves in a form of Pulmonaria saccharata called Mrs. Moon. Elsewhere, it is only angustifolia, I fear, as often in Britain where we all miss a chance. The Pulmonaria is twenty times better in a named form, usually originating from a great gardener. Bressingham sell and export several good ones, of which I would praise the deep Highdown Blue to the skies; Bowles's Red is another winner (cheap from Careby Manor, Lincs.), but the best two are sold by E. Parker-Jervis, open to visitors only at Longworth, Oxon but willing to provide health-certificates and export-forms for orders over $30 from foreigners visiting the city of dreaming spires. Among many border plants peculiar to her list, she offers a superb deep blue (Lewis Palmer), a good pale Cambridge Blue, the true Bowles Red and a clear Sissinghurst White: Cambridge's name has never kept better company.

One difficult corner is beginning to catch the joys of spring. Even more robust than Spotted Dog is Brunnera macrophylla, a plant like a forget-me-not in flower and colouring, but unmistakably borage-like in its rounded coarse leaves which become an eyesore later in the year. I tear them off as soon as they become offensive, but their absence does not seem to deter it. As it is some 2 feet high when in flower, it is well able to poke up through the spring grass of an orchard or the tangle of a dark and weedy border: there, the leaves can be overlooked and in grass, mown without harm in high summer. Its near relation Mertensia virginica, the Virginian cowslip, is less rampageous but much more lovely. Commonly called blue-flowered, it combines shades of indigo, purple and lilac, while its leaves are a study in themselves. First, they are black; then, they are smooth and green, delicately traced with the lines of their lurid youth. Brunnera is a common plant (Weston, or White Flower), but in Britain, Blooms sell a lovely cream variegated form which is emphatically not for difficult places, but belongs in a well-watered bed, where I love its cream

49

leaf. Mertensia is such a common wild plant in America that visitors from Virginia to Sissinghurst's great garden used to wonder how V. Sackville-West could possibly want to grow it. In Britain, it is still quite rare and unfamiliar: to and fro across the Atlantic, our awkward corners can well be eclectic.

I cannot omit the yellow-green Spurges or Euphorbias. Some of them, like the tall and lovely palustris, are too fine for a difficult under-nourished corner, but there is one which is indestructible, and another which is invasive. Euphorbia polychroma is so tough that even I have not killed it on a slope which has killed most things in the past ten years. There it sits, a lovely mound of yellow-green bracts in late spring, neat leaves thereafter and noticeable colour when the leaves turn in October. It resists drought, thunderstorms and cats. In spring, it has a beaming look of freshness, not quite so harsh as the yellows of alyssum and Leopard's Bane: about a foot high, it mixes well with the emergent green and yellow growths of the garden in spring. It grows readily from seed (Parks or Thompson and Morgan), but it is too woody to divide conveniently. Otherwise you can buy a few plants from, say, Bressingham Nurseries or Wayside who emphasize its resistance to drought and say that "it is rated by one of the world's outstanding nursery experts as among the ten best perennials".

My other spurge grows wild in East Anglia and is, I admit, a potential menace. However, menaces have their uses and shade, even dry shade under small trees, will suit the rampant, low-growing spurge called Euphorbia cyparissias. It is so free-growing that the faint-hearted might fear it as a nuisance, but its excesses can easily be controlled by firm use of the spade. It is about a foot high with masses of stems, whorled and fuzzed with leaves like miniature Mare's Tails; they are of interest throughout the summer, and they colour a brilliant yellow-orange in autumn before dying down to a nest of small green buds, like the growths of a stonecrop. In late April and May, this spurge is covered in clouds of green-yellow heads, each containing twenty or more flowers like frogs' eyes. The flowers are wide-eyed but not so heavy as the bigger and uglier spurge varieties. The cypress spurge will grow under trees or as a filling in a narrow, difficult bed. Provided that nothing delicate is within range, it can be given a narrow bed in a difficult corner and allowed to colonize it.

Into this mixture of blues, yellow-greens and yellows, we ought to allow for some white. Lily of the valley (Convallaria) is an obvious possibility, as it likes dry semi-shade and flourishes if you top-dress it with a thin layer of balanced garden fertilizer and leafy compost in early spring. The scent from its white flowers is heavenly. Scentless, but earlier, is a bold white-flowered Bergenia called Silver Light (Silberlicht in Germany where it was raised). Bergenias are indestructible plants with that rather grim combination of dark brown stems and leathery evergreen cabbage-leaves, but they do exclude weeds, grow almost anywhere and save no end of trouble. Normally, people buy the rose-pink forms which are rather drab in the company of the leaves: I noted Silver Light as something special twenty years ago in a German Botanic garden and since then, it has reached discerning gardens. (Bressingham Nurseries sell it in the U.K.; Westons, Mass. in the U.S.A.) The flowers are a clear white and raise the tone of the leathery foliage without detracting from their vigour. Silver Light is a great stand-by near rubbish-bins, outside back doors, by drainpipes or in those cold alleyways between the shaded wall of your house and the neighbouring fence.

Among this mixture, you ought to find something for any odd corner in a difficult site. What about the next level, the bulky four- or five-foot-high masses which give the impression of luxuriance? These are by no means easy to find. I would try the golden elder, because a brightly coloured leaf is a bold retort to the challenge of dark gardens. Sometimes it is said to be too out of the way to be grown in unpromising beds or backyards but I have not found this to be so. I have a flourishing plant in full shade where a cracked gutter pours water down the wall behind it. It has been happy there for ten years.

Perhaps the name of this elder deters gardeners: the only worthwhile elder for shade is Sambucus racemosa plumosa aurea, available from Wayside or John Scotts, in Somerset. It can be pruned hard in March or allowed to grow up to seven feet high: the gold is noticeable, even in shade and I like the brightness of a green and gold colour scheme with this elder, the tough Euphorbias and the Leopard's Bane in a group together. All this suggestion needs to complete it is a tough and reliable climber. In light shade, away from the drip of trees, I would use flowering quinces, or Chaenomeles. These favourite wall plants flower thickly on leafless branches in April, adorning their nakedness with ruffs of pink, red or white flowers like hawthorn. It is important to prune them in May after flowering.

Behind my golden elder, I would try the pink-and-white form called Apple Blossom: its name is self-descriptive. In extremely heavy shade this

51

would not be likely to flourish. I would therefore pick up the elder's colouring by planting an ivy behind. Hedera colchica, from Anatolia, has the biggest leaves, but it is not as hardy as some: in America, Wayside sell it for zones six to nine. In England, that climate is more or less available and so we can also grow the best of all, the variegated form with cream markings. This ivy is at home in the ancient land of Colchis where the wicked Medea kept company with the Golden Fleece. In all but the coldest districts, it is as bewitching as she was and much less bother to the family.

Some Sentimental Scenes

To see spring through the difficult corners in shade is to miss its familiar appeal. Spring flowers have always touched a soft streak in human nature: I would like to turn to two sentimental plantings before picking my way through some special associations. They are fit for the haphazard scattering of flowers which still satisfies the eye in the early season of leaves and growth.

The first of them stands on a significant site, the grave of a neighbour's long-lived dog. For the sake of my garden, I wish it commemorated her cat, but I can only commend her skilful planting. Above the grave, a large urn had been planted with two double-flowered alpine clematis, the pink and slate-blue forms of Clematis macropetala which had been allowed to intertwine before falling forward over the stone slab.

In this unlikely site, the two Clematis made a pair of harmonious colours and had a suitably melancholic air. Too seldom we plant two differently-coloured varieties of the same plant and allow them to mix naturally. These clematis have smaller flowers than the familiar hybrids and open earlier than most of their relations: in America, Blackthorne Gardens supply the two colours, calling them Pink and Blue Fairy Ballet and I suppose there is an airy gracefulness about their flowers. I cannot, however, agree that they are like "graceful fairy ballet dancers with swirling skirts and pantaloons, high kicking and pirouetting to the symphony of spring breezes". Their colour has that touch of grey which gives it a Victorian tone: in Britain, Treasures of Tenbury Wells sell them in a more restrained manner. I recommend the pair together.

Not far from this dog's urn I know a second sentimental planting, composed entirely of that sentimental flower, the forget-me-not. Romance runs through this plant's past, so I will briefly tell it.

It all began at the end of the fourteenth century, when the future King Henry IV was still living out his Part 1 and most Englishmen at court had time to be romantic, the more so since they often travelled and fought in France. To please his supporters, the young King Henry, then Earl of Derby, began to wear the flower called Souvenez Vous de Moi, the French for our forget-me-not. Wearers of the flower, he told his barons, would never be forgotten by their lovers, and such was male vanity that the thought of a lasting memory among so many women attracted the nobility and made Henry's suggestion into a fashion. He even ordered his tailor to embroider him a robe with a collar of blue Ss, standing for Sovereign and Souvenir, remembrance, therefore, of the blue forget-me-not.

Silver thread was used to suggest the plant's leaves, and so distinctive was the result that the emblem S became a recognized proof of allegiance to the House of Lancaster. The Lord Mayor of London still wears a collar of Ss in remembrance of a Lancastrian benefactor. However, was Henry's French forget-me-not the same as the plant we call Myosotis, meaning mouse-ear, because the leaves once reminded some botanist of such an unlikely piece of nature? There are those who insist that Henry's emblem was the blue speedwell, but in the margin of a manuscript copied in his reign, I was once much struck by a long border of forget-me-nots, and I suspect that this emblem had been chosen to suit the king's new fashion.

The forget-me-not which we all grow from seed and bed out for spring flowers is not the same as the flower King Henry patronized. He had been charmed by the Water Forget-me-not, a perennial plant for the edges of ponds or damp gardens where it looks charming in late spring. I recommend Myosotis scorpioides and its little yellow eye: in England, Hopleys of Much Hadham, Herts sell a good Mermaid form and in America, Wayside have a semperflorens form for any damp places in zones three to eight.

By growing this plant, you attach yourself to a royal legend. Henry, however, was only the beginning, and the sequel makes his fashion seem an example of English reserve. Three hundred and fifty years later, when men were searching their romantic souls and arguing that only wild feelings were genuine, the forget-me-not had made a home by the banks of the Danube. Splashed by the river's current it spread by the thousand into a sea of uninterrupted blue. There were many romantic oak trees, of course, moss and a recognized corner where lovers could tie up their horses. A young couple, said a suitable romantic legend, came for a walk there at a great moment in their lives; they were due to be married next day and things were already not going too well. She was telling him that marriages last briefly, and she was not sure that brevity was right for her; she would rather call it off.

As he protested, they saw a forget-me-not being swept downstream on the Danube's current. She took it as a sign and remarked that marriage was as swiftly and easily swept away as one blue flower. How wrong you are, her intended answered, and to prove it he dived into the river and saved the flower with which she had diverted the argument. But the current caught him, too, and away he was swept to his death by drowning, calling all the while 'Forget me not' to the lady he left on the bank.

Poets and musicians have made great play with this soulful German story: to gardeners, forget-me-nots are no longer plants of the river, but bedding-plants to be grown from seed and massed in spring. I have two tips, here. Remember to sow the seed early, at least by the first week in June, so that the plants can build up strength before being transplanted to a rich flowerbed in the late autumn. Forget-me-nots will seed themselves freely, but the seedlings revert to a pale sky-blue. I much prefer the dark blue varieties, the deepest of which is Compindi, sold by Dobies of Clwyd: in America, Park's sell the neat deep Victoria Blue which is almost as good. Keep the flowers away from passing brides-to-be; whether he or she forgets you, a carpet of the deep blue form with white-flowered tulips is always a consolation.

Snakeshead Fritillaries

I come now to my own favourite, the flower which I myself might rescue from the riverbed. As it is the finest wild flower in Oxford and at its best in the meadows of my first College, another touch of sentiment is in place. It derives from memoirs of the 1890's, before the motor-industry had raped the outer city and the fellows of the University had spoiled their own colleges with ill-planned buildings.

'In our perambulations we had come to a place where the Snake's

54

ULIPS AND ROMANTIC FORGET-ME-NOTS AT COURT FARM, BROADWAY

VIOLA ODORATA: *SWEET VIOLETS*
LILIUM REGALE: *REGALE LILIES*

HELLEBORUS NIGER: *CHRISTMAS ROSE*

FOENICULUM VULGARE: *COMMON FENNEL*

Head fritillaries hung their chequered bells. Every Oxford man worth his battels knew them in the month of May round Iffley village or the meadows beneath Cowley, a symbol of the best of the year, the best of the years maybe. In my time the most unlikely sorts of men would pick them from bunches glowing among the grass like green fire. We would come laughingly down the tow-path with our spoils; they may do so still when Finals are afar, the boat runs well and ladies are coming up for the Eights'.

"Unlikely sorts of men" still abound, but the practice, I am happy to say, has changed. An age which harps on "student-vandalism" should remember that its wild flowers are no longer picked indiscriminately and that vandalism also occurred in the past. The snakeshead fritillary still flourishes where the damp meadows persist: its greatest enemies have not been students since the 1890's, but their teachers and the city-"planners" who have built on many of the bulbs' natural homes.

No flower is so mysteriously lovely as our native fritillary. The legends say it grew from the blood of people massacred in France on St Bartholomew's Day in 1572. Nobody would believe that, but in fact a young English apothecary from the Midlands did pass over the field of the massacre soon afterwards and was much impressed by the wild 'snakeshead lilies' which he saw there.

He had some bulbs shipped by a French merchantman to England and later grew them successfully in the garden. Had he known better, he would probably have found them growing wild already in this country; certainly they were known to the Tudor herbalist Gerard, 25 years later, who was at a loss to describe their unique quality. Aptly, he remarked that they were finer and more curious than the best of paintings: fritillaries do indeed have an artistic air about them, a colour and texture that would be well at home in the foreground of a Carpaccio painting. This colour is notoriously hard to describe and varies from bulb to bulb. Generally, they are 8 inches high with one, or even two, hanging bells of six petals, each marked inside and out with a chequered pattern of purple and white alternating squares. Inside, the colour runs more darkly round two central yellow stamens; the stems and very thin leaves are a flattering shade of grey-green. The petals are of a solid texture that feels like close-cut apple peel.

Any description is bound to be clumsy, for the fritillary has such a mixture of qualities. For once, the Latin name is more instructive: Fritillaria (from the Latin for a dicebox), meleagris (from the Latin for a guinea-fowl), a subtle compound, as the flowers do hang down like a dicebox and have the colouring of a guinea-fowl's feathers. The Germans, less appropriately, call them Plover's Eggs, which are a different shade. Country people once feared the fritillary as a plant of doom and gave it rude or ugly names like Weeping Widow or Toad's Head. But standards change, and keen gardeners now value them and their Far Eastern cousins as the most distinctive May-flowering bulbs.

In the garden they must have a wet soil to give their best. They are happy on lime: in a waterside meadow beside a stream or in a wild wet garden they will run and spread freely in hundreds and thousands. They can compete with the toughest turf. If you have a damp place, plant a few dozen bulbs 2 inches deep in autumn. They could hardly be easier to grow. Slight shade suits them better than sun: in America, good stock is available quite cheaply from Weston Nurseries in Massachusetts.

I live on a hot, dry soil which fritillaries do not enjoy for long and I have had to grow my favourite bulbs in pots instead. Here, it needs excellent drainage and some leafy earth in a deep pot, for the roots become long very quickly. Plant the bulbs 2 inches deep in autumn and leave them in a cool, dark place for at least eight weeks. Then, gentle heat will bring them into flower in late March. Though bulbs in pots last well for only a year, it is worth bothering with the more expensive varieties. Aphrodite is a very large white; Charon is dark purple; Artemis a pretty pink-grey and Poseidon a rather unreliable white marked with maroon. All are worth trying, except the contorta varieties whose flowers are shaped like tubes and seem to me to have lost the charm of old meleagris.

Essentially, however, these are not bulbs to be confined in captivity, as anyone who hs seen them in nature will know. In a pot, the flower's markings can be admired at leisure, but in the rare English meadows where they grow wild, the massed effect of thousands is amazing. One of the principles of good gardening is to plant in generous groups, but nature can be more generous than even the most extravagant gardener.

In a meadow in the middle of modern Oxford they are still growing in their thousands, possibly the most dramatic sight in the world of English wildflowers. All around, lorries thunder down their smart new ring roads and 'planners' have tried twice to put concrete in a fritillary-meadow. Protest stopped them, to their surprise. After another seventy years' technology those fritillaries may not be there to remind the 'most unlikely sorts of men' of the very best of the year.

Crown Imperials

Snakeshead Fritillaries are not the only beauties in a huge and beguiling family. I have experimented with others, the jade-green acmopetala (from Amands in London) which is exquisite if grown in a pot, and the rare citrina and pinardii, neither of which I recommend. One variety, however, cannot be so negligently treated, Fritillaria imperialis, better known as the stately Crown Imperial. Dictionaries still refer to it as a common plant which thrives in cottage gardens, but as cottage gardening is fast becoming a myth (though books are now being written on its range and history) I feel justified in urging you to reconsider it.

Among spring bulbs, it has the supreme advantage of being tall, reaching 4 feet by mid-April and thus providing a statuesque background to primroses, anemones, dog's tooth violets and other smaller flowers which grace the ground at the same time. This habit gives it architectural quality and I do not know where else you find it so early among flowering plants. As a result, I like to group Crown Imperials in threes at intervals down a small spring garden, surrounded by sentimental forget-me-nots and the various types of auricula which you can raise from seed.

Not only is this fritillary tall: it is extremely striking, with an exotic air which befits a native of Persia. Its stem is thick with green fleshy leaves, set so like a lily's that early botanists included it in the lily family, a classification which still holds good. At the head of the stem, the leaves are gathered in a thick top-knot, reminiscent of the top of a pineapple but less rigidly arranged. Beneath this green top-knot, the flowers hang in bunches, shaped like the diceboxes from which the fritillary took its Latin name. It is best known in two colours, either yellow or brick-red, though many intermediate shades of pale lemon to outright orange have been selected and named. I prefer the brick-red sort, especially as daffodils provide enough yellow already in spring.

All hanging flowers, especially fritillaries, tempt us to reverse nature and hold the petals up to peer inside. The Crown Imperial is a mixed blessing; as soon as you brush against it, it gives off an extremely strong scent of fox. If you do not flinch from the smell you are rewarded for your troubles. Inside each hanging bell, in the roof of the flowers, are set six white spots in a dark surround. Botanically, these are the nectaries of the Crown Imperial, but historically, they have been fair inspiration for some charming speculation. Like many flowers, the stately fritillary has gained more from our imagination than from science.

Most famously, these spots have been seen as a punishment for atheism. It is said that alone of the flowers at the Crucifixion, the Crown Imperial refused to bow its head in sorrow, feeling that Jesus had got what he deserved. When proved wrong by the Gospel tales of Resurrection, it lapsed into an eternal blush, changing its colour from white to orange, hanging its flowers earthwards, and retaining six white tears of repentance inside as a confession of its error. This slander was mde up in Christian countries; the Crown Imperial reached Europe through Constantinople, being distributed in the mid-sixteenth century by the Duke of Florence's personal doctor. It originally came from Persia where it was eaten as food, and dignified with a more favourable legend.

An Empress called Atossa was wrongly suspected by her husband of infidelity — faith was clearly not the Crown Imperial's strong point — and was changed into an Imperial Fritillary instead. As a symbol of her unjust treatment, she shed six tears which are perpetuated at the base of her flower. Gerard the herbalist even believed the spots were made of imperishable water. He cannot have looked very closely.

Crown Imperials are living monuments to our capacity for unscientific thought. They also pose a problem to scientific study. It is well known that they prefer sharp drainage and a good loam: they are not happy if the soil becomes waterlogged in winter. To help their drainage, you are advised to plant the large bulbs at a slight angle, so that they rest on one side without creating an air-pocket round their base. Nonetheless, for some odd reason, one Crown Imperial will flower quite freely while its neighbour, a foot or so away, will only send up leaves. There is no knowing which bulb will go blind and deny you its flowers in any one year.

Nobody can explain this habit, but perhaps I can reassure you by adding my personal confirmation. I have seen this superb bulb growing wild in mountain-valleys in Iran and even there, it is evident that some groups flower while others restrict themselves to leaves only. If this blindness occurs in your garden, console yourself that it also occurs in nature where the conditions have otherwise sufficed to keep the bulb growing wild since long before its arrival in the West. Do not blame the suppliers: in America, red or yellow Crown Imperials are offered by Westons and in Britain, I buy from Amands, along with other species. May not, after all, the heavens be punishing the Crown Imperials for some historical sin?

Spring

Oriental Cherries

Early May is dominated by the enormous flushes of flower on cherry-trees which we have imported from the East. There is no particular advice to give about their placing, because they are much the same in their vices and virtues, one superb show of flower, then dullness for the rest of the summer. Avoid the flat-topped varieties and be very wary of the weeping varieties, because they are so difficult to place in a convincing context. The upright vase-shaped forms are also tricky: I prefer those which have spreading branches, but not so upright that they look stiff. The whites are vastly preferable to most of the sugary pinks.

We are still rather coy about our Eastern imports. If I asked you to a party to come and see my cherries, you would probably refuse, suspecting a double entendre. However it was not always so. Parties in honour of cherry blossom were the height of civility in Imperial Japan, where a fine show of flower was the test of a gentleman.

'From five to six miles I walk every day in search of you, cherry blossoms', wrote Bashō, the most sensitive of Japan's travelling poets three hundred years ago; nowadays, a walk for five miles around my garden would only reveal a mass of raspberry-pink blossom, mostly of the kind called Kanzan which was never prized in the East. Our nurseries stock only a fraction of the varieties grown in the East and depicted in paintings, on pottery and on finely-worked fans.

But were there ever bullfinches in Japan? I would very much like to know, because an Englishman's sense of melancholy on seeing a cherry in springtime is caused more by the raids of the sparrow and bullfinch than by the brief life of its flowers which so moved the Japanese. It is almost worth growing a cherry tree in order to see a bullfinch set about stripping off the buds, an extraordinary effort of acrobatics, mischief and skilled application of a curved beak.

To be fair, the bullfinch does also destroy insects, which we call pests. In the garden I never bother with any of the commercial bird-repellents because they have to be applied regularly from autumn until early summer and if they fail, as they do, it is always because on a chilly afternoon in March you happened to miss the topmost cherry-branch, thereby spoiling the tree's defences. Instead, I would be inclined to try mothballs. Hang a few on prominent branches during February, and the smell of naphthalene is probably the reason why two growers who use mothballs tell me that for the last three years they have not been bothered by the bullfinch. 'On seeing mothballs hanging in a white-flowered cherry tree': I leave you to compose a suitable Japanese four-line poem, perhaps with the help of a translation of the admirable Bashō, which explains the simple rhythms needed.

The choice of a cherry tree is never easy. I know I hate Kanzan, that blowsy, street variety of raspberry-pink which has as little elegance as a geisha girl in full cosmetics and face powder. My favourite, of the obvious kinds, is Tai Haku, the largest-flowered cherry grown in gardens. Being white, it is also the most sensational. It is said to be less prone to the plundering of birds. It also has a nice story.

Tai Haku, or the Great White Cherry, as its Japanese name means, was still thought to be lost to cultivation only seventy years ago. On a visit to Japan, the British king of the modern cherry tree, Captain Collingwood Ingram, was being shown antique paintings by a Japanese collector, and was much struck by a 200-year-old picture of a white cherry which his Japanese friend admitted had never been seen in Japanese gardens. Artistic fancy was being invoked, when Collingwood Ingram remembered some cuttings which he had taken from a particularly large white cherry in a Sussex garden; the size of their April flowers had seemed a mystery. The Japanese drawing and the Sussex survivors were compared and identified. From one English cherry tree, whose arrival from the East remains obscure, the world's entire stock of Tai Haku has been raised. Of all the large whites, it is the best, but it does need space and it flowers only for a fortnight. Tai Haku has a span of at least twenty feet and matures quite rapidly. It is a glorious tree with which to mark an entrance-way or gate: it is readily available in England and is best planted with the long trunk of a full standard. In America, you must try Wayside, though there are restrictions on shipping Prunus into Arizona, California and Washington.

I am not the best person to recommend a pink-flowered variety, because I find them too opulent or too reminiscent of fussy confectionery. Instead, I will tell my favourite tale of a pink-flowered Prunus, a tale which reflects well on a ruler, even if you do not altogether share his taste.

One of the most noticeable upright pink cherries is called Mikurama Gaeshi. There is a reason for this name. The Emperor of Japan was going to take tea with a lady whose fine handwriting had impressed him. Out drove the Imperial coachmen, postillions and Masters of the Fan down one of those bumpy roads which limited a day's travel to a mere five miles and made Japanese court-life as enclosed as life in a modern city at six o'clock in the evening. On a bank on the Emperor's right grew an upright sort of cherry, ungainly had it not been for the way it bore its apple-pink flowers. Each bud lay close to the branch and showed no stem; the Emperor, who had never seen a forsythia or a delphinium bearing flower branches in the same sort of way, noticed it and ordered the carriage to reverse.

Tea with the ladies was as nothing to an unusual pink show of blossom; the coachmen coughed discreetly, the horses were reined back over the ruts, and His Imperial Dignity, Child of the Chrysanthemum, Son of the Sun, inquired the cherry's name. It hasn't got one, they told him, and when he ordered them to find one, they suggested Mikurama Gaeshi, the Royal Carriage Returns. On drove the Emperor, resolved on a cutting; tea was late and although his pink Prunus is not the most beautiful in flower or shape, it still holds up passers-by in several botanic gardens.

Gardening in Gravel

By May, we have to think more carefully of the balance of shapes and colours and the interplay of formality and informality. My first thoughts arise from the emergent crops of weeds: they tilt in the direction of informality. In May, a wilderness is still fresh and controllable.

Looking at my gravel paths, I feel they could be usefully turned into a garden. Every spring they do their best to sprout seedlings for the coming summer, whereupon I do my best to stop them by soaking them in sodium chlorate; the wind blows the weedkiller on to the lawn, while unpredictable showers wash the remainder where I do not want it. By mid-June the paths are sprouting all over again, and I have to repeat the ritual. But if plants are so determined to seed themselves into gravel, why not let them do it?

I can imagine a gravel path looking pretty, unusual and healthy. There is nothing like a dose of grit and gravel for giving a plant sharp drainage. In nature, of course, it is an obvious accompaniment to plant-life on a mountain. When the last spring snows are melting high on the Dolomites, the more particular sorts of cushion-plant, the androsaces and drabas and rare saxifrages, are saved from being swamped because abundant grit and

61

chippings lie around and beneath them, through which this sudden spate of water drains safely away.

Intense mountain sun and quickly draining rainwater are the combination gardeners struggle to repeat in order to please alpines in the foggy and damp climate of a lowland garden. Gravel, at least, is one alpine ingredient we can distribute generously. A surfacing on a flowerbed helps to stop the moisture evaporating, while handfuls laid underground help those frightful summer storms and winter fogs to drain away. Large plants, shrubs even, will grow in beds of almost pure gravel: the deeper their roots, the less they need to be watered in summer. You probably know that large heaps of gravel remain cool and damp in their centre, even during a heatwave. A bed of pure gravel is too arid for small, shallow-rooting border plants but if it is made to a depth of two feet or so, with good soil beneath and a small proportion of earth inside it, it makes a happy home for evergreen shrubs, rosemary, cistus, daphne, the many hebes and grey-leaved accompaniments. The great English nursery-garden of Hilliers in Hampshire uses deep beds of gravel for just this purpose round the main house and its terrace. Gardeners have been slow to realize the possibilities.

At this point I seem to be hovering between gravel paths and gravel gardens. The difference, I suggest, should be more one of planting than of planning. In the path I would sow or set the many free-seeding rock plants which do not mind being walked on from time to time, though heavy and continuous trampling in nailed boots is more than any carpet-plant will stand. I am thinking of thymes, soapwort, sandwort, the very smallest cotoneasters, sun rose, mints, bugle, golden marjoram, Creeping Jenny, and generous sweeps of self-sown erinus, that most prolific of 3-inch-high tuft-like plants, which brightens up any wall or paved garden in late May with its small spikes of rose-red flowers.

I would not mind if passers-by trod several of these plants to death. Ready replacements would come from seed, their own and other varieties': the best way to grow the little erinus is from seed, which any English catalogue lists. Seeds and gravel go surprisingly well together, leading to some happy reproduction. Since describing the apple-green flowers of the Corsican Hellebore, I have been watching how my own plants of it have seeded themselves abundantly into the adjacent gravel of a path. Interestingly, no seedlings have appeared in the surrounding flowerbed; the stoniness of the path appeals to the hellebore's Corsican origins. I notice, too, how dark blue lavender, spring crocuses and many of the plants on the wall above have made similar second families in the same gravel-path. There are even some young self-sown hebes.

If plants will reproduce in gravel of their own choosing, I am sure this habit could be encouraged where we happen to want it. Perhaps the yellow-green flowered Alchemilla, or Ladies Mantle, is too vigorous for you, but there is no doubt that its seeds will germinate in any gravel which gives them a free run. I can never have too much of this remarkable plant, which first became familiar in English gardens of the 1950's, crept into Europe in the 1970's and is now making an appearance in the better American catalogues (White Farm; Weston). Its fault, however, is the vigour and speed with which it develops tenacious roots and a hard, woody rootstock. If you plant it near gravel, it will colonize it gratefully, but if you leave seedlings where you do not really want them, they will have to be prised out like little sycamores or elders after one season. Control the Ladies Mantle, then, but combine it with other, gentler colonizers, foxgloves, pale evening primroses and the various aquilegias whose common lilac-pink form is detested by exhibitors but always strikes me as a discreet and unusual colour, willing to seed itself anywhere. In an informal gravel bed, you need not worry about the purity of your plants' breeding. Each spring, I would help the seedlings' population grow by broadcasting hardy annuals directly from seed-packets into the gravel. If watered in their first six weeks of life, they will grow away contentedly: to date, I have failed with clarkia, agrostemma and larkspur and succeeded with the glorious deep blue phacelia, cornflowers, toadflax, red flax (Linum) and primrose-coloured Californian Poppies (Eschscholtzia). I have also grown some stunted, starving Love-in-a-Mist.

Not that the main planting in gravel need be seedlings and annuals. To give it shape and bones, I would use several of this book's architectural plants for a permanent setting: bold yuccas at emphatic points in the gravel, elegant acanthus, the fast-seeding fennel, thistly eryngiums and the glaucous-leaved Sea Kale (Crambe maritima) which is neater and greyer in poor soil and produces its honey-scented flowers more freely. In between these emphatic clumps I would scatter the smallest wild geraniums, their close relations the erodiums, any amount of silver leaves, especially the smaller artemisias, campanulas, hebe and, for future benefit, mounds of the silver variegated box, perhaps the most aristocratic of all silver-marked shrubs. Anyway, you catch the idea from these suggestions.

63

The gravel, I think, would be the smaller pea-sized variety, mixed with half its weight of sand and a very small proportion of rich earth and leaf-mould, about four-fifths gravel an one-fifth earth. I would spread this to a depth of a foot below the path's usual surface, and water well after planting. If you like the informality of a garden which seems to be wild and natural but if you do not want the bother of uncut grass and meadows, colonize your gravel paths, set aside a small area of flowering gravel and limit your yearly use of weed-killer. Admittedly, you will have to be careful with the hoe and busy with the hand where previously, you sprayed Pathclear only once a year. In gardening, however, you never get something for nothing.

Horizontal Emphasis

By the middle of May, the weeds are sprouting heroically and at once we all want them out of the way. Can we stop them appearing in the first place? I am sceptical of much that is nowadays promoted as ground-cover: often, it is a plant which begins to weaken after a few good years or else is so coarse and unrestful (like Borage) that it is not much better than a weed itself after flowering. For an easier life, I recommend you to look for shrubs with wide-spreading horizontal layers of branches. If you space them at a proper distance, clear the intervening ground with hormone-based weed-killer and keep it hoed and poisoned till the horizontal shrubs meet, you will eventually have a lasting canopy which will flower, exclude weeds and show that constant theme of this book: a contrasting outline of leaves and branches.

In late May, three horizontal shrubs for this purpose are at their best: two evergreens, one deciduous, each of them easy and floriferous in almost any garden. They are not in the obvious American lists, but the Sunset Guide for Westerners commends them all, so they ought to be available locally in good garden-centres. The first is a newish sort of cherry-laurel, Prunus Otto Luykens. Do not confuse this plant with those awful yellow-spotted "laurels" which parks like to plant round their public conveniences: Prunus Otto Luykens has dark green pointed leaves which shine enough to reflect light. It fans them out on flat horizontal branches, reminding me of a bird which is fanning out its wings on the ground to protect its nest. It only reaches a height of 3 feet. It is evergreen, of course, though that means it sheds a few leaves in spring; it also flowers, bearing short spikes of white flowers in May, which are pleasing but not sensational. Suppose you have wide steps in the garden, perhaps descending from an open gravel space or terrace to sit out on: one or two of these laurels planted beside the stop of the steps would be most emphatic, especially if contrasted with an upright spiky shape, like a yucca or two, so splendid in town gardens, whether gravelled or not, or the admirable Phormium tenax for slightly sheltered gardens. The phormium's variegated form is particularly desirable. Horizontal laurel against a vertical shape is an elementary sort of contrast, but I have never seen many other gardens try it. Admittedly, the phormium is not a plant for zones of climate with frosty winters, but it is tenacious in drier, warmer regions. Elsewhere, I would use the upright Fatsia whose green, fingered leaves are another contrast, much less vulnerable to frost.

You may, perhaps, think that all the blue-flowered ceanothus are vulnerable and that there is therefore no point in considering one for horizontal cover unless you live in California or the drier parts of America where the ceanothus frolics memorably in the wild. No ceanothus is totally winter-proof, but the nearest is indeed a horizontal grower, the remarkable Ceanothus thyrsiflorus repens, sometimes sold for convenience as Blue Mound. I can see no obvious difference between Blue Mound and the Latin-named variety whose flower-colour is anyway variable. The important point is that they both spread rapidly sideways into handsome layers of glossy evergreen leaves, eight or nine feet wide, whose shoots are covered in powder-blue flowers during late May. I have come to value this vigorous plant as a weed-proof layer in the front of shrubberies and tall shrub roses or along the side of driveways where previously, we had to think of periwinkle. In the milder zones of America and on the West Coast, try the similar Ceanothus Yankee Point which is, if anything, even better.

Evergreens tend to be slightly sombre, but leaves are not the primary distinction of the king of horizontal shrubs, at home on very limy soil but also willing to grow on acid ground among azaleas: I refer to the great Viburnum plicatum tomentosum, either Lanarth variety or mariesii. This shrub loses its leaves in winter but brings late May to life with a massive display of white flowers, born flat on upright individual stems along horizontal branches. It is an original shrub which owners of wide spaces must consider before any other deciduous plant. It often turns a vivid colour in autumn and in some Octobers it bears red berries, like its relation the compact Guelder rose. I do not know why the berries occur in some years, not others, but you must be patient, no less than with the deceptively small specimen your nurseryman will send you: this shrub, at least, is readily available in America, from both Westons and Wayside. After five or six years it will be well on the way to a big shrub, some 8 feet tall and perhaps 12 feet wide. It will stand boldly in rough grass, but I like to underplant it with the grey Senecio laxifolius, an infallibly easy shrub in sunshine, where it makes large low mounds for those who wisely trim it back and pinch out the tips of its shoots in late April.

Blue-blooded Violets

I take my leave of spring with a suspicion that the Englishness of English gardening lies partly in its reflections of social class.

Princess Mary, the Princess of Wales, the Duchess of Sutherland, Comte de Brazza, the Duchesse de Parme, Governor-General Herrick, Mrs David Lloyd-George, Admiral Avellan, John Raddenbury, Mrs Norah Church and Mrs J.J. Astor looking as pretty as ever ... No, not a list of those society figures, among others, whom I met at a very enjoyable tea party in the president's tent at Chelsea Flower Show. Instead, they are an extract from the Who's Who of the English garden violet. No other country could have given such exclusive names to the slight variations in a tiny flower. Whatever the botanists do to their Latin, in the English garden there are always society names to be dropped.

At first sight, few flowers seem less blue-blooded than the violet. In woods and hedgerows all over England, six varieties grow wild where they please; in the says of flower-girls, violets sold for a penny, the least aristocratic of bouquets. Nevertheless, this commoner can trace its family tree far back in time; 2300 years ago, Theophrastus, pupil of Aristotle and father of botany, remarked that the most skilled gardeners of his day could persuade the violet to flower in every month of the year. He was referring to our native sweet violet, Viola ordorata, and though we do not have the climate of ancient Greece, in the West Country, at least, this charming wild flower is often out as early as November, continuing until April and early May, the months with which it is more usually associated. Those of you with room to spare in cold frames and greenhouses can still imitate the ancient Greeks and plan your violets to flower whenever you wish: slight heat forces them along very quickly indeed.

However, these wild commoners have no claims to a place at the violets' high table. The plants on its social roll-call are a very different matter. The Duchess of Sutherland is an upper-class beauty: long and spindly in habit, rather fussy about where she goes, insisting on rich food but rewarding her friends with magnificent semi-double flowers. The large outside petals are a pure uncompromising blue but the middle ones are a subtle shade of pink. Like many violets, she has extremely good leaves of dark green. The Germans have renamed her Pride of Frankfurt. She still has the edge over Princess Mary, another semi-double, whose outside and central petals are both rich blue. Mrs David Lloyd-George is easier to please and prepared to put up with poorer soil; her semi-double flowers are an attractive mixture of blue and gold.

Fine though the semi-doubles are, the full doubles are even better. The Duchesse de Parme has light green leaves and flowers of that shade of lavender which reminds me of old ladies; the Comte de Brazza (who sounds like her hot-blooded lover) grows exuberantly with double flowers of racy white. Neither of these foreign grandees beats Mrs J.J. Astor whose dusky pink colouring is indeed unique: she is not too easy to please and is happier in a shady place.

The others are not so well-bred but they flower earlier in the year. Governor-General Herrick is regularly out in February and is extremely easy to grow. Like all these named violets, his flowers are bigger and more clearly coloured than the wild hedgerow varieties. Like the Princess of Wales, he is royal purple, but he also has a very good scent, which she does not. If you want to try violets in pans in a cold greenhouse, he is the variety I would recommend. Outdoors, he flowers so early that he needs protection for foul winter weather. In a cool room indoors he makes an original alternative to the poinsettias and cyclamen of early January.

Of the early varieties, however, Admiral Avellan is the best. It grew excellently in the late E.A. Bowles's great garden near Enfield, where its purple-red flowers on long stems stood clear of their leaves and spread their true violet scent far and wide on clear February days. It is always known as an extremely easy variety. Mrs Norah Church (who does she think she is, anyway?) is more ordinary with dark violet-blue flowers; John Raddenbury is a clear scented blue.

At this point, you must be wondering where you find these high-society names. My list is the result of twenty years' watching and noting in other people's gardens, catalogues now defunct and sources of limited supply. Some, but not all, of these violets I have grown myself: not all of them persist. In Britain, the widest collection I know in a catalogue is offered by Careby Manor Gardens, Careby, Stamford, Lincs: they have the Admiral and the Princess of Wales, Norah Church, John Raddenbury, a good Rothschild and the estimable Elsie Coombs. Herrick turns up quite often and Princess Mary is not extinct. But the other names are keenly sought and I cannot direct you to a willing seller.

All violets are better for some leaf-mould and fertilizer rubbed into their mats of leaves after flowering. Between paving stones or in cool places they are especially good because the earth round their roots is kept damp. None of them objects to shade: all the aristocrats are evergreen, can be divided with care and thus make first-class edging plants in any garden. The advantage of named varieties is that the stems are longer and the flowers are not hidden in masses of leaves.

'When violets grow on brambles ...' was a Greek poetic proverb for an impossibility and with the blue-blooded beauties I have suggested, one can hardly imagine it being fulfilled. In their absence, there are others, unnamed double whites and blues, a pink Coeur d'Alsace, and a long-stemmed red called Windward, but they belong in a more egalitarian world. In America, of course, the choice is more democratic: White Flower have the purple-blue Royal Robe and the healthy White Czar, but Wayside stop at Red Giant and the worthy pink Rosina. A blue-spotted violet has been found in Baraboo, Wisconsin: it is named, quite simply, "Freckles".

SUMMER

Summer

By June, gardens are potentially heavy with scent, the particular fruitiness of heavy-petalled Bourbon roses, the first of the season's stocks, lilies, white tobacco-plants and the pungency of catmint's ash-grey leaves and the cistus's resinous foliage.

'Scents are the souls of flowers: they may even be perceptible in the world of shadows''. Philosophically, this fantasy has little to recommend it: it is no surprise to find it was written by an elderly Frenchman. In a gardener, logic is seldom a virtue, and I would like to believe that the Frenchman had right on his side, for scents are the very essence of the garden. It would also mean that orange-blossoms are destined for immortality.

In high summer, Orange Blossom (or Philadelphus) is the scented shrub which I could least abandon. It grows fast and smells gloriously. All its different varieties have lovely white flowers. Wherever it is, it forces its presence on us: one small gust of wind, and its scent of juicy tangerines, not oranges, is spread for yards around. At night it is almost luminous in its whiteness and among trees or semi-shaded woods it is a surprise that never fails to swamp a visitor's senses.

The only problem is its name: old gardeners sometimes try to call it Syringa which is the proper name for lilac, whereas others know it correctly as Philadelphus. In Greek, the latter means 'fondness for one's brother', a name so appropriate for this friendly plant that we should put up with occasional confusion. Philadelphus coronarius was grown in Elizabethan times and I still think it is among the best. It has four points in its favour: its creamy flowers are small; they are produced earlier than

PHORMIUM TENAX: *NEW ZEALAND FLAX*

ANEMONE BLANDA: *GRECIAN WINDFLOWER*

most other sorts; their smell is not too sickly; it is retained even when the flowers are well faded. This last virtue makes it a wise and unusual choice for pot-pourri. In the seventeenth century it was very widely grown in Italy but there seem to be few traces of it there nowadays. It is extremely easy to grow in sun or shade and can often reach a height of 10 feet. In gardens, coronarius is not the showiest variety, but it has a particular use: it will grow nearly wild among trees, against boundaries, in semi-shade or woodland. It is almost indestructible and tolerates quite a dry soil: in England, Sherrards of Newbury and in America, Weston Nurseries of Hopkinton, Mass. supply good plants, the latter offering stock five feet high which you can never buy in Britain. There is also a golden-leaved form, coronarius aureus, which grows more slowly. It is very striking when in leaf but has fewer flowers and I think it thrives and looks best in semi-shade, unlike many golden-leaved plants. There, it can be massed to give a clump of fresh leaves in early summer, three or four feet high, which are scented from the inconspicuous white flowers on its stems. Its moment of glory is late June, when the leaves are in their golden youth. Afterwards, they fade to a duller, more predictable green and the plant loses its particular charm. Coronarius aureus, in short, is good of its type, but not better than other possibilities: it has not, commercially, crossed the Atlantic.

Nor, I fear, has Beauclerk, a better specimen shrub which grows in an arching manner and has masses of larger cup-shaped flowers of pure white flushed slightly in their centres with a tinge of pink. Most usefully, it begins to flower as coronarius finishes. Eventually, it reaches seven feet and covers itself every year in sweetly-scented flowers.

Good as Beauclerk is, it is not necessarily the best. There are two superb upright forms, one old, one new, both of which have sweet-scented double white flowers. Beauclerk is a possible shrub for an avenue or a large, loose hedge: the two doubles are tall individuals for dominant places in a border, isolation in shrubberies and orchards or emphatic places where walls or paths meet. The older one, Virginal, is too sweet-scented to ignore, although it does grow bare at its base and tends to sparse, unevenly-flowered branches of darkish green leaves. Nonetheless, I love it wherever I have hidden its lower legs. In America, Weston Nurseries and others sell it, rightly emphasizing its fondness for a rich and slightly damp soil, although it will grow quite well in a drier sunny place; Westons also have a shorter form called Virginal Glacier which stops at five feet and which English gardeners would very much like. We have just begun to see the value of another Transatlantic double, the ice-proof Minnesota Snowflake. It combines a heavenly scent and clouds of snowing, scented flowers along its rounded shape, rising to eight feet and curving to the ground. This tough variety is a great Transatlantic discovery, and we ought to see more of it soon in Britain too. Again, its scent is heavy and the effect is as luminous in early evening as a white light. I have chosen to repeat this variety as the main vertical feature of a classic long border backed by a high stone wall.

If you prefer the scent of pineapples to tangerines, you should try the wonderful, purple blotched Belle Etoile instead of Beauclerk. Indeed, I prefer it to all other singles, noting that it has just reached American commerce too, where it is hailed by Wayside Gardens in South Carolina as a long-awaited rarity. In fact, it grows absurdly easily from summer cuttings and is one of the toughest of the entire family: like Beauclerk, it would make a lovely informal hedge or walk.

Ideally, I would plan these orange blossoms for continuity: a splash of coronarius for early June, then Belle Etoile and Virginal and finally, Beauclerk with its chalice-shaped flowers which sometimes last till the third week in July. I often think how well they could be massed in hedges on either side of a rough-mown walk, with a statue, perhaps, at the end: the pity is that none is evergreen, and they lack the firm shape for a mass in a formal garden near a house.

All this imagining sounds rather grand but there are smaller Philadelphus too, Manteau d'Hermine (three feet high with tiny double flowers), Sybille (up to five feet, and my favourite, though British only in commerce) and Silver Showers (a close second, up to four feet and also very lovely: German by origin, it is sold by Wayside and Weston in America too and suits gardeners all over the world). These smaller plants mean that even the small garden has room for a continuity of orange blossom: each is very sweetly scented. I like to try them in a big hole in paving stones with a seat nearby from which I enjoy their wafting scent. And there I sit and wonder whether, after all, their scent is not so strong that it will indeed be perceptible in the world of shadows. For the next world, the Greeks promised us meadows of that dingy asphodel, the Romans agreed and Christianity confined its flowers to members of Paradise only. How nice it would be if Monsieur Joubert were right and scents like the scent of orange blossom did await us all.

Strawberries from the Woods

In case scent is taking over from the other senses in this book, I would like to develop an unfamiliar summer taste. It is not for those who judge what they eat in terms of quantity, as the fruits I will recommend are not a dish to make you feel full. Everybody knows the big fat strawberries of June, but it is their small alpine relations which I urge you to try. They bear fruit almost continuously from June to October and are the least fussy delicacy to grow. Unlike the inflated varieties, Royal Sovereign and others, they need no nets and none of those ugly layers of straw which protect ordinary strawberries from birds or wet earth. For me that is a blessing. One year, we tried to festoon our strawberry bed with a skein of much-publicized nylon thread, and as a result every strawberry we picked brought a train of whispy white 'wool' with it. Nylon is not on its best behaviour in a gusty spring wind.

Alpine strawberries need no protection, because the chattering blackbirds are too stupid to realize how well they taste. They carry their small fruits on upright wiry stems as much as one foot above the ground, and so there is no danger that they will rot on the earth. They are easier to pick, as you do not have to rummage for fruits in the leaves. I have never known them catch a disease and that is a rare recommendation for a strawberry. They need two encouragements: plenty of water, as much as a hosing a day in spring and summer, and plenty of well-rotted manure, especially on light ground. If they are thirsty or starved, they will not fruit properly. I cannot blame them for that.

So much for my panegyric: now, the drawbacks. To enjoy a good helping for four people, you need a lot of plants. Do not think of their crop in terms of weight: half a pound of their nut-like fruit goes a long way. Each individual berry is about the size of a hazel-nut, so you must pick plenty in order to make a meal. The trouble is that they are expensive. In French gardens, you can sometimes find varieties which spread by runners and which would be easy to increase for yourselves. In the trade, there are two varieties, neither of which have this virtue: in England, Baron Solemacher and in America, "Fraises des Bois" Charles V from White Flower Farm, Litchfield, Connecticut, who claim that the French king Charles V in the year 1360 first brought strawberries in from the woods to the dinner table. As a matter of fact, they are wrong. We know from accounts of the English king, Edward III, that "silver paid for the strawberries" was already a royal extravagance in 1328: admittedly, Charles V's staff brought 1200 wild strawberry plants for planting near the modern Louvre in Paris, but they were not the first patrons of the fruit.

It is fashionable to complain that our range of plants is narrowing and that nowadays, we have to buy highly-bred 'standardized' varieties, ignoring good natural forms. There is truth on both sides, but disputers seldom allude to the strawberry's remarkable ups and downs. I will discuss the wild European strawberry, Fragaria vesca, offered as such in America by White Flower Farm: it alone survived in commerce, because its long season could be developed and popularized. A related form, the famous Hautbois, has disappeared from the trade, although it grows wild in Europe and has usefully long stems. Our forefathers would be disgusted: in Jane Austen's Emma, Mr Knightley would touch nothing else, only the "Hautboy, infinitely superior, the finest sort. ....".

The Chilean strawberry has also gone from the market, though admittedly it was not hardy: odder still is the fate of the famous Virginian, Fragaria virginiana, which was the most admired fruit found in Virginia by the early settlers. Plants had raced back to France by the 1620's; the Indians had called its red fruits "wattahimneah", and the first 'New World' travel-books enlarged on its attractions. Even in the 1830's, you could buy twenty or thirty varieties of this form in Europe. Nowadays, I can find none. Fraises des Bois are alpine 'European' Fragarias, and nothing else: we have dropped half the strawberry's history and only maintained this small branch-line.

When planting these small alpine strawberries, you should think in terms of fifty or a hundred plants; as they pass their peak after three years, an alpine strawberry-bed becomes expensive if stocked with pot-grown plants from these sources. The answer, I have found, is to sow seed, available to any country from Thompson and Morgan, London Road, Ipswich: they now offer the golden-fruited alpine strawberry too, a charming visual contrast, so I recommend their easy Fraise des Bois mixed strain. Sow the seeds, for best results, not in spring (as T. and M. suggest) but in September and prick out the seedlings in the next month, wintering them in a cold frame or greenhouse. Plant them out in their bed in early April leaving about 15 inches between each plant and about 3 feet between rows. Miraculously, they fruit well in their first year, but by their third they will need replacing. Their seed is very fine, so you must not bury it in earth. Water a box of firmed seed compost and allow it to drain;

mix the strawberry seed in its packet with a little sharp silver sand; scatter the mixture evenly over the box; dust another thin covering of sand over it and water the whole box once more from a can with a very fine distributor, swinging it to and fro to ensure a light, gentle flow before applying water to the seed box itself. By this method, you will not dislodge the seed with heavy drips of water: continue to water it sparingly until the young seedlings appear by the hundred. Two or three packets allow you to raise hundreds for very little cost.

Alpine strawberries make a stylish edging, underplanting or cover against weeds. They are native to woodland and will flourish in light shade; they are completely hardy; they will grow in towns. They also breach the needless distinctions of accepted taste and practice. Never be afraid to mix the many beautiful fruits and vegetables among your flowers. Much of modern gardening is a battle against the artificial divisions of rose, shrub, herbaceous, fruit and vegetable gardens: all are plants and plants belong in profusion together.

I have only two warnings, one horticultural, the other culinary. Alpine strawberries are extremely hardy and will flourish in climates as harsh as southern Canada, but they are then prone to a habit which a friendly correspondent, Mrs J.M. Dexter, has drawn to my notice. After a frost, they are given to 'heaving'. This habit pulls them up out of the soil, loosening their roots and leaving them exposed to the weather. Each autumn, you should top-dress your alpine strawberries with bracken, pine-needles or débris so that they are safely protected. When frost or snow melts, go round the plants, pushing those which are 'heaving' back into place. Then, they will bear an admirable crop for their three fat years, however cold the winter months.

The culinary warning is that alpine strawberries must not be judged by the taste and shape of garden strawberries. First impressions seem to be powerful, here: either you like their pungent stickiness or you do not. Two small tricks may help to persuade you. Soak your alpine strawberries in caster sugar overnight before eating. Do not spoil them with cream but given them a dash of sweet white wine and serve them in tall glasses. I am sorry that sounds so house-and-garden, but it is an excellent recipe. It is also a very old one: in seventeenth century herbals, I found exactly the same advice, recommended as excellent for "swelling spleen". Myself, I owe it to a great American gardener in exile, who even made alpine strawberry jam from the plants which edged his Irish kitchen garden. On a hot

June afternoon, he silenced us all with the ultimate strawberry-pudding: alpine strawberries and fresh blueberries, mixed in equal parts, enlivened with a heavy dressing of lemon.

Travelling Weeds

At this point, weeds and their profusion force themselves back to my attention. Scents and strawberries are not the sole marvels of a summer garden: weeds are there too, sprouting in impossible places, multiplying in a month's absence and never leaving flowerbeds alone. I remember a thinly-floored cottage which started to crack and move one summer as the great white bindweed thrust up through the dining-room floor, sending trailing stems through the carpet's underfelt and buds between the skirting-boards.

Nonetheless, movement, we are told, is one distinction between plants and animals: animals move, whereas plants do not. Personally, I have never thought of my garden as a zoo, although the herbalists used to class flowering mandrakes as animals and John Parkinson, in the 1620's, classed a unicorn's horn hopefully among objects for a herb-garden. Plants cannot walk, although there is a puzzling, squishy substance called Euglaena which bothers the botanists: it feeds through the walls of its cells, like a plant, while moving about, like an animal. However, plants can certainly travel, spreading in a summer drama whose script is constantly being enlarged.

On calm summer evenings, gardeners can forget what a scramble for position is going on beneath their flowerbeds. Textbooks claim that a single birch tree produces about seven hundred thousand nuts with wings each year. Only one seedling must survive in order to keep the birch-population constant: you and I are on the controlling end of a fight between plants' unwanted progeny. Annually, six hundred and ninety nine thousand birches must fall by the wayside or shrivel on stony ground. Whatever you believe to be the moral of the Parable of the Sower, "many are called, but few are chosen" is a lesson for us gardeners. Chick-weed, groundsel or the puffball fungus are equally prolific, while family-planning among foxgloves is a lost cause.

While so many children are going to waste, some are sure to travel: horticulturally, we live with a constant mobile surplus, like the exposed babies of antiquity or the middle ages. When they appear in our gardens, we should be thankful that there are not more of them, and we should think twice before blaming the usual culprits: dogs, or the neighbours. Quite probably, birds have been the innocent vehicles. Once, Charles Darwin trapped a red-legged partridge and rescued a ball of mud clinging to its leg: when sown in a box, the mud produced more than eighty different seedlings. Birds' messes have produced similar results.

Not that men are absent from the story. In the nineteenth century, a rampant type of marigold, the ill-named Tagetes "minuta", escaped in Australia through the agencies of a visiting Mr Rogers. It is still known locally as Stinking Rogers. It then travelled with cavalry horses from Australia, finding a home in their bales of hay: when their ships put in at the Cape of Good Hope, "Stinking Rogers" hopped from the manger and naturalized itself up-country. Its European arrival was more cautious, as the climate was much colder. It took rumour to spread it, when botanists began to believe that chemical secretions from its roots would help to drive out perennial weeds from cultivated ground. To this day, it is tested in British research stations and displayed in Dutch botanical gardens, where it is thought to kill ground-elder.

Seeds are not essential to these great escape-stories: some of the most reluctant foreign travellers have colonized their new homes, nonetheless. The blue speedwell, Veronica filiformis, arrived in Britain by 1770, having been collected from its native Caucasus. It sets seed very seldom and can only travel by root. It faced a land where speedwells were already established, where every inch of soil was being fought over by countless surplus seeds, and yet by 1950 it had spread all over the British Isles, revelling in Ireland and only faltering in very dry soils. Wherever a scrap of root touched the earth, it flourished. At first, gardener passed it to gardener as a useful alpine plant. Once they discovered its rampageous nature they passed it despairingly to friends. When there were few ignorant friends left, they slung it on to rubbish heaps. From rubbish heaps, it crept to hedges and roadsides, where it now sits, mocking the farmer and the passer-by.

Man, in fact, does as much to spread his own weeds as does any animal. Plants are not always the passive victims: butterworts, sundews, goosegrass or tumbleweed are catchers and clingers, sticking and hooking themselves on to passing feet and hitching a lift elsewhere. Willow-herb and balsams are catapulted from their exploding seed-vessels. Gummed to man's boots or tractor-wheels, the pineapple weed has spread itself all over the country. Yet it only arrived from America a hundred years ago.

This casual transport thrives on man's major disturbances of nature: in the last century, the most extreme disturbances have been bombs and railways. During the Second World War, people in Britain even started to wonder if the Germans were adding flower-seeds to their bombs, and if somebody, somewhere in the Ruhr had a guilty ecological conscience. One night, two bombs dug a huge crater on Box Hill, near Dorking, not far from the old heart of Surrey which Miss Jekyll, the queen of gardeners, had loved. Within six months, its freshly-turned soil sprouted foxgloves and thirty different kinds of foreign plants, mainly European, so that people suspected a chance addition to the bomb itself, a sort of botanical broadside from Germany. This implausible theory was widely believed, until a man admitted that he had sown the seeds from packets while on a walk, because he thought the crater needed cheering up. His interference infuriated field botanists who had been trying to keep records of Surrey's "pure" native flora: in field botany "native" is a shifting concept. After causing botanical chaos, the man's idea came to nothing: the surrounding hazel trees colonized the crater and swamped his wild-flowers within two seasons.

Well-meant efforts at colonization have seldom been so effective as pure chance: I once had a friend who decided to broadcast seeds from seed-packets out of the windows of railway-trains. His particular theory was that the ground between the tracks had been well-manured by generations of passengers, using the lavatory on their journeys to and fro. Perhaps he can still be found on some branch-line in the south, flushing love-in-a-mist through the cistern and maintaining his fight for natural gardens on railway-embankments. Even so, I doubt if his results will compete with nature's railway-marriages: the best gave us a new plant, the rare London Ragwort. This weed is a hybrid child of two exuberant parents, one of which is the squalid or Oxford ragwort, whose story begins in the seventeenth century, when it was sent from its home on Sicily's Mount Etna to the Oxford Botanic Gardens. By the nineteenth century, its prolific seeds had blown far and wide round the city. Then came the Great Western Railway. The trains created a rushing draught, the racks supplied congenial pebbles and the ragwort raced on a one-way ticket to Paddington Station as its seeds blew down between the sleepers. It arrived in time for the Second World War, waited till the bombs had piled up the rubble and then moved into the new open spaces.

Down on the Southern Region's railway, meanwhile, the British sticky groundsel had also decided to move. After years of inactivity, she broke with the green fields and hedgerows, took an Excursion Fare to London and found that she liked the waste-space on bomb-sites, so much so that she, too, spread all over them. On one such site, she met the visiting Ragwort; they mated and produced a hybrid child, Senecio londinensis, or the rare London ragwort: as a penalty for its parents' morals, the London ragwort is sterile.

If the weeds begin to depress you in the full flush of June, you might like to reflect on the forces which you are trying to oppose. They travel on birds and boots, in hay-bales, on tractors and on trains, if not in bombs. A rough Sicilian arrived once in Oxford and took the town by storm: it then caught the railway to London in time for a bomb-site romance with a visiting British female, up from the Southern Region: the sins of the parents were then visited on their sterile offspring. The travels of weeds have an operatic quality which you and I will never contain: check for stray white roots on your boots before you board the next train up from the provinces.

Albion's Roses

A flower which was chosen by Botticelli to be painted round the goddess in his famous Birth of Venus, a flower from which Britain itself was once believed to take its name: if anybody ever offered you the plant behind this evocative history, I hope you would welcome it into the garden even if it ran about like bindweed and looked only slightly less ugly than edelweiss. In fact, ugly is the last thing you could call it. Despite its stirring history, it is in no way a rarity, although surprisingly few gardeners grow or know it now. It is none other than old Rosa alba in its many delightful forms.

Rose alba is the old white rose of York. It has the strongest claim to be the national emblem of England too: the Roman Pliny in the first century AD mentioned that Britannia was also known as Albion and explained its second name by the masses of white roses known to grow there. As alba is the Latin for 'white', it was not an idle guess. It is very possible that what we now call Rosa alba was the rose he meant. Roman Britain suggests many images nowadays, dull ditches and unexplained walls, Caesar taking men from the rear, minor gentry swapping bad Latin over Home Counties' home-grown wine, governors cynically "creating a desert and calling it peace". Historians forget the roses: perhaps a posting to Hadrian's Wall was not such a botanical banishment for men of taste.

In England, there are several old bushes of Rose alba still growing wild, particularly, I believe, in Cheshire. You will see some in rose-collections in America, and there are a few available from Roses of Yesterday and Today in California whose stock, however, is not grown in conditions that always favour transplanting to the different climate of the East Coast. Here, you might as well import your plants directly from England: Peter Beales, of Attleborough near Norwich, Norfolk is a leading supplier with many albas and is willing to arrange export and advise on any necessary documents.

The alba rose is worth this trouble because it is extraordinarily tough. I have never seen Rosa alba with disease and if you prefer the old roses to the latest scarlets from the floribunda breeders, you will know how valuable that virtue is. Many of the most luscious old Bourbons, Hybrid Perpetuals and so forth suffer recurrently from black spot or mildew and only nostalgia induces us to try them. But alba is different. It even thrives in semi-shade or, better still, against a cold north wall. I have seen it as a wonderful summer hedge or as a bush, centuries old, fighting its way into flower among a wilderness of weeds. There is much good sense in growing the plants that are known to like life in the wilderness.

The most beautiful form is alba Celestial, one of those roses which looks its best when still in bud. It is the most remarkable shell-pink, a very pure shade even when the small double flowers are open. It grows into an elegant shape, upright and with branches of exquisite silver-grey foliage which go so well with every shade of pale pink. 'Ah', say the sceptics and the lovers of hybrid teas, 'but it only flowers once'. Maybe, but so do magnolias and it would be a good thing if roses as strident as the red and yellow Masquerade were restricted to one short burst too. Better to have beauty once than harshness all the summer.

Queen of Denmark runs Celestial a very close second. Its fault is its straggliness, but if alba roses are pruned very hard in late December, this failing can be overcome. Its flowers are luxuriant, showing a darker pink at the centre and a paler pink at the outside but always heavy with ruffled petals, the sort of colour you contrive if you mash raspberries with cream. The leaves are grey-green and look excellent if the bush is trained against a wall.

Two close relations have the same range of colouring, but unlike

Queen of Denmark, they do not combine it at one time in one flower. Felicité Parmentier is cream when in bud, turning to double white when first open and a pale pink when ageing and about to fade. Its flowers are the smallest of the alba roses, but they have an exceptionally charming form, like a perfect pom-pom. The leaves are also very handsome, another distinction of this class of rose: when choosing roses for one of the most prominent beds in Oxford, I took my starting-point from the setting of Georgian architecture and exquisite wrought-iron railings and picked Felicité Parmentier as the most classically-formed alba rose available. She has rewarded my trust, flourishing without any disease among dark purple Lavender Hidcote, silver-grey shrubs and artemisias and pink and white penstemons for the autumn season. On bigger bushes, the same range of colour is spanned by an alba rose called Great Maiden's Blush: the French call it Aroused Maiden's Thigh, untranslatably, and Vita Sackville-West adored it. It does have the freshness of its name and no old rose enthusiast should omit it.

These later varieties are not the plants which Pliny knew or which Botticelli or Giotto decided to paint: the nearest to their old roses is alba maxima, a taller bush with double pure-white flowers which are as charming as their history. The semi-double semi-plena is well worth growing too, for it has a very distinguished history. The story goes that this was the rose which the Scotswoman Flora Macdonald gave as a farewell present to Bonnie Prince Charlie, the "Young Pretender" to the throne of Britain in the eighteenth century. Certainly, it is still seen in Scotland and the story may well be true.

It goes without saying that all those old albas are deliciously scented especially if they are planted in the sun. For three weeks in June you can revel in their scent of honey and spices for very little trouble indeed. Six hundred years ago, a gardening monk in Britain remarked how his white roses, surely Rose alba, made bushes with trunks many times thicker than a man's arm. Cultivation has improved since then and Albion's rose should do even better in your gardens.

Wilson's White Lilies

Except for the pointed stake, the use of the motor mower or the wonky ladder, gardening is a relaxation, a pleasure which has little to offer to those in search of danger. Nothing is more satisfying than a well-grown garden in midsummer with flowers to delight the senses and the problem of why we enjoy them to occupy the mind. Beside me now, there stands a clump of white July lilies, Lilium regale. Overwhelmed by their powerful scent and the purple exteriors of their trumpet flowers, today, at least, I vote them to be my favourite flower. Nothing could be more peaceful and nowadays regale lilies are familiar friends. But it was not always so. Behind their innocent white flowers stretches a tale of high drama. What I am now enjoying derives from one man's bravery in the face of extreme danger.

A regale lily may look as though it has been in our gardens for centuries. In fact, it was not discovered until 1910. In that year, Ernest Wilson, the noted plant collector from Chipping Camden, had been sponsored by Americans to return to China, the happiest of hunting grounds for enterprising botanists of the day. He headed for the Min Valley, on the borders of Tibet, an ignored area known only from native rumours. One midday, descending into the river gorge, he was met by a sight which has guaranteed his gardening reputation. All over the banks of the precipice grew Lilium regale, as we now know it. 'Surrounded by mountains of shale and granite', he later wrote, 'whose peaks are clothed with eternal snow, the regale lily has its home, not in twos or fives, but in hundreds, in thousands — yes, in tens of thousands'.

Ernest Wilson liked to travel in a sedan chair; halting in the ravine, he sent his Chinese coolies to collect the bulbs as abundantly as they could. Thousands were dug up until, ominously, the shale began to slip and the rockface slipped forward in an avalanche. Over went the sedan and Wilson was crushed by a boulder on his leg, while his men scattered in horror.

He lay trapped for hours until his servants returned to his rescue, prised him free and stretched him on the road to inspect the damage. While they did so, a train of local mules ran by; Wilson was in no condition to be moved. The only road was so narrow that he had blocked it, and all fifty animals clattered over his body in order to go past before the avalanche began again. Despite the shock of their hooves passing inches above him, Wilson clung on to the remaining bulbs, determined to bring them to safety. Ingeniously, he set his broken leg in the remains of his camera tripod and was hoisted on to his bearers' shoulders to be carried for three days back to base. There the leg festered and was nearly amputated, but the lily bulbs, some six thousand, were shipped at once to Boston. Wilson recovered and was fit enough to walk for another twenty years, but his valley has never been revisited since. From that original stock all the regale lilies in our gardens are now grown, one of the great collections which American patronage first brought to the "Englishman's garden". It is still widely available in the U.S.A., being well supplied by Breck's Bulbs, Illinois, among others.

Few bulbs have been so harrowing to collect, but no lily is so delightfully easy to grow. For any garden, big or small, it is essential. In a town, if space is scarce, it can easily be planted in pots, three bulbs to a width of 7 inches, and put outside on pavings or terraces. It needs a covering of 4 inches of soil above the top of the bulb; a top inch or so of mulch is a good idea and it does not mind lime.

This lily's home, as described by Wilson, explains its toughness: it grows in terrific heat in summer with sudden thunderstorms which are too violent for man or beast. In long dry spells it can be disappointing, growing shorter and flowering very briefly. Obviously, lack of water is to blame. Like most lilies it is happiest when sited with other plants around its roots. Its 4-foot stems look especially fine when emerging from silver leaves. Try planting a grey artemisia like splendens or discolor above it and allowing the lily to come through this curtain each year. The grey leaves stop it looking naked and are an excellent foil to the flowers, which are wine-purple outside, white inside, and yellow in their middles.

Its particular merit is the ease with which it grows from seed, a fitting recompense after the trouble of introducing the original stock. You can easily collect your own seed when it ripens in August: sow it at once, preferably in some heat. By late September the seedlings should be transplanted 6 inches apart in open ground. They may well flower in their second year and will certainly honour you thereafter. By sowing a little seed each year you can build up a big succession of lilies for no cost at all. Like every lily, regale moves best in the autumn, not when dry in spring, for no lily bulb is ever dormant. Unless you grow your own, you cannot contrive this type of move: no nursery will supply you with bulbs when they are still in leaf. In the U.S.A., Park's and in the U.K., Thompson and Morgan sell good seed of the regale lily.

On a summer's evening this lily is the most soothing of flowers and its scent uplifts the gloomiest corner of the garden. Its loveliness is an added reason for remembering Ernest Wilson; peaceful though a garden is, it too has been bettered by the efforts of brave men.

Lesser-Known Lavenders

Lavender is a plant which everybody knows and many people grow but its popularity has never made it common. It is as well to remember that this can be so, as gardeners tend to divide themselves into two groups: those who like to grow what they see repeatedly in other gardens (the motor car has had some influence here, as it has made it possible to look out of the window at nothing but forsythia and floribunda roses) and those who only like to grow what others will find difficult to recognize.

The connoisseurs look down on the copycats; the copycats become aggressive in defence of their marigolds and I have known old friends become quarrelsome about the relative merits of stocks and sarcococcas. Each side has a firm hold of part of the truth but they are convinced that the part which they hold is the whole. Yet there are plants to bridge their differences, none more appropriate than the lavender, a familiar flower, often planted, but still a choice for the connoisseur. Lavender has a long and respectable history, spreading westwards from the Mediterranean to the medieval gardens of the monks, and from their monasteries to the formal parterres of the seventeenth century. The white variety was much favoured by Henrietta Maria, the 'blue' by Miss Gertrude Jekyll, most perceptive of garden planters in the Edwardian age. This Mediterranean origin suggests its use in the garden. Lavender is a plant for an aromatic border, breathing the smells of last year's summer holiday; in a small garden, many people plant drifts of lavender along the path to the house. Beneath the house I would mix the less common varieties of lavender with aromatic cistus and the pungent helichrysum, allowing a few golden marjorams and lemon-scented thymes (called citriodorus) to spill forwards over the path. A daphne for spring, either the Somerset variety or the sweet odora aureo-marginata, the wide-spreading, golden-leaved hardy Fuchsia Graf de Wit for autumn, and I would have a planting to be enjoyed throughout the year. The winter iris (called unguicularis) could be added beneath a south wall to brighten the heart in January.

In this company Lavender has a rare freedom of flower, an appealing range of colouring and a gentleness of outline. There are those who complain that for three-quarters of the year it looks spiky and awkward, but this is a view which I do not share; the different varieties should be used differently and only in the wrong place do their faults become too obvious. Lavenders do have one maddening habit against which you must be warned; after six years or so they begin to grow leggy and sometimes catch a disease which makes them die out in bits and pieces, leaving a healthy branch or two to encourage you to spare them for another season. A hard trimming after the bushes have flowered can help to delay this degeneration but even so, you can only look on lavender as a short-lived feature. As soon as the plants become patchy, throw them out. When planting them on heavy clay soils, I dig in a liberal dose of sand, as the lavender is a native of the seaside and thrives in the lightest earth. Even on sand, cuttings must be kept to replace the middle-aged parents. Never waste money buying lavender in dozens or hundreds. Short cuttings taken in April or August are absurdly easy to root and are ready for their permanent home within nine months of leaving their parent.

In order to enjoy lavender, you should know the varieties to suit your purpose. As a drift between evergreen shrubs and topiary or an edging to gravel paths, the neatest kind is the dark lavender Hidcote, 18 inches tall and grey-green leaved. Although it is rather desolate in winter, it makes a very subtle picture in July when thick-set with its spikes of indigo flowers, like coloured ears of wheat. In England, I like to buy my lavenders from John Scott, The Royal Nurseries, Merriott, Somerset, a reliable source of all varieties; in America, Hidcote and the paler blues are offered by Weston, Wayside or White Flower Farm, so there should be no problem.

The paler blue varieties, Munstead or the open-spreading Twickel Purple, are taller and less emphatic: they have their uses where you want a higher hedge or softer colour, perhaps beneath the alba roses which we have just discussed. Below the white flowers of the Philadelphus, I prefer the deeper indigo-blue of Lavender Hidcote; among the pinks and pinkish-whites of the old roses, the softer more traditional "lavender" is more effective. The plant is particularly precious because it comes into flower in early July when the blues of lupins, veronicas and delphiniums are fading. One of my favourite plantings has been the vigorous orange-red Lily Enchantment among Munstead lavender: this lily is the strongest and most lime-tolerant variety which modern breeders have raised.

If you hunt around, there are, as always, other good forms. I particularly like Lavendula alba, the 'white' lavender which is really a special shade of grey-white. In its smallest form, known by one nursery as Baby White, it is only 9 inches high, very slow growing and extraordinarily aromatic. Its branches are easily broken, and as soon as they are rubbed,

84

they smell of the strongest lavender bags. The place for this obliging plant is a hole in paving or a dry wall; there, it will spread very slowly to a width of a foot. Even after nine years, my oldest plant shows no sign of disease. This, I believe, refutes those who think lavender can only be massed for the sake of its flowers, for this small shrub is always tidy and one specimen suffices on a terrace or in a wall.

One of the simplest tricks with lavender is the least used: try mixing the lavender-blues with a pink form, Loddon Pink or the vigorous pink-white Jean Davis, available in America from Wayside, South Carolina. I first saw this combination in the garden of a great connoisseuse who had deployed it on either side of her gravel paths: it was so elegant that her children, I later discovered, had copied it when they had gardens of their own. She recommended one lavender-blue to every two pinks, as the pinks were the paler colour, especially true of the American Jean Davis form whose vigour is still neglected in England. Like all lavenders, these varieties grow very easily from cuttings taken in the month after flowering: anyone can root these plants from short tips of their own growth, as I will shortly explain. A secret of successful lavender-gardening is to keep a store of young rooted cuttings growing on as replacements each year. From two or three bushes, you can quickly develop your own economical hedge.

Lastly, there is a special, eccentric lavender for gardeners with warm walls and a low incidence of frost. Lavender Stoechas is the lavender of southern France which smells powerfully of seaside pines; it is barely two feet tall, but its regimented heads of purple flowers are softened by a tuft of upturned lavender bracts, like coloured leaves. It looks rather impudent and it pays for its insolence in very severe winters by being cut to pieces by frost. I like it very much indeed and when in flower, it reminds me of a flight of deep violet insects, hovering above a bush of grey-green leaves. Cuttings allow you to perpetuate it, if you winter a few indoors: it is much less hardy than other lavenders, as I can best emphasize by remarking that in the United States, ordinary pinks, whites and Hidcotes are rated as hardy in Zone 5 of the climate map, whereas Stoechas is hardy in Zone 9, four zones above them. So you have all been warned.

Inspiring Visits

While the lavender is in flower round the disease-free alba roses and

SCENTED CYTISUS BATTANDIERI WITH SOLANUM CRISPUM
PHILADELPHUS BEAUCLERK: *MOCK ORANGE BLOSSOM*

PHILADELPHUS BELLE ETOILE: *MOCK ORANGE BLOSSOM*

your self-sown clumps of regale lilies, you may not feel like leaving your own garden and wasting your weeks of triumph on a journey to anyone else's. This feeling is best resisted. In high summer, we can all learn from other people's golden moments, realized in different gardens: even if they have nothing to suit our particular site, we can still learn by wondering how we would have gardened in these new surroundings. Comparison stretches the imagination.

Over the years, I have learned most from a garden which is a famous series of gardens, none too grand to be applied in principle elsewhere. Sissinghurst Castle, in the Weald of Kent, has been made famous as much through the pen as the spade. Its slow accumulation of features and firm outlines was described for ten years in the finest of all gardening columns by its creator, Vita Sackville-West. If there are still gardeners who do not know her writings, after the hundreds of thousands who have read them in books and newspapers and visited Sissinghurst as a result, there is a recent, broad selection, published by Michael Joseph and Athenaeum in 1986, which I had the pleasure of editing.

The gardens at Sissinghurst now belong to the National Trust and are visited by over 100,000 people each year: in June and early July, it is the place to which I would go before all others in order to see the variety of a classic "English" garden. On a recent visit, as I walked under the first of the castle's old brick arches and watched the white pigeons flap off the lawn like a pack of cards, I was at once struck by how much of this great garden has been stolen and copied by others. Old-fashioned roses, white gardens, informal planting in formal design, roses up fruit trees, fruit trees in borders, broad-headed onion flowers in beds, again, of old roses: I dare say there were models for most of these ideas before Miss Sackville-West applied them, and certainly she owed some of their detail to the general influence of the great Miss Jekyll. But I am sure that her writings and the success of her own garden are the reasons why they recur in other great "English" garden plantings, from Kiftsgate to Killerton, from Cranborne to Crathes Castle.

The Sissinghurst style, with a few Versailles tubs and a few of the newly-fashionable green flowers, has become the ideal of gentlemanly taste, the copse and serpentine lake to the twentieth century's Bathursts and Burlingtons. There have been few artists since Poussin who have laid down for so many people what a particular sort of landscape should look like; imitators usually simplify, and the pupils of V. Sackville-West seem to me to have overlooked one necessary part of Sissinghurst.

It is not just a garden of pale restraint and civility, although it is closed to French marigolds and scarlet salvias. The cult of the pastel colour and the sensitive sweep of grey and silver seems to me as much a proof of deficient taste as the beds of bright blue lobelia and china pink asters which the country-house class disdains as too common. Most of history's civilized tastes have also drawn on an exotic strand, a bold expression of all that their civilized ideals of restraint and balanced harmony would otherwise deny them. V. Sackville-West valued warmth and generous richness in colours of her flowers. Just as the patrons of classical Georgian houses had a taste for Oriental romances, for gipsy tales and poems set in the East, so this planter of a classically formal garden drew on the gorgeous store of the East for the comparisons and combinations which made her garden and her writings so distinctive.

A mass of pansies seemed to her like a Persian carpet; wine-purple roses suggested damasks and Isfahan: she planned for the peacock colours of the tigridia and the columbine as much as for the silver-leaved pears and the white climbing roses which others now copy and admire. Her passion for the old roses, which she did so much to revive, was mixed with a love of Provençal sunshine, tapestry and the romantic colours of the Crusades. She would have understood that some of the finest roses that I have seen were not in Queen Mary's rose garden in London but wild, white and single-flowered in the Afghan foothills north of Kabul. Her garden was not an "English" garden at all.

Sissinghurst is well known as a garden of compartments, of yew-hedged rooms for different seasons, privacies and firm straight lines. It is less often seen as a bright carpet of warmth and colour, though much of it was planted in order to develop this idea. The cottage garden of reds and yellows is not just a small variation in a grand, sober plan. It is central to the colour-sense and style of the whole place: the mixed colours of the ordinary Aquilegia or columbine, which we can all grow from a packet of seed, are to my mind the emblem of Sissinghurst in summer. A courtyard filled with columbines was one of Miss Sackville-West's ambitions, but it is not the one which many of her followers still copy as her example.

Under the care of the National Trust, Sissinghurst is astonishingly well gardened, so that one takes it for granted that there are no weeds, only the rarest sign of mildew on all its countless roses, and that every old rose bush is trained on stakes and pinned perfectly to walls. But it is not a daunting garden, too perfect to be an encouragement. At all levels, it is a source of subtle groupings and pairings of shrubs, leaves and coloured flowers, the dimension in which gardening becomes an art. To achieve the best, you have to see an idea of it, in order to fire your imagination and show you the possibilities. Shrubs, especially, are plants with a long time-span and you cannot be sure, when picking them at random, how they will develop and fill out.

At Sissinghurst, I would like to pick out two plantings at either end of the scale, one dark, one white, both of which are adaptable to other sites and purposes. The dark planting springs first to my mind when I think the garden over, and I suspect it began with the owner herself. It is very simple and obliging.

Beneath a pink brick wall of the front courtyard the dark velvet flowers of the purple-black Pelargonium Lord Bute shows through a group of the navy blue-purple Cherry Pie or Heliotrope, in its deepest and richest form. Beside the pair of them grows the ash-grey and pink-leaved Fuchsia tricolor in its tough, variegated form. This small shrub changes the shading of its leaves from pink to grey-green throughout the summer, according to the youth of its shoots and the diligence of the bugs which obligingly eat the leaves as they age and become drab. These three plants have the warm opulence which their owner loved, and the heavy scent of Cherry Pie in sunshine gives the planting an even richer tone. To copy the idea, sow Heliotrope Marine, available in England from Dobies or Thompson and Morgan; in America, from Park's or Burpee.

At the other extreme, away behind its dark green hedges, Sissinghurst's white garden has made more impression on the British gardening public than any other planting of the past thirty years. Even since Vita Sackville-West conceived it, survived the doubts expressed by her correspondent husband Harold Nicolson, and turned it into the effect she outlined in her first note about the idea, white gardens have been very much in the night air of English country gardens. I can think of fifteen, at least, only two of which are suited to their surroundings. Such is the power of photographs and prose as entertaining as Miss Sackville-West's. I was prepared for a disappointment when I first saw the mother of them all.

Disappointment was not a possibility: the effect of Sissinghurst's white garden on an evening or early morning in July is indeed astonishing. By close inspection you can see how art has softened and varied the original idea of whiteness.

There is scarcely as much white in the garden as silver, not only the silver of the magnificent silver-leaved weeping pear tree (Pyrus salicifolia pendula, which you should place carefully) but also the silver of small Convolvulus cneorum, the marvellous cut-leaved Senecio leucostachys and the felted grey round leaves of Helichrysum petiolatum, both of which are excellent accompaniments to a summer border. The easy-growing Lambs Ear, or Stachys lanata, is another fine accompaniment, supported by the silver of tall Onopordon thistles, the lovely carpet of Artemisia schmidtiana and a new form of Hebe called Quicksilver which will, I hope, become prominent in future nurseries' catalogues. Grey-green Eryngium giganteum has seeded itself charmingly and there are mats of the grey-green Hebe pagei, a readily available plant for any dry soil: we, too, can raise the ghostly-green Eryngium with ease from seed, sold by Park's or Thompson and Morgan.

Among them, of course, there are also the white flowers, the tall white haze of the imposing kale (Crambe cordifolia, so bold in early July), easy white Galega and the neglected Eupatorium, white everlasting pea (Lathyrus, from seed), several hardy white geraniums (especially the forms of pratense, the Meadow Cranesbill), the white "pink" (Dianthus John Gray or Mrs Sinkins, though the new long-lasting Haytor would be even better) and tall delphiniums which could be the huge white Swan Lake variety. White tobacco plants and other daisy-flowered annuals reinforce the impression, while the garden's centrepiece is a famous cascade of white. Originally, it had been composed of four white almond trees, but when they died, they were replaced with a pleasing frame of iron on which roses and white climbers could be trained. The central rose Bobbie James is memorable, commemorating a great forgotten English gardener whom Miss Sackville-West particularly admired. White clematis keep it company, the lovely Marie Boisselot with her huge flowers, elegant Henryi and the August-flowering viticella alba which even the experts tend to overlook, to their cost.

Perhaps anyone could have amassed these and other white-flowered plants, but by a stroke of genius, they are matched with the deep green of clipped Box edging, pretty frames of Box for the undersides and arms of a garden-seat and a subtle use of glaucous leaves and grey-white flowers for contrasts. Whoever suggested the slate-white hanging flowers of a campanula called burghaltii deserves a prize for ingenious planting. In full flower, this abundant plant takes the edge off the bright whiteness of the main theme, for white is itself a very strong colour. This grey-white campanula is well mixed with the glaucous leaves and flowers of hostas, and the grey-white spots on the leaves of the ordinary spring-flowering Spotted Dog or Pulmonaria, a plant which is untidy elsewhere but improved beyond recognition by its surrounding of bright white flower and dark green yew hedges.

Like grey, some greenish-yellow flowers and dark evergreen leaves bring the best out of white which is concentrated in small, bold groups: I suspect I am right in accusing the National Trust of introducing too many white Iceberg roses into the original off-white design, as Iceberg was barely in commerce when Vita Sackville-West died. It is an interesting warning that in a white garden, two-thirds of this white rose would be better removed for being too blatant. I would rather see the white valerian, a plainer and softer flower.

But there could be no question of moving the garden's glory, surely planted in the first design, a thriving clump of the lily-like Cardiocrinum, whose glossy rounded leaves rise to a height of seven feet. They bear enormous downturned trumpets of sweet white flowers and sum up the whole strength of the garden's whiteness. There is no more spectacular plant, but I have never made it grow, perhaps because I own no shaded woodland. This giant lily is happiest in leafy soil.

The charm of this famous white garden, in fact, is that it is not entirely white. By all means imitate it, but the one idea of whiteness, blueness or pinkness makes only a collection, not a garden. You may feel that it is timid to copy others' ideas; you may wonder whether a garden based on black-purple against a grey-leaved hedge might not be an alternative. But if you go white by night and enjoy your own small Sissinghurst on a summer evening, I cannot blame you for copying something so lovely. I doubt, however, if you will balance the result so beautifully again.

Down with Herb Gardens

When a lady first comes into possession of a country garden, she begins to think she wants a patch of herbs. Near the kitchen, she thinks, so that she can hurry out and pick bunches of fennel for her boiled turbot; plenty of variety, she hopes, as books are always talking about hyssop for the honey, tansy for head-colds, rue for brown bread sandwiches, and lashings of penny-royal, which is said to cure depressions. So, next Christmas, her husband gives her a novelty pack of herb seeds from the huge range of Park's or the U.K.'s Chiltern Seeds in Cumbria; he clears a patch near the kitchen and leaves her to learn that weeds are determined, winters cold and recipes often misleading.

Herbal lore and country remedies are two fields of knowledge which I have no wish to master. I would rather buy jam and have time to raise more seedlings than spend three days in making jelly from home-grown fruit. Cans save the bother of bottling; peppermint tea seems less effective for headaches than a dose of aspirin. Count me out, if it is old wives' cunning you are wanting, as one of the twentieth century's achievements is to have killed it off. Morris dancing still lingers but, on the whole, we have taken the olde-tyme merriness out of the countryside. About time too, and as a gardener, not a cook, I feel the same about most herb gardens.

Herb gardens have a way of intruding into designs by default. You have placed the roses, the herbaceous, the lavender edging and the blossoming cherries, and you are left with an awkward rectangle behind your newly planted hedge, preferably not a hedge of brilliant green conifers if you value this book at all. Somebody mentions herbs as a romantic addition to every country garden, so you seize on the remaining rectangle and begin to plan camomile paths, small thyme lawns and a clump of heart's-ease to keep out visiting witches. Dressed in a frilly sunhat, madam will be able to trip down to cull basil and strew it in her trug, while fumitory protects her from pixies, the scent of tarragon deals with her neckaches and the valerian gives her cat the amorous time of its life. A small adjustment of the bodice, and we might be back in the fifteenth century.

No, most emphatically, a herbery is not for me. Obedient to recipes of the great French chef, Boulestin, I have eaten rue sandwiches and tried to pretend they were helping my eyesight. I have picked the candied angelica off party cakes and wished, from the earliest age, that this green-flowered garden plant was kept out of the pâtisserie. Dandelion wine is a perversity; less so, nettle soup, but I would never choose to pick the ingredients. For gardeners, herbs mean hard work, frequent renewal and, usually, a patch of unkempt ugliness.

As a general garden rule, I do not like segregation: gardens for herbs go against the grain. I like to see vegetables among flowers in the front garden, and I would only consider a rose garden if I was allowed to underplant it, a habit, incidentally, which does not harm the rose bushes as long as they are heavily fed with liquid manure. Most of the herbs are rank-growing and floppy and at their least tidy when flowering or flowered. In an exclusively herbal corner, they often look boring rather than romantic. I prefer to separate them and put them to their different uses.

Take tarragon, for instance; this seems to me to be a culinary necessity, if only for roast chicken or tartar sauce, and yet it is lanky and extremely dull to grow. It insists on a well-drained warm soil, and together with basil, another undistinguished plant, it is as difficult to please as any herb. In a herb-garden, it cannot compete with tansy, one of the bitterest and least sympathetic plants, or with wormwood, so much uglier than the other artemisias and useless unless you are being crucified, or with woad, which dyed our fore-fathers blue but is quite incapable of turning us green with envy. Yet herb gardens often combine all four of these herbs in one bed. Naturally, I do not ban all herbs. It is just that so few find their way palatably into cooking, and it is sentimental to pretend that the rest are of such garden value that they deserve a corner entirely to themselves.

Among the exceptions, I include fennel, so decorative in youth and middle age: once you have it, it does its best to stay with you, as its yellow-green flowers quickly set seed and then spill seedlings far and wide. The leaves of young fennel are charming, but the roots are a serious menace. They develop as rapidly as carrots: they fork, thicken and put out anchors so that you can hardly extract them. Fennel is a plant which typifies the quality of so many herbs: charming, in an odd way, but almost uncontrollable.

Less arguably, rosemary is a herbal necessary, for its appearance as much as for roast chicken (you must be thinking I eat nothing else); the finest mint is the white variegated form, which can hold its own in any shady border, besides adding flavour to the new potatoes. Hyssop is a charming autumn shrub, although herbally futile unless you keep bees. It is not that I am hostile to herbs but rather to herb gardens and the useless recommendations which herbalists try to foist on to gardeners. I quote, for instance, the virtues of cumin, one of the washiest of purple weeds. It 'occurs in the Bible, heals the eyes; adds pallor to the cheeks and prevents fickleness in love'. You can stop your cumin, as far as my garden goes: give me a myopic, weathered face and an inconstant heart, but please keep these Scriptural weeds away from gardens which have any sense of style.

Taking Cuttings

"When all is said and done, is there any more wonderful sight, any moment when man's reason is nearer to some sort of contact with the nature of the world than the sowing of seeds, the planting of cuttings, the transplanting of shrubs or the grafting of slips? It is as if you could question the vital force in each root or bud on what it can do, what it cannot and why".

So thought St. Augustine in one of his less intransigent moments as a north African bishop: in his later years, it did not occur to him that faith, too, can be propagated as gently and peaceably as an oleander. Some 1500 years later, keen gardeners still share that contact with nature which he had the insight to appreciate; gardening is seldom more satisfactory than when it raises new children from old.

Midsummer, perhaps especially the early weeks of July, is the moment at which to be busy. Many good shrubs have flowered and are sending out the right kind of young wood: anything which roots can be potted up and coaxed into a separate life before winter interrupts it. In my garden, the process runs continuously from late June until late October: I begin by trying to propagate shrubs, roses, pinks and spring-flowering alpines; I move on to the less hardy plants of which I have already written for terraces, scented corners and odd accompaniments. October sees a flurry of cuttings from silver plants, penstemons, verbenas, fuchsias and a host of half-hardy daisies and pelargoniums, including Sissinghurst's dark Lord Bute. They must all be stored safely in cool frames before the frost starts to spoil them: next year's summer garden is created in the previous autumn.

For some reason, amateur gardeners are scared of cuttings. They think the business is beyond their talents, and when you offer them a piece of Ribes or willow, they decline, saying that they will never be able to root it. In some families, multiplication by cuttings is ludicrously easy. Last March, I sowed different kinds of violet in an old kipper box and as I had to keep each variety in its own compartment, I partitioned them off with thick twigs of yellow dogwood, cut haphazardly and shorn of its leaves. None of the violets came up, but in their place I had four new plants of dogwood. They had rooted along the twigs which were lying flat on the seed box for two months. I now discover that some types of cuttings do not even need any soil. In April, I cut a few branches of the red Ribes, or flowering currant, and put them in a vase: when I threw them out belatedly, they had already begun to root in the water. Each October, near-hardy shrubs like fuchsias or hebes are combed for cuttings by gardeners who do not wish to risk losing them to a sharp frost. These cuttings, too, can be sunk up to half their length in a jar of water, just like Ribes, and allowed to make underwater roots: the water soon turns green, but it is no hardship to change it and keep it sweet by putting a piece of charcoal at the bottom. The jar can be stood on a light window sill where any roots can be kept under observation: I am enjoying six lilac-pink penstemons at the moment which rooted in a kitchen glass during the latest British power strike.

Compost, however, is the usual substance in which cuttings like to find their way. Here, there is a routine which I have long used and like to think has been responsible for my successes. Like Adam and Eve, I have no mist propagator. My cuttings go into pots and boxes, thickly spaced but never so close that their leaves touch. Their earth is mixed to an unforgettable recipe which is called one, two, three; one part by bulk of sieved garden soil, two parts of peat and three parts of coarse silver sand. Builders' sand is useless and all peat of a poor quality is a waste of money. I water this mixture until it is damp throughout, but not boggy: usually, I begin by watering it too heavily and have to leave it to drain itself for a while. I aim at a consistency familiar to those who make their own cakes and scones: a damp but open mixture, like flour into which you have rubbed butter, but not any milk or eggs.

Once you have a damp mixture, the art reduces itself to two essentials: sharp, clean cutting and a swift and sensible transfer from plant to earth. For the sake of the swift transfer, take your box or pot across to the parent-plant you have chosen. If you have a choice, always prefer the young and healthy parent which is known to flower freely. Cuttings off older, weary specimens tend to root more erratically and grow with less vigour.

Let us assume you enjoyed my earlier praises of Orange Blossom and that you have looked up Philadelphus in a catalogue and found that a plant costs as much as a hot meal. As you liked the idea of a Philadelphus hedge, you hunted around for a friend with a good bush of Belle Etoile and asked leave to take a few cuttings. In July, the plant is thick with next year's flowering shoots, young, not too sappy and springing from a hard branch. I take one young shoot near where it joins old wood and pull it gently away with my fingers, trying to bring a 'heel' of old wood off with it; the heel must be short and thin. Pessimistically, I take twice as many as

I need. As each is taken, I slip it into the propagator's secret weapon: the polythene bag. Once inside, a cutting will not wilt dramatically; if it does, seal the bag with a few drops of water inside it and wait till it recovers.

The advantage of the bag is that it allows you to deal with a cluster of cuttings one by one, keeping them fresh until the moment when you wish to trim each one and plant it. If you begin to handle wilting cuttings, you are wasting your time: they will never revive and go on to make roots. Arm yourself with a very sharp knife or a razor-blade, not with secateurs or pruning-shears which crush a plant's stem. Then, take the cuttings one by one from the bag and trim them carefully.

If you are planting cuttings in a box or a pot, you do not need to retain a long piece of the stem. A shoot trimmed to fifteen centimetres is quite sufficient. Nor do you need a thick profusion of leaves. I slice all the leaves off at least one third of the stem's length. If there is a skill in this pleasant art, I suppose it intervenes at this point: you must be very careful to cut the leaves and stem cleanly and not to leave a grazed area on the surviving cutting. Also, waste no time: the longer the trimmed fragment is exposed to air, the more water it loses.

After trimming, I dip the end which is to be planted in a standard brand of hormone rooting-powder. Certainly, this powder does no harm, but I have never tested to discover how much good it also does. It does not retain its power for ever, so do not buy a large pack and reckon to use it cannily over the next ten years: small tins are a better buy and should be matched to the plant you are rooting: shrub, border-plant or tree. In Britain, I have always used Seradix.

Now comes an easy little trick. I plant each cutting near the side of a pot because the drainage is usually better there: cuttings placed in the centre tend to perform less well, although you cannot avoid them if you are using a large box. I make a hole with the blunt end of a pencil, suiting its diameter to the girth of the cutting. I bury one third of the cutting's length and press the earth firmly round its lower half, trying not to handle the cutting or bruise it. When the earth is firm, I test the cutting by a gentle pull to see if it is packed into position. If it stays firm, it is correctly planted.

I find that four cuttings to a standard five-inch pot give the right density: be certain that no leaves are buried or left in contact with the soil. On most varieties, they cause rot, although there are a few alpine plants, the blue Lithospermum, especially, which do prefer to be buried with a pair of leaves still in place on the stem. Once the little hopefuls are in place, I use one of two methods. Either I place the entire pot under one of the convenient plastic hats which garden-shops now sell as a cheap covering for seed-boxes. They give them grand names like "mini-propagator", but they are simply a rectangular roof of thick plastic with a small air vent in one corner which you can open or shut. In Britain, I use the Stewart Propagators, from garden centres or Stewart Plastics, Purley Way, Croydon, Surrey (c. £1.85 each). If these hats are unavailable, I wrestle with a polythene bag instead. Slip a bag over the pot, head downwards, and tether it by leaving the pot to stand on the open end, packed underneath it. The bag should be quite wide as it must not touch the cuttings: contact with condensation will cause them to rot. To avoid this contact, you may have to bend a piece of wire into a hoop across the pot so that the bag can rest on it. Obviously, this hoop is best made before you try to plant the cuttings, as it is most easily tethered by being poked down into the pot's compost. My problem is that most of my spare bags either began life holding woollen sweaters, and are therefore too big, or are pinched from the spare-parts bag for the incorrigible vacuum cleaner, and are too small. To hold them securely, you can also slip a rubber band round the middle of the pot or box's girth.

Under hat or bag, the cuttings are left to sweat without any opening or fresh air. They should be stood in semi-shade, if possible, and best of all, in a cold frame: the heat of a greenhouse is not necessary. Watering will not be needed very often, but you should inspect the earth every four days and decide accordingly. If any cutting shows any sign of rot, fungus or black squelch, pull it out and destroy it immediately. Otherwise, you should wait until the others show signs of new growth. These signs may be slow to appear, but usually, they emerge in the end. On no account pull the cuttings out of the earth in order to see how they are getting on; curiosity is forgivable but if you must inspect them before they show signs of growth, tap the entire ball of earth out of the pot and see if there are signs of roots down its side. If the cuttings are firmly planted and the earth is damp before you dislodge it, the cuttings will probably not fall out during this interference. It is better to leave them well alone and resist impatience, the enemy of all forms of gardening. I once rooted an osmanthus after 14 months of neglect.

When signs of growth show, how do you bring the new children back into our daily atmosphere? Here, the art is to acclimatize them by stages.

Open the vent in their plastic hat and allow a little air inside: then, slide the vent fully open after two or three days: then, remove the hat altogether. If you have used a bag, not a vent, cut a slit in it at first; wait a few days and only then remove the entire contraption. It is a severe shock to emerge from a polythene bag which has been over one's head for several weeks. After a further few days, the new young plants can be potted on into individual pots, hardened off and planted out into the garden in the following spring or autumn. By growing your own cuttings in the one, two, three mixture and then in a good garden loam, you avoid one of the modern planter's primary perils: the soft, fine peat-compost in which nurseries hurry along their seedlings and cuttings under mist and on bottom heat. I have given up planting these fragile root-balls directly into my tough garden-soil. On receiving them, I re-pot them in a bigger pot, half filled with the sort of earth a plant meets in outdoor life. When it has rooted out of the nursery-sponge into this solid diet, it is fit to go outside. If you give dead plants a post-mortem, you will often find that after a year or two, their roots have failed to cross the great divide between the ball of soft peat in which they arrived and the soil into which you placed them. Obviously, nurseries use this soft feather-bed for speed and cleanliness. When raising your own young plants, you can treat them roughly from the start and greatly increase their chance of future survival.

So much, then, for the broad procedure; next I will fill in a few details and suggest those shrubs which are most likely to succeed. Even St Augustine would not have been so enthusiastic if he had tried to root the common but obstinate lilac. Wonderment is the privilege of the successful. It is here that enthusiasm gets the better of ability; not just one of my neighbour's pink ceanothus, I tell myself, as it dangles enticingly against her wall; why not take ten or twenty and hedge my bets against the killing frosts it so detests? A forest of philadelphus, a grove of ginkgo and among them, honeysuckles of every kind; where parents are waiting for the propagator, it is easy to think in lavish terms. Three months later sense returns, as every rooted cutting needs repotting and there is never room for them all. They do, however, make excellent presents for Christmas and birthdays.

I must insist that it is often no harder to root a shrub than a border-plant. It depends which varieties you choose. At first, avoid lilacs and viburnums, camellias, and most mahonias, as they are either rather slow or rather difficult; the perfect beginners' cuttings are sun roses (Helianthemum), orange blossom (Philadelphus), honeysuckles, cotton lavender, thymes and most of the grey-leaved plants which lift any garden out of a rut. Buddleia, Japanese quince, honeysuckles, Rubus tridel, caryopteris, ceratostigma and senecio are equally easy. So, too, are the popular shrub potentillas if you are aware of their nurserymen's trick. Those who root them in cold frames take cuttings in late summer when the flowers are still open on the tips of the shoots. Certainly, I find the lovely yellow-flowered Potentilla Elizabeth roots very quickly at this season.

Adventure, however, can bring more surprising rewards, especially from shrubs with firm fleshy stems. If you see a flourishing bush of the mexican orange (Choisya ternata) in the next few weeks, be sure to ask permission to cut a few young shoots beneath the point where they show a rough join on their stems: roots sprout more quickly from cuttings taken just below a callous. Slip a few choisyas into a polythene bag and they will root within weeks in the bag-or-hat system. So will the glorious Daphne odora in its plain or golden-leaved form: I have not been praising an expensive and inaccessible plant, but one which any gardener can multiply. Such is the sweetness of its scent in early spring that everyone should have it, either outdoors against a sunny, warm wall or indoors in a pot. To secure plenty of plants, visit Daphne odora with a polythene bag in mid July; take short cuttings just below one of the many nodules on each stem and set them in the one, two, three mixture. They root with remarkable ease.

If your garden is too cold for this daphne, try cuttings off the evergreen skimmias instead. These plants are the ones with elegant leaves, sweet-scented off-white flowers and red berries, if you arrange the sexes carefully: they have all the virtues which you wish you could find in a low-growing laurel, and none of the vices. They are not very cheap to buy, but they are elegant shrubs for courtyards near the house-door, that enclosed area which great garden-designers have often seen as a green oasis of cool, calm leaves, not over-colourful flowers. Skimmias break easily into short lengths, ideally suited to cuttings. They also root very quickly, a willing-ness which you would not guess unless forewarned.

Even within the same family, different varieties will root with differing ease. Every summer, I realize this odd fact from my adventures with pinks, or Dianthus. In July, I am swept away by thoughts of edging the entire garden with pinks. The familiar strawberry-pink Doris roots very easily, as do many of the single crimsons or carnation-yellows. The laced varieties, patterned with white and maroon, are mostly more difficult, though I find the old London Brocade quite obliging. Some of the most delicate patterns of scarlet, white or crimson elude me entirely, while I have never had much luck with fringed lilac and related colourings. A great connoisseur assures me that she is no luckier: from cuttings, the many old garden pinks vary, and we should not blame ourselves. Nonetheless, they are all worth trying, preferably a fortnight after flowering when you can plunder the robust young shoots which would otherwise bear next season's flowers. It is tempting to pinch out the cuttings with your fingers, but a sharp blade gives neater, firmer results. The difficulty with a pink's cuttings is that they tend to come away with a hollow tube at the end of their stem. No roots will ever form on this outer coating, and you must try to cut cleanly at an obvious joint in the stem. Too often, you will find you have severed the outer layer only and broken the inner core rather higher up. These hollow ends are perhaps the chief cause of failure in the types of pink with thin stems.

From a good day's work, you could expect a hundred or so new pinks, and as many violas: for violas, clip the plants' stems back after flowering and then take cuttings from the young growth which follows a month later. Penstemons are yours for the taking, as are buddleias or hebes.

How confident this advice sounds and how close to becoming too sure of the job; one night I walked in through the shadows, pinks in polythene behind me, and suddenly caught the scent of the year's first flower on Magnolia grandiflora, lemon-scented, spice laden, as cool as an empty church. Its crumpled white petals defied me to try my luck with them. The razor blade advanced, steadied, then withdrew; ten years had passed before that magnolia had flowered, and it did not seem right to meddle with its long glossy leaves. Even to the propagator, certain shrubs remain private. Magnolia grandiflora, though willing in principle to root, made my polythene bags seem very humble affairs.

Climbing and Rambling Roses

Throughout June and July, one of the glories of the garden has been the climbing and rambling roses. They flower with extraordinary profusion, up walls, houses or even through the branches of tall trees and hedges. They 'climb' only because we help them with pins and wire. In nature, they cling and sprawl, using the thorns which they have developed for this purpose. In gardens, too, roses can be used informally, to fall off a bank, hook themselves into a boundary's hedge or grow through the tall shrubs beside a drive-way.

Among their profusion, which varieties are always worth choosing? Here, I am brought up against the good fortune of the English garden. Our rose-nurseries, Beales, Austin, Harkness and others, list dozens of civilized climbers, allowing our gardens to be swamped with their curtains of summer flower. In American lists, there is hardly a climber I would want, except Golden Showers: most of them belong in the low third class, although there are so many in our lists which will survive cold winters and hotter summers. Only by comparing and looking at other countries do you begin to define where the Englishness of English gardens lies. Climbing roses, I find, are central to its effect and for what follows, I can only refer you to the lists of Peter Beales in Norfolk or David Austin in Albrighton, Wolverhampton, devoted rosarians who will export or advise customers in odd climates. Our sterling prices are low relative to other countries and I doubt if their stock is much more expensive than a local climbing misery like "White Dawn".

If you have plenty of room and want something to grow quickly I do not think you can do better than the warm pink rambler Albertine. I would say that I have never known this fail had I not planted one recently on a corner of a house where it is shaded by a high yew hedge and scoured by a north-west wind which comes through the gap of a nearby garden gate. After two years it looks very scrawny, proving that no worth-while plant is tough enough to grow anywhere. Against an ordinary north or east wall. Albertine will ramble rapidly. It is quite a business to wire back the new growths which it makes with great speed from May until autumn. Albertine is a wichuriana rose, one of a group whose new shoots appear with the vigour of a fruiting blackberry. It flowers on its old wood of the previous season and by mid-June, this wood is often left behind by the latest tangle of young canes. I find it best to prune Albertine in mid-July after it has flowered so that all the flowering wood for the next season begins at the same length. I never touch it in winter or spring, the usual time for rose-pruning, as by then, I am cutting off wood which is set to flower in the summer. Only an emergency or unmanageable tangle persuades me to break this rule. You can use the bag-method on the bits of Albertine which you cut off in midsummer: bury them up to half their length in a trench dug in shady open ground and filled with a mixture of sand and earth. If watered and left in peace, they will probably root within a season. Two Albertines, or one, are enough for most gardens, so you can give away your other plants as prickly Christmas presents.

No rose is ever perfect and Albertine, admittedly, flowers only once. That one season, however, is unforgettably generous. The flowers impress by their quantity, not by a classic shape: their promising buds of a dark shaded pink open to a rather loose and fluffy flower whose pale pink looks as if it has been dipped in a cup of tea. It does not smell of teacups, I assure you, in case you fear that particular scent of a somnolent office in the late afternoon. In fact, Albertine has a sweet smell, but not a heavy one. It also has a charming leaf which shines in the light, at least when it is not attacked by mildew. In late summer, Albertine does sometimes show mildew on its leaves, but as the attack comes after the flowering season, I ignore it. It never seems to do any serious harm and the plant is strong enough to shake it off.

Profusion and vigour are Albertine's characteristics. She is not a rose for a small pergola or a low wall, but she has a magnificence wherever she can spread herself. So does her close neighbour in catalogues, as in origin: another wichuriana called Alberic Barbier. This rose is even tougher and quicker. It is white-flowered with a yellowish tinge and although the individual blooms are no more shapely than Albertine's, they appear in such profusion that they transform any wall or broad arch with room for them. Alberic Barbier has two particular virtues. It will often keep its glossy leaves well into early winter. It will also grow cheerfully in shade. I find it a superb rose for north walls behind shrub- or mixed-borders where it has the height to be visible and the stamina to cope with half-light and competition. Old Alberics develop thick trunks with age and become the great event of each summer when they bear, once only, their thousands of white flowers.

In warmer areas, I am extremely fond of another white scrambler called Rambling Rector. This rampant variety makes much quicker headway than any of the church dignitaries after which it is named. I consider it the best of the romantic white rambling roses for growing into trees, over ugly sheds and garages, into hedgerows and over hideous areas of corrugated iron. Let the white-flowered Rector ramble on your hot tin roof: for several years, he raced up ivy which intrudes from my neighbour's wall, waved cheerfully beside the guttering and sent out long growth over

LONG LASTING RED PENSTEMONS AND SILVER LEAVES

CARDIOCRINUM GIGANTEUM: *HIMALAYAN LILY*
TREE LUPIN AND BLUE FLAX AT DOWER HOUSE, BOUGHTON

her beastly roofing on an old, decrepit barn. In late June, the entire area, twenty or thirty metres square, was a sea of small white roses, one of the prettiest effects I ever contrived. Then, in a very fierce winter, the Rambling Rector returned to his maker and left me with a sad gap. Nobody knows there the Rector came from: parentage is unknown, but this waif was left to stray in gardens, perhaps with some blood of the wild musk rose in his veins. The winter which killed mine was remarkably cold, but with that one warning, I would send for the Rector nonetheless and enjoy his abundant, single crop of flowers.

Enough of the vigorous ramblers: I must name my favourite climbing roses which have well-formed flowers and better manners. For me, the season begins in late May with the generous Maigold, a strong coppery yellow, but never too strident and always reliable on walls of any aspect, north included: once-flowering, I admit, but a heavy flowerer at an early date. Among the dark reds, I name Etoile de Hollande unhesitatingly as the best, although the flowers fade sometimes to purple-red: she has the vigour and shape and depth of colour which other more modern varieties never combine. Among pinks, I stand by old Caroline Testout, a rose of incredible fullness and richness, silvery-pink, heavily-petalled and very vigorous with its pretty grey-green leaves. Among whites, Climbing Virgo has an exquisite shape and subtlety of shading; my favourite yellow is the single-flowered Mermaid, a prickly rose but a persistent flowerer, even on north walls, with the one proviso that hard winters (15°C or more below) will usually kill it off. Otherwise, I stand by the modern Golden Showers; its flowers are not the most shapely but they appear persistently from June till late autumn and the plant is always healthy.

I leave two particular favourites to the end. The first is the matchless New Dawn, the pale pink-white rose which ages to a pure blush-white. It is extremely strong and will grow in half shade: the winters never bother it. It flowers only once, but its season is two weeks later than most other ramblers and climbers, beginning in July when other roses are past their peak. To see its colour at its best, place it where it shows up in your nightly vista as dusk begins to fall. New Dawn belongs on a summer's eve, when its paleness looms through the shadows and acquires a particular depth.

My other favourite is not so vigorous, but its flowers have a rare shape and colour and in most autumns it will flower a second time. Bred in 1853, Gloire de Dijon will also grow in a north or eastern aspect. Its shape is sparser and taller than New Dawn's and without careful pruning, it will become bare and gnarled in its lower parts. It is also prone to black spot and mildew, neither of which do permanent harm to it. Why bother with this ancient rose? Because its flowers have such a fine fullness, flat, quartered and heavy with petals of a unique shade of buff-apricot. Gloire de Dijon will grow and flower almost anywhere, but it flourishes to the full almost nowhere: I rather think it prefers hot summers. It is a worthwhile rose, because its flowers have a weary, well-bred quality in a rare and sensuous colour. At that moment of unintended comedy, when the gamekeeper Mellors has just seduced Lady Chatterley for the first time, D.H. Lawrence draws back to describe the effect of her ladyship's nakedness after sex with one of the estate's servants. In the sunlight, he remarks, she seemed like a Gloire de Dijon rose: plant this buff-apricot rose on your shaded walls and look, like a literary voyeur, on the effect of its suggestive blooms.

Late Summer Trees and Shrubs

Trees are our permanent memorials, beetles permitting, but in late summer they are beginning to look rather tired and dusty. What trees should we best choose for a good effect in August and early autumn, between the climbing roses and the brilliant colours of the fall?

I have one particular favourite which thrives in poor soil and a warm summer, although it is also hardy in any winter. Koelreuteria paniculata is a cousin of the horse chestnuts, but much less familiar. It has pretty leaves, fine flowers and good autumn colour. It is tough and not too obstructive. After twenty years, it is about twenty feet tall and can be encouraged to make a single straight trunk. It is a tree with a bold and interesting leaf, pinnate, as botanists call it, or feathery as I describe it, in the way that an enlarged acacia leaf or a shortened Tree of Heaven leaf would be feathery and elegant. When these leaves appear in spring they are a reddish brown for a week or two before taking on a normal green. Flowers appear in dry summers during late July and August; they are pretty, discreet and, to my eye, thoroughly charming.

A popular name for this tree, which few gardeners plant, is the Golden Rain tree because the strings of small yellow flowers hang like raindrops from the branches. In Britain, they appear only in a dry summer, but in warmer climates they are visible from an early stage in the tree's life. The yellow flowers have a red centre and are hung in clusters like a neat bracelet: after they have faded, they leave bronze seedpods shaped like a bladder, as on some of those late summer shrubs which are cousins to the pea family; these are worth studying, but the Golden Rain tree's autumn colour is far more noticeable.

It grows into a pleasantly open shape and shows its yellowed autumn leaves to great advantage; I had always assumed its natural home was China, for the Rain Tree had that unusual grace which is commonly found in inaccessible Chinese plants. So indeed it proves; the gardener who has the patience to wait for ten years will prize the Koelreuteria, a tree of so many differing qualities, known and neglected since 1763. In America, Wayside and Weston both sell it readily; in England, I have had good plants from J.H. Chichester, The Mill Yard, Beaulieu, Brocken-hurst, Hampshire.

Nobody could say that Horse Chestnuts, or Buckeyes, were under-patronized. They are the supreme specimen trees for late spring and early summer. Their leaves open to a particularly lush and vivid green, like spring's unfolding pocket handkerchiefs. Within weeks, they are set with red or pink or white spires of flower, like the candles which as children, we clipped each year onto the green branches of Christmas trees.

In gardens, however, these trees are a mixed blessing. They grow much too tall for a modest space and even if grown as an avenue for bigger country properties they have an annoying secondary habit: they drop their big seeds, or conkers, all over paths and driveways, leaving them to be squashed by traffic or stolen by invading schoolboys. If you intend to plant these noble trees down a driveway, choose either the sterile pink-flowered Aesculus Carnea Plantierensis, a conker-free hybrid, or the double white British Chestnut, Aesculus hippocastanum Baumanii, a valuable tree which sets no seed. In England, buy with confidence from Notcutts, Woodbridge, Suffolk; in America, from Weston, Massachusetts.

It is not, however, for the grand gardener only that I mention the family here. While your Koelreuteria is pouring Golden Rain in early August, your American Buckeye could be blossoming in an unexpected season, not a tree but a useful three-metre shrub, as wide as it is tall. Aesculus parviflora will grow anywhere, but it is grossly ignored. It is a shrub Horse Chestnut, a beautiful Buckeye from south-eastern America, happy in any East Coast garden, yet seldom seen, even by connoisseurs. It flowers profusely, bearing the short, typical candles three months after the big trees have finished with them. The flowers are white with red middles, the leaves are recognizably a Buckeye's, but the shrub's third virtue is the brilliance of its burnt red autumn colour in any soil or site. Aesculus parviflora is perhaps too broad a shrub for all but the biggest mixed border, but it is a superb sequel to the shrub roses and philadelphus of less formal planting where the garden merges into an orchard, rough grass or a well-loved wilderness. In England, Sherrards of Newbury, Berks can supply it; in America, it is offered as the Bottlebrush Buckeye by Wayside, South Carolina.

The Golden Rain tree reached gardens in 1763; this shrub Buckeye was introduced in 1785. Both plants have a sequence of handsome features, yet for two hundred years, we have stared these merits in the face.

Architectural Acanthus

In late summer, especially, gardens ought to strike a balance between their permanent bones, the architectural plants of which I have written, and their temporary, transient flowers, "gaily-coloured hay", as that great landscape-designer, the late Russell Page, described them fondly. On holiday, I always find one type of bone most handsomely in evidence: the classical leaf of the Acanthus, thistly, supremely architectural and the bold type of feature which the summer garden needs.

The shape of the acanthus leaf inspired classical architects who designed the ornate leafy capitals of the distinctive Corinthian column. They took the design from Greece to the borders of India; it expanded westwards to Italy, Spain and Gaul when Greek art and ideas were diffused by the Roman empire. Even now, in Rome it is hard to escape the acanthus for long. The leaves persist throughout the winter in southern Italy and last well into December in my own coldish garden.

In Italy, the acanthus seldom has flowery neighbours, as the flower-border is not an Italian feature. It looks even better for their absence. If you have never met an acanthus but have looked at classical architecture, you will know what it looks like, as it has been carved on pillars for two thousand years. Long, glossy green leaves, prickly and similar to those of a globe artichoke, reach a height of above two feet and then throw up straight spikes of hooded vanilla and white flowers in August, equipped with a thorny hook which has earned them the unattractive name of Bear's Breeches. You will like them if you do not handle them, but it is the leaves, I hope, which will most catch your fancy. Usually, they are concealed in a late-summer flower border and placed for their flowers only. Their outline is lost in a mass of phlox and daisies and visitors wonder why anybody bothered to plant them.

But the place for an acanthus should be special, a bed of its own where it can be viewed from all sides, or a place of emphasis, at the bottom of a statue or on the corner of a path or at the foot of a wall where its flowers can be cut off if they look too tall for the glossy green of the leaf. In Italy, it appears at the foot of old box hedges, beside an ornamental flower-pot or even in the formal paving of a country villa's terrace. It is one more evergreen brick from which Italian gardens are built.

There are several varieties, but your choice will depend on availability: the cheapest source, as usual, is seed and here, Thompson and Morgan supply and export seed of the kind I most enjoy, Acanthus mollis with huge soft leaves of a glistening deep green. Allow three years before you have a proper plant which can develop into an impressive clump, but the delay is worthwhile. Plants of Acanthus spinosus are also available, the other variety which I recommend: the leaves are slightly less imposing than mollis's, but the plant is tougher.

The point about these Acanthuses is that they are so firm, solid and unfading when a hot summer has begun to take its toll of lesser flowering plants. They will grow in semi-shade as well as in sun; they tolerate quite dry conditions because their roots are long and fleshy, their leaves are glossy and their flowers are so curiously set with spines. I have come to rely on groups of three or five, strategically placed near steps, at corners or turning-points in my garden's plan. They unify the late summer jungle of annuals, summer hyacinths (Galtonias, grown from bulbs), emergent Japanese Anemones and the sombre blue Monkshood (Aconitum Sparks's Variety and Bressingham Spire). The Aconitum is my particular favourite as a companion for Acanthus, because it has similar hooded flowers and finely cut leaves, but its features are less bold and softer to the touch. Like Acanthus, it will flourish in sun or semi-shade, but unlike Acanthus, it is not a plant for dry soils. It likes to be damp and although visitors have sometimes queried its hardiness, I must emphasize that Aconitums of all types are extremely robust. They break up the frequent yellow and orange of late summer gardens and grow from three to four feet tall, depending on the dampness of the soil. In Britain, the best range comes from Bressingham Nurseries, Diss, Norfolk, who raised some of the prettiest, including the violet blue Bressingham Spire; they will export, but a range of Aconitums is now offered in America too by White Flower Farm, Connecticut. In case you think they are awkward or tender, I note that in America they are suitable for climate zones 3 to 9: as tough as common Mallow, but much less often grown.

Decorative Daisy-Flowers

My last impressions of summer are the yearly jungles which I have contrived between the architectural plants, acanthus and the silver-leaved artemisias, fatsias and the unstoppable fennel, a self-seeding exception to my reservation about herbs: even if I disliked it, I could not now dispense with it. One plant, bought ten years ago, has bred as rapidly as any travelling Ragwort.

In the yearly jungle, I am enjoying the annuals whose ordering and sowing we noted in winter, but in warm years I notice how the daisy-flowered varieties and the marigolds do best. "Marigolds obey the sun", wrote the captive King Charles I, in his English prison, "More than my subjects me have done". I am on the side of disobedience: most marigolds are too stiff and harshly-coloured to find any place in my garden. I dislike their smell of stale tea-leaves and their compromised shades of orange and yellow. You may think that perceptions of "harshness" in a colour are too personal: I note that even the critical eye of Charles Darwin noticed that marigolds appeared to give off a particular bright flash of light from their petals on clear evenings after a sunny spell. He believed it might be measurable, so there is science in my taste.

My own feeling, when marigolds are flashing most brightly, is that this is a season in which we should be growing annuals from South Africa. When the marigolds signal fine weather, the brilliant daisies from the veldt and lower hill-slopes are set fair for the summer. Their names deter the unadventurous: Gazania, Dimorphotheca (a botanical word to mean a flower with two shapes of seed-vessel), Ursinia, Arctotis and Mesembry-anthemum (or Livingstone Daisy).

All these long names have flowers like a large and exotic daisy and are half-hardy, needing to be sown in a greenhouse in early April and to be pricked out three weeks later and planted outside in early June. Devoted dead-heading will keep them flowering from late June to October and while away the slow, spare hours of a Sunday evening, to great effect if you are careful to remove every single one of their faded flowers. In dull weather they close their petals tightly, like an umbrella held upright. These petals are attached to a dark daisy-disc in their centre which contrasts prettily with their outer shades of pink, orange and flame.

Seeing them last year, a keen visitor told me that she so envied English gardeners their annuals, but that this range of colour would never be possible anywhere else. Again, the remark was proof of the "Englishman's Garden" disease, a condition which leads outsiders to attribute all manner of un-English ideas to English greenfingers and explain to themselves why their own gardens are less exciting: "We could never grow it at home". In fact, these annuals are not 'English' at all: they grow better in American or Continental climates than in ours and in one case, the best seed-mixtures come from America, not Britain, where all but one of these plants can be ordered anyway.

The exception is the little Ursinia for which you can turn to Thompson and Morgan, London Road, Ipswich, wherever you happen to live. I like Ursinia because it grows so easily and flowers so freely: you can sow it directly into the ground in mid- to late-May or start it earlier in a box indoors. If you dead-head it, it bursts into second or third crops of flower: it is a clear silky orange with a chestnut-brown ring at its base. It grows 9 inches high, flowers unforgettably freely and would make an unusual edging in place of those mats of white alyssum.

The Livingstone Daisy is lower-growing, more familiar and many-coloured. Its fleshy leaves of grey-green are marked with small crystals, like grains of sugar, and hold the drops of water which they need in their arid home ground. This fleshiness should persuade you to plant them on top of dry walls or at the edge of gravel paths where there is sharp drainage and little water. They spread into a mat about a foot wide and flower very brightly. It is a mistake to sow their seed too soon in a greenhouse or warm room. A mid-April sowing times their season sensibly, or even an early May one. Do not be talked into starting them in March, for they will damp off as seedlings or suffer a check when they have rooted and grown on too early. They never fully recover. They are worth a little trouble because they are such superb performers in dry conditions: you see them massed in those awful crazy-paving walls which prop up new

108

tavernas in arid southern Greece and you can even grow them out on the American prairies, as my prairie-authority, the late Claud Barr, used to report to me by letter from the Dakota ranch on which he tended the flowers he made famous as 'prairie gems'. Burpees Seeds of Warminster, Penn. 18974 and Park's Seeds (under 'Ice-Plant') supply them on one side of the Atlantic; Thompson and Morgan and everyone else, on the other.

The other three varieties are not much more difficult, but are more artistic and less crude. In America, you can order them all from Park's Seeds, Highway 254N, Greenwood, S.C. 29647 whom I, too, have used, as I will explain.

The Arctotis, or African Daisy, likes to be dry but not baked: Park's alerted me to its preference for 'cool dry conditions', a fair description of some English summers and as a result, I am careful to shade the young plants when I set them outside in early June. Once they are rooted and growing away, they are not difficult. They are extremely pretty, having flowers nearly three inches wide in shades of bronze, pinkish-rose, orange and white. Again, take off the dead-heads and their stems, back to a pair of leaves, and Arctotis will flower elegantly until the frost.

Dimorphotheca is more of a mouthful, but it is an easier plant and so long as the sun shines, its flowers remain open. In England, we do, admittedly, have selected ivory-white strains which are useful in a sunny white garden, on the Sissinghurst circuit; elsewhere, the admirable "aurantiaca mixed" is universally on sale, and quite rightly so as it has such a range of many-petalled daisy-flowers, from peach to orange, white and lemon. You can sow this mixture directly into the ground in mid-May and still enjoy flowers in August. The seed-heads are easily saved for subsequent years, and if I had to begin with one of these annuals, I would choose this one: the family is undergoing a name-change (Osteospermum) and a new interest in its perennial relations, but the results have yet to make it unrecognizable in seed-lists.

From this dependable daisy, I suggest you progress to the infamous gazania. I say infamous, because this plant is dependent on fine weather and careful gardening. Its tones of colour include a pink-grey, a pink-orange which wallpaper makers call sunset and a selection of tangerines, buff-yellows and raspberry pinks which I do not think you will find in any other plant. A green-grey leaf displays them to their full advantage.

The answer, I have found, is to send off to America. Park's seeds offer much better strains of gazania than any in England and if the summer is hot, as it was in 1983, you will amaze yourself with the results. I recommend three of their strains: Sunshine (superbly striped in pink, yellow and red), Fire Emerald (more rounded and the easiest, I found), Sundance (the biggest flowers, some striped, some pure self-colours). In America, these types are sown directly into the ground in late spring and rank as 'easy to grow'; in the Englishman's garden, they must be coaxed along from seed in a cool greenhouse and given the hottest, driest spot in order to succeed. Do not confuse the mature plants' liking for sun and drought with the young transplants' needs: they must be watered and shaded for a week or so after moving outdoors if their silver and grey-green leaves are not to collapse. Their flowers are truly distinguished, rich in colour and velvety to the touch: here, English gardeners do not have the best of things and have to look further afield to do the plants justice. In front of dark acanthus, a mat of these gazanias is a charming postscript to high summer.

AUTUMN

Autumn

The first intimations of autumn reach me every year when the flowers open on the border phloxes. They are an early intimation, opening by August in most gardens, but they have a mature scent, almost smoky at times, which introduces a note of bonfires and ripened growth. Blindfolded, I think I would know where I was in the year, if left to find my way down a border full of good phloxes. I prefer the pale blues and lavender-blues to the sugary pinks and carmines: I also make full use of the pure whites among groups of flame-coloured Montbretia and the splendid Crocosmia Lucifer. I pick the white Everest, the clear-coloured Lilac Time and the pale pink Dresden China with its darker eye: Scotts in Somerset or Bressingham in Norfolk are good suppliers, while Blackthorne in Holbrook, Mass. sell these three and several others, including the tantalizing Blue Ice which is a special bonus for East Coast gardeners. Phloxes like water and richly-manured ground: they have a second season of flower, shorter-stemmed but very welcome, if you pinch out their first heads of flower as they fade. Cut them back to a lower pair of leaves. Then, in September mists, you will have heads of pale phloxes showing through the dew and damp, a common bond between British gardens and areas in New England as the year begins to turn.

As September advances, other indicators point me to the cooler evenings. The clematis returns to the centre of my interests, the lovely yellow-flowered tangutica which turns to silky seed heads and the admirable smaller-flowered viticella forms which I set beside the well-known purple-violet Jackmannii. My favourite viticellas include the deep velvety red-purple Royal Velour, so prominent at the end of the famous

111

red border at Hidcote Manor, Gloucestershire, the 'English' garden of Lawrence Johnston, the American genius who learnt so much of his art from the gardens of Italy and southern France. I also learned to love Minuet, another viticella, in the gardens of another American emigré, Mrs C.G. Lancaster at Haseley Court in Oxfordshire where it flowered for months on the honeyed stone walls behind a border on the edge of her box-edged 'Virginian' garden. Minuet starts to flower in July and hangs down the rounded flowers which make up its great tangle of blossom: each flower is purple with a rounded white centre and as you look up into their dangling petals, you see the combination from a perfect angle. As a third partner, I grow the white viticella alba luxurians, the climber on the back wall of Sissinghurst's white garden, not an American garden, this time, but not altogether 'English', as we have seen.

These viticellas are extremely easy to grow. Minuet runs up a wall; alba can tangle through a lightly branched shrub, a Corylopsis perhaps, whose season has fallen in early spring; Royal Velour is best grown flat, running horizontally on a low wall or beside steps, so that you can look down onto the full beauty of its dark velvet flowers. Because they are 'small-flowered', many gardeners ignore them and popular garden-centres seldom display them. They are not odd extras. They are healthy, prolific and extremely showy because of the quantity of their flowers, not their individual size. Treasures of Tenbury Wells, Shropshire sell them and display them well in their Burford House Gardens; I am pleased to see that Blackthorne offer my favourite three and others to New England gardeners, so that these clematis can be enjoyed by fellow-countrymen of the planters who first drew them to my notice. Blackthorne also sell the yellow Tangutica, which I much prefer to the more attractively-named 'Orange Peel Clematis', orientalis.

Colour Contrasts

After the phloxes' intimation of autumn, the true season arrives with the emergence of the bronzes and bright colours of the last flush of border plants. There is an acrid smell about autumn's Michaelmas daisies and bronze-yellow heleniums which I always notice on the green canvas of the flower shows' stands. Heleniums do not come high in my list of plants, because they lack the scent, subtlety of colour and virtues of leaf or architectural form which appeal to me. Most Michaelmas Daisies are rather transient, lasting only two or three years at their peak, but I make exceptions for two: the remarkable Alma Potschke, a glowing cherry-red of rare vigour, and the subtler Aster frikartii Glory of Staffa which flourishes and becomes a jungle of single lavender blue daisies for two or three months if you feed it very heavily and give it rich soil. I grow mine best in a bed which is made up of three parts of rotted pig-manure and one of garden loam. The wonderful Alma is a recent discovery and still unknown to most Aster-growers whose older Eventides have mildew and beetroot-red Winston Churchills are beginning to revert and go wild. Both are sold by Bressingham Nurseries, Norfolk and Wayside in South Carolina.

Autumn is a time for these bold colour-contrasts: I have several favourites. I like shocking pink Guernsey Lilies, or Nerines, in sunny, sandy soils beside the tall 'Plumbago', the cobalt-blue Ceratostigma willmottianum, a marvellous shrub which is pretty hardy: American lists seem to be limited to the low-growing form, plumbaginoides, which flowers less freely in Britain but colours a good red in its leaf in October. "If you can't grow Ceratostigma, give up gardening!", say Wayside Nurseries, but why, then, do they not sell the taller form which is even more floriferous? I can grow the smaller one, but I confess that it flowers very sparsely and yet I do not intend to give up my gardening life.

I also like the cherry-red of Aster Alma Potschke and the blue of the quick-growing Caryopteris (Scotts; Weston; Wayside and so forth) whose little plumes of flower, the 'Blue Spiraea', appear so freely as the year ends. A cold winter cuts the Caryopteris right back and usually kills it: it roots, however, so readily from cuttings taken in summer or autumn that there is no excuse for losing it, as you can protect its pieces on a windowsill. There is no reason to buy more than one parent-plant. It is one of those shrubs which will even put out roots from sprigs left in a glass of water.

Blue and pink-purple, again: try the creeping half-hardy Convolvulus mauretanicus, a well-behaved carpet plant, among the stronger purple colchicums, or large autumn 'crocus', which will poke up through its outlying runners. Sandwich Nurseries, Dover Road, Sandwich sell the convolvulus among a host of other half-hardy autumn perennials and will export worthwhile orders: the combination was devised by a great plants-woman, Mrs Fish, in her informal garden in Somerset. I added a postscript recently by mixing the brilliant rose-carmine Verbena Sissing-hurst, a half-hardy perennial of vigour and great cheerfulness, with my favourite blue autumn crocus, common old Crocus speciosus. Sandwich Nurseries sell and export the Verbena, a fine summer filling for the front of a border, and bulb firms (Peter Nyssen, Manchester, U.K.) or nurseries (Westons, Mass.) sell the crocus with its bright contrasting orange pollen. Both plants grow very easily, but only the crocus is hardy if left in the ground.

Late-season Shrubs

Blue and pink or shocking pink may be too strong for you, so I will remind you of the cooler blues and whites in the calmer reaches of the hydrangea family and put in a good word for the fruits, seed-heads and berries of other earlier flowers. I much prefer the tapered plumes of flower on the oak-leaved Hydrangea quercifolia and the flat plates of fertile and sterile florets on the 'lacecap' varieties to the heavier balls of colour on the conventional mopheads. If lacecaps tend to prefer the milder and damper parts of England, the West Country and areas touched by the Gulf Stream, the oak-leaved quercifolia, found by an American, seems to be much more obliging in American zones five to nine than it is in most English gardens. If so, bless your good luck, because the red autumn colour of the oak-leaves is enviable and the white pointed heads of flower fade to pinkish-white in August and are easily placed in any mixed border as they last for two months or so. Wayside are displaying a new variety, Snow Queen, which has interesting bark, orange buds, good autumn colour and (in photographs) very heavy, tall trusses of white flower, held well clear of the leaves. In the right zone, it looks a winner and I am ordering one on sight.

On a more English note, I am very fond of a planting of the one truly repetitive old-fashioned rose, the modest-growing Comte de Chambord. Its flat flowers of pink are in the Damask, or Portland rose, branch of the family and I find that they are the one which always flowers in autumn, unlike many which are said to do so. Peter Beales in Norfolk sells and exports it and for some reason, it simply is the most persistent form. Otherwise, I rely on the superb Musk roses, bred by an artful clergyman after the First World War. The great bunches of buff-yellow flower on Buff

Beauty repeat their season very well: like Comte de Chambord, it is a rose I like to place within sight of my favourite Buddleia, the informal alternifolia argentea whose long wands of lavender-mauve flowers sweep forwards from the tall branches in June. This elegant Chinese Buddleia is very hardy and grows easily in the open, but it also looks charming against a wall, even in a tall, enclosed yard. Please remember the 'argentea' part of the name, so that you have the best of all, the form with shining silvery leaves. Sherrards of Newbury and White Flower Farm, Connecticut list this variety specifically, having seen the greater value of it.

Fruits and Seed-heads

As the year has advanced, the garden's scope has broadened: in autumn, we have flowers, scents, architectural leaves and stems as before, but also the possibilities of seed-heads, fruits and early berries. It has become a commonplace that these features should be valued, but gardeners do not often act on what others like to write. I have already alluded to the wonderful silky seed-heads on the yellow-flowered Clematis tangutica, one of my favourite later-flowering climbers for a sunny or semi-shaded place. I have also learned to tolerate the early dullness of leaves on a group of Callicarpas. Five or six feet high, they then cover themselves in brilliant purple-blue berries during October, signs of their satisfactory sex-life. They like a deep, rich soil but do not object to lime: try to plant at least one male to fertilize the females even if you have to send away to a supplier like John Scott, The Royal Nurseries, Merriott, Somerset for good stock. In the U.S., Wayside sell a fine form, Profusion, and advise it for zones six to nine.

More accessibly, I wish to emphasize four other fruits and seed-heads: the ornamental onion's, the rose's, the mountain ash's and the flowering quince. The onions to which I refer are the paper-brown seed-heads of the ornamental bulbs called alliums. The flowers are mostly rose-purple or lilac-purple, though there are some blues which are needlessly unpopular; in autumn these flowers have disappeared, and careful gardeners are left with dried brown seed-heads like a major's drumsticks, in which the black onion-seeds glisten and rustle, ready for collection.

The seed-heads can be cut and used in vases for winter decoration, along with autumn's teasels and grasses: some of the most effective heads are borne by a 4-foot-high allium called schubertii, after the composer, I like to imagine, because it is very harmonious in its rose-lilac flower and dried brown old age. It is becoming very fashionable, and the branches in its seed-heads are as clearly defined as the struts or girders in an architect's designs. A valuable autumn contrast can be enjoyed from this ornamental onion among late bedding-annuals. It is matched by others: albo-pilosum is more magnificent in full flower in June, while afflatunense is slenderer and slightly cheaper. Their flowers smell of onion, but the dried heads are quite unscented: J. Amand of Beethoven St., London W.10 and Dutch Garden, P.O. Box 400, Montvale, New Jersey 07645 are two suppliers with a good range of varieties.

If a dead-head seems depressing, it can be cheered up by the colour and enticing shape of rose-hips. One of the many disadvantages of growing modern floribundas is their lack of this sensational second season; they do not fruit brightly, whereas the shrub rose called moyesii in its several forms enlivens September with masses of scarlet hips, as prominent as any autumn crop of rose buds. This is a vigorous shrub rose for tough grass, orchards or the edges of lightly shaded woods where it will arch prettily into a wide and tall specimen. I have no woodland, but I have placed the best form of Rose moyesii, called Geranium, in a circular hole in surrounding grass and greatly enjoyed its single scarlet flowers, like roses from an antique tapestry, which open in early June and are followed with hips as bright as sealing-wax. It is a splendid, accommodating shrub, a good pair to my other choice for rose-hips, elegant Rose rubrifolia. Its leaves match almost anything and so, like moyesii, it has a double interest; you do not really want a rose for hips alone.

Red fruits and berries, of course, are autumn's familiar attraction; how many gardeners, though, take the yellow-green fruits of their spring-flowering quinces (or japonicas) seriously? I have resolved to pay more attention to this second effect of a shrub which has few equals for massed wild planting or decorative woodland thickets. We should all plant, too, for the scarlet berries of viburnums, especially the enormously heavy trusses of a kind called betulifolium and the bright bunches on forms of the Guelder Rose, Viburnum opulus. I am especially fond of the tall Xanthocarpum, whose bunches of shining fruits are nearly a pure yellow: it bears the typical bunched heads of white flower, scentless, alas, in late May or June and soon reaches seven or eight feet. My favourite, however, is the smaller-growing opulus Compactum, which reaches only four or

TRADESCANTIA VIRGINIANA

ACANTHUS SPINOSUS: *BEARS BREECHES*

five feet and has a superb autumn season of glistening red fruits, like fine currants, above reddening leaves. This plant is extremely hardy; it loves lime; it will grow in shade and even in a wet place. The great Miss Jekyll used to place Guelder Roses beside doorways in her walls and grow the rampant Clematis montana up the stonework above. The two plants flowered charmingly together on a verge of summer, and then she had the shrub's berries. I value the compact form in any mixed border or small urban garden's shade: Scotts of Merriott always sell it and the compact and yellow-fruited forms are both available from Wayside in South Carolina, who keep a good range of all Viburnums.

Lastly, remember the bunches of fruit on the Sorbus, or Mountain Ash. I like the pinkish white marbled fruits on hupehensis, which has grey-green leaves, but all the varieties are handsome, even the scarlet-fruited Rowan which appears in streets. I leave you to choose what is available, emphasizing the value of this second feature in a Sorbus family which has fine leaves, autumn colour and earlier, some respectable white flowers.

Concluding Scents

When the bonfires begin, the scents of flowers retreat from my awareness. I value, therefore, two clematis which both climb vigorously: rehderiana, whose little off-white flowers smell of cowslips, and flammula, which grows over ten feet a year in a good soil and has white flowers like vanilla-scented snow, followed by fluffy seed-heads. Both are offered by Treasures of Tenbury Wells, but only the latter, the 'Fragrant Virgin's Bower', in America by Blackthorne, Mass., who praise it highly. Other-wise, one of the clearest divisions between gardens in August and gardens from winter till the fading of the first roses is this matter of smell. In winter, sweet-scented flowers are almost the only flowers which are open; in late summer there are butterflies, fermenting apples and the season's leakage of oil smoking sharply on a tired mowing machine. So I wondered what I would have to do to deserve a scent if I was turned into a summer flower.

It would all depend, I find in my botany books, on my attar. Before you joke about Mother Nature scenting roses attar stroke, I remind you that attar is a Persian word meaning smell and that it applies to a plant's essential oil. This oil is puzzling, hence the word 'essential' to deter

117

further inquiry: it is also said to be secreted, another metaphor to put you off the scent. But the first points about it are easy enough.

Attar is stored in leaves and petals, not in a plant's sexual parts, and is released by evaporation. The cooler the air, the more gradually it evaporates, one reason for the richer smell of night-scented stocks in gardens after dark, and (I imagine) winter iris and winter sweet in chilly January. Lush petals which feel like velvet are slow to lose drops of attar, hence velvety roses do smell more gorgeous, quite apart from our romantically natured noses. Double flowers have more petals, hence more attar, which they also lose less rapidly.

From here on it is very much a question of explaining a familiar quality in terms of equivalent but unfamiliar chemistry. Attar is secreted as a waste mixture of sugar and oil, usually an alcoholic oil; alcohol is still used by scent makers to dissolve the chemicals of scent. This delicious sort of refuse is piled up because of the plant's chlorophyll, the magic green mixture behind so much plant growth whose origins and nature I cannot discuss here. Chlorophyll piles up sweet-scented oils in so far as it is not impeded by the pigment in a petal's colouring. This is a text-book fact which gardeners have to take on trust, for it explains more effects in our gardens than it confuses. Heavily-pigmented flowers such as scarlet tulips or orange Super Star roses have very little smell because their colour hinders chlorophyll's part in producing attar. White flowers have no pigment and thus smell strongly, so a white garden of lilies, cream-white honeysuckle and rose Blanc de Coubert is not just an illogical exercise in good taste. There is science in Sissinghurst's success.

There are two lines to the inquiry at this point. Either we can explore the chemicals and discuss the scent of mock orange blossom, my favourite summer scent, in terms of methyl anthranilate. Or we can ask whether plants have a reason for storing waste oils in the first place. These questions of function and design have always been dangerous. Our great-grandfathers used to dodge them by answering in terms of God's will, and now that ecology has become a cult, we answer in terms of a mystical balance of nature. The main reasons for scent concern insects and pollination, but they cannot always explain how the two matched themselves so neatly together. When I consider the only available reasons I am happy to think that their match was divine.

Like intelligent advertisers, flowers often suit their scent and appearance to the presumed preferences of their clients. Hawthorn smells of stale dung and wears a brown look on its white flowers in order to attract dung flies; moths go for the clove-scent of night-flowering campion which is released only when the air temperature falls quite low, usually, therefore, at night in its summer flowering season when moths are on the wing, able to pick out a pale colour like this campion's pale pink. Perhaps moths are common in winter in the home countries of the scented shrubs of a winter garden. On the other hand, there is no powerful scent to flowers which rely on the good old birds and bees. Birds have no sense of smell, so they do not pollinate my lovely Lilium regale; bees do not visit scents so much as colours, although they do not see colours as we do; they prefer blue and purple flowers but they see them more in terms of purple and red. White, to a bee, has a yellow suffusion, though how any scientist knows this for sure without being bee-minded himself I cannot say.

So the answer to my question concerns moths, oils and fertility. As with flowers, so too with leaves; the resinous scent of the Mediterranean cistus and helichrysum serves to deter grazing animals; the oils of thyme and rosemary leaves are strongly antiseptic and kill off germs. The sequence of these effects is more of a puzzle; which came first, the pungency of the sage's leaves, or the browsing goat? The theme of scent has wound through this book, from romantic fancies about jasmine through praises of Daphne odora and plans for scented lilies to this conclusion, that it would never exist so strongly without butterflies, bothersome moths and molesting animals on the move.

Wild Cyclamen

In late autumn, I look to flowering bulbs, not only the bulbs which have to be planted for the following spring, but those, too, which flower in these declining months of the year. There are the hardy Guernsey Lilies, washed up in legend from their shipwreck to the foot of a sunny wall and a sandy soil: there are the butter-yellow flowers of the lovely Sternbergias, no taller than those of a large crocus and popular candidates as the biblical "lilies of the field": they, too, like a sunny place and have flourished and multiplied for ten years or more, if not with me, at least with my brother on a stony, alkaline soil. They are totally hardy and emerge suddenly, like yellow crocuses, in early autumn.

These "lilies of the field" prefer special south-facing beds, always a precious position. However, the entire south-facing aspect cannot be given over to autumn bulbs. It is here that the hardy Cyclamen come into their own: one of the essential attractions of any garden, large or small.

Everybody loves these small flowers and their popularity is world-wide: in the 1930's, the import of cyclamen into America was still prohibited under a ban on possible disease-carrying plants and the bulb magazines and handbooks reacted with the indignation of whisky-drinkers, confronted by a second round of prohibition. Prices went up vertically: "Why should we be starved, having been tantalized?", asked Louise Beebe Wilder, an influential writer on bulbs and corms: the whole episode is witness to the hardy cyclamens' hold over gardeners. Yet in my experience, gardeners are still nervous of growing them. They know the half-hardy varieties because the shops push them at them, and they think the wild ones are for specialists only, something to admire, not grow. I think the truth is the other way round: the hardy forms are easier than most of the plants you buy in a florist.

If you decide to buy them, you have the choice of whether to buy the corms dry or in green growth and potted up. The potted corms are easier to establish and you cannot really fail with a hardy form unless you stick a fork through it when it is dormant: in Britain, W.E. Ingwersen of Gravetye Nurseries, East Grinstead, Sussex are good suppliers, as are Potterton and Martin of Moortown Road, Nettleton, Caistor, Lincs. who will also export very efficiently, cyclamen not being banned any more to Transatlantic addicts. Necessarily, these potted growing corms are more expensive. As I wish to suggest liberal uses for cyclamen, as edgings and groups, I will spend some time on the problems of dry corms, a cheaper source, In America, I recommend Blackthorne Gardens of Holbrook, Mass. who do a special collection of cyclamen, and supply all the hardy varieties (but not persicum) which I discuss. For the past two years they have had to cancel varieties from the Middle East, due to political disturbances in the supplying areas: the cancellation looks set to run for a few years yet.

When planting a dry corm, the danger is that you will plant it upside down. Not long ago I was potting up some rare fritillaries and confronted the same difficulty. The whole surface of the bulb was cracked and wrinkled like an old man's skin; what the books like to call basal roots seemed to be sprouting in all four directions. In the end I trusted to luck and hoped that the young shoots would right themselves if they were upside down. Fritillaries usually do, but cyclamen are not so obliging. The shapes of their dry, dormant corms are particularly perplexing.

I will discuss the most common variety, neapolitanum, first. It is the well-known form which flowers from August onwards and is distinguished by its reflexed petals and the silver marbling of its leaves. Usually, the flowers are pink, but the rarer white form is quite lovely: its corms are more expensive, but a few whites should always be included in a planting of pinks so that they can seed themselves and develop over the years. Pink and white neapolitan cyclamen develop roots from the tops of their corms, unlike other types of flowering plant. How, then, do you find the top of a corm? The answer is to look for the bottom first: the bottom is hollowed out into a concave pattern. Even so, it is not immediately obvious. The whole corm is saucer-shaped and expands with age until after twenty or thirty years it begins to resemble a plate. Its top surface may well be disfigured by cracks or dents, but it must not mislead you. You need to find a concave hollow and then you plant the corm on it, cracks, scars and other irregularities uppermost. Do not take fright at the sight of last year's roots and assume that they must go on the underside, whatever my advice. Cyclamen are perverse and happily keep 'roots' on their upper surface.

Despite this habit, hardy cyclamen do not need to be deeply planted. Sometimes, in the wild, you may find them anchored way below the surface of the soil, but you should never be trying to excavate them and steal them; please leave them to their firm anchorage. In gardens a covering of two inches of soil above a corm is quite sufficient. Their tendency is to move upwards, not downwards. Sometimes, after a few years, a huge old corm will rise to the surface, amaze you with a girth up to 6 inches across and still produce its 3-inch-high flowers quite happily. The best time to plant neapolitanum and indeed any other variety is early July, when the corms are all but dormant. Always handle dry corms very carefully. If you tip them out of the packet and plant them where they fall, thinking you are achieving a more natural effect, you will probably break the little surface roots that matter most.

Neapolitanum has such lovely flowers. They remind me of Ernest Shepherd's drawing of Piglet in a high wind, with his ears streaming out horizontally behind him, like the flowers on a wavy cyclamen. Like a crocus, the cyclamen has a scent which gardeners usually ignore: in warm weather, you can catch it if you kneel down to it, the source of the scent which has been bred back into tender greenhouse cyclamen, now absurdly named 'Scentsation'. Unlike Scentsation, the wild neapolitanum needs no heat and gives you a fine carpet of marbled green leaves when the flowers have died; the leaves last from October to April. After flowering, the stems coil down and lie flat against the earth as if they were taking a bow. They are full to seed which is worth saving. If you sow it at once and leave the pots outdoors in winter to freeze, there is a strong chance that it will sprout in the following spring or summer. Alternatively, if you leave the seed alone, it often germinates beside the parent. Sometimes cyclamen will spread far and wide, a habit which is helped by friendly ants who convoy the seed between their front feet and drop it at a distance, where it often germinates.

Above all, neapolitanum is a cyclamen which really flourishes in dry shade. Some of the biggest corms are found among the roots of huge old trees: I have dined in cyclamen-fields, growing wild among the bone-dry pine-trees of Greece and the Aegean; in captivity, the corms flourish in arid conditions, even in a garden on the prairies. My favourite planting runs in a ribbon beneath a long green hedge of the useful evergreen Thuja: it fills that awkward space between the hedge and the edge of a lawn and produces a long line of Piglet's ears each autumn. Under yews, junipers or the ghastly Cypress leylandii and macrocarpa, this cyclamen is in its element. It actually chooses such places in the wild: members of the family are wedged magnificently among the among the antique Cypresses, yews and ilexes of central Italy.

Nonetheless, it is extremely hardy. It survives any winter anywhere in Britain: I have had correspondence with contented growers as far north as Ontario; Blackthorne comment that visitors to their nursery are "delighted and dumbfounded" to see the "proud pink blooms bravely holding their heads above a blanket of snow in December". So you can trust them to survive. A lime soil is much to their liking: their one awkwardness is their frequent reluctance to flourish in polluted city-gardens. I cannot blame them, but I would never rely on them in a window-box.

Neapolitanum alone is good enough but there are many other varieties, which are as lovely and prolong the season almost the whole year round. Coum is a Greek one, from the island of Cos, which is extremely tough and really does flower every year in winter: admittedly, its flowers are a harsh shade of rose-pink, but I admire its stamina and greatly enjoy it. Hiemale is a rarer companion, slightly later into flower: I then have the pinkish-lavender Atkinsi in late spring; a brief gap, unless I am lucky with the Greek graecum in July; then, one of my special friends, cilicium, which comes from southern Turkey and is very obviously scented in its soft pink flowers. One of the easiest forms with the most marbled leaves is europaeum, an essential companion to neapolitanum: together they bring you almost back to coum and a second round of the cyclamen-calendar.

That last paragraph is almost more Latin than English but each of those names refers to a very individual beauty. Each has its idiosyncrasies and I like them all. I would need a hundred tongues to describe them or complain how the florists have blown up the persicum varieties into those huge pot plants we give out at Christmas. The real persicum has long reflexed petals of blush-white with a dark spot at their base: it smells deliciously and flowers in March. I do beg you to try it in gritty, limy earth in a shallow pan. It takes up little room and unlike its forced, waxy children, I have never known it wilt within a week and die. It comes from Rhodes and Cyprus, the drier hillsides of Asia and the sparse slopes of inner Iran. In captivity it is happy in an unheated greenhouse, a conservatory or a cold frame, happy homes for all the potted cyclamen I have mentioned. I like to see the neat leaves and perfectly shaped flowers above a surfacing of gravel, easily contrived in any pot or pan. Some of the best cyclamen I ever saw were grown by a friend in those matchless gardening containers: plastic margarine-boxes. Naturally, you have to empty out the margarine before planting.

Of all the ideas in this book, wild cyclamen are probably the one which has given me most pleasure. If you are still undecided, perhaps I can settle the matter by reminding you of their historic virtues. To find these properties, you have to look to the old books of herbal wisdom, compiled three or four centuries ago when the art was at its height. They are rare books, but good libraries have the originals or one of the later facsimiles.

Among the herbalists, the most accessible are two Englishmen: John Gerard (1597) and John Parkinson (1629). Gerard wrote a famous Herbal, Parkinson, an Earthly Paradise (Paradisus Terrestris) with a Latin pun on his name (Park In Sun: Paradisus In Sole). As Parkinson usually disagrees with his predecessor, it is all the more amusing to compare them: on the topic of hardy cyclamen, they excel themselves.

Gerard begins by reminding us what a network of local knowledge passed to and fro between inquisitive men in Tudor England. 'Men of good credit', he says, have told him that the cyclamen grows wild on the hills of Wales and Lincolnshire, and in Somersetshire; also upon a fox-burrow not far from Master Bamfield's farm. Charming though his geography is, he may have been mistaken (he often was). Sixty years later, Parkinson said that he had very curiously inquired of many whether or not the cyclamen grows wild in England and they had all affirmed that they had never seen it and that it did not. Nowadays, there are a few naturalized clumps of the neapolitanum variety in the south, but they have escaped from gardens. As the name shows, the wild plants belong in Italy near Naples.

But Gerard has more to say. Cyclamen is known to him, as to some people now, by the English name of sowbread: in parts of Greece, indeed, it is still used as a good for pigs. In the 1870's, primitivists like Ruskin wanted to change all Latin plant names back to their English equivalents; they had to pretend that they preferred to admire each other's Sowbreads, rather than comparing their Cyclamen. Kyklos is the Greek for a circle and 'kyklamen' refers to the spiral shape of the flower-stem after flowering. It is a prettier idea than pigfood.

Back, however, to the herbals: besides feeding sows, cyclamen were also valuable for male chauvinist pigs. According to Gerarde, cyclamen (hot and dry in the third degree) should be beaten into little flat cakes and is then 'a good amorous medicine to make a man in love if it be inwardly taken'. Poor old Parkinson obviously tried it as he found that 'as for its amorous effects, they are mere fabulous'. He was not using the word in its modern exclamatory way: he meant they were stuff and nonsense. Certainly, he was never happily married, but if he had been, he might still have kept cyclamen in the cupboard. In the first century A.D., the Latin author, Pliny, had remarked in his Natural History that cyclamen were useful for childbirth. Anything said by Greek and Latin authors was treated with excessive respect by the sixteenth century's naturalists, and Gerard was quick to act on the advice. It gave casual employment to his wife and quite changed the shape of his flower-beds. Mrs Gerard, he tells us, had become a dab hand with cyclamen-leaves: she had had 'great success in placing cyclamen leaves on the secret parts of women in travaile', while he himself was taking no chances in his garden. So strong is the pull of cyclamen leaves on a woman with child that he had to counter their natural virtue by 'fastening sticks on the ground and others also crossways over them lest any visiting women should by lamentable

124

experiment find my words to be true by stepping astride the said cyclamen and delivering long before their day'.

Much has been said about life in Tudor England, its haphazard justice, its Court, its theatre, its sudden millionaires, the habits of its Virgin Queen. But it was also a place where people knew cyclamen on fox-burrows, where a visiting woman might come and wrap cyclamen-leaves in your underpants and where you had to be careful while looking round gardens in a maternity dress. This 'knowledge' had a long and wide-spread life. When Parkinson's book appeared, Gerard's was promptly revised by Thomas Johnson and his edition, Johnson-upon-Gerard, appeared in 1633: ten copies are known to have reached New England with the early boat-loads of settlers. From Virginia to Norfolk, people had to watch where they trod in the flower-bed: I dare say that the cyclamen-suppliers can still provide a protective frame of sticks if you are on the route of expectant mothers.

Strong Maples

Even in Britain, autumn is a time of changing colours, red and yellow leaves and a fall which is more of a slip or stumble compared with the great displays of America's East Coast. Maples are more of a matter for gardeners in Vermont than in England's Home Counties, but we do have one, and access to another, which I think we all underestimate. They are tough, reliable trees, one for hedging and screening, the other for a prized place in any garden which is not too dry; surprisingly, I cannot find them in the lists of major American nurserymen who work by mail-order, so perhaps the great maple-growers, too, may be needing a nudge.

The British Field Maple, or Acer campestre, is a tree for which I have a particular fondness. Its shape is very decisive, as if it knows its place in the plant world and is determined to take its stand there. It is round headed, a sturdy 20 feet high, and graciously equipped with five-lobed leaves. It is often to be seen as a young bush, encroaching on a crab-apple tree or competing with the Traveller's Joy which enlivens our hedgerows even in November, smothering them with its greying seed-heads as if a flock of sheep had left their wool on the brambles underneath. It will put up with any cold wind and will flourish on chalky soils: in Britain, it is at home on the exposed prairies of East Anglia where the farmers of Norfolk, Suffolk,

Essex and Cambridgeshire have turned the countryside into a bleak plain in the past thirty years. Field Maple is one of the few screening trees which will put up with the wind and the rising dust off these miserable apologies for 'farming'. Trees, like prophets, tend to be ignored in their own countries: to see Acer campestre's potential, you should go to Austria. In the old imperial gardens of Schloss Schönbrunn, in Vienna, there is a magnificent hedge of our field maple, thick, regular and beautifully matured. In a grand setting, on limy soil, it would be fitting and rewarding to plant a future rival.

Snakebark Maples are trees of an altogether higher quality. Their trunks tend to have a hint of olive-green in their grey wood and characteristically, they are marked by snaky, vertical stripes of white on their bark. Snakebarks are not native to Britain, but they are one of those interesting types of plant which divides its habitat between the Far East and America. To my eye, there are three especially good forms: capillipes (a Japanese form), pennsylvanicum (American, naturally) and rufinerve (Japanese). Pennsylvanicum is the most readily available and grows quickly, so I will concentrate on this American native, remarking only that rufinerve is perhaps marginally my favourite: you can recognize it by its glaucous young shoots, as I discovered some years ago in the Glasnevin Botanic Garden, Dublin where the Irish have a rufinerve nearly fifty feet high. It must be on sale in its homeland, but the mailing lists somehow fail to specify it.

Pennsylvanicum grows quite rapidly, but it is a specimen tree for a modest garden's lawn or boundary. It flowers in May, but the yellowish flowers are not conspicuous: its three virtues lie elsewhere, in its leaves, bark and habit. Its maple-leaves open with a pink tinge, grow to quite a handsome size and turn a pleasant yellow in the autumn. As the tree ages, its bark improves, like a vintage port: a snaky line of white runs in a zig-zag down the trunk and branches, taking over from an earlier reddish brown phase in the wood. Snakesbarks look their best in those variable lights of March or April days, when sun and rain-clouds alternate, or the particular serenity of clear October afternoons. Pennsylvanicum, finally, has a rather upright habit which allows you to fit it into a fairly confined space. I think of it as a twenty foot tree after fifteen years, developing more slowly afterwards. When the Far Eastern Snakebarks were found in China and Japan, our grandfathers forsook the Pennsylvanian Maple and pursued the newcomers instead. I am not sure they were right: on my view, in England old or new, this Acer is a tree of great distinction.

Rapid Trees

When a man grows old, Dr Johnson once remarked, he begins to plant trees. I have often observed this effect of the passing years, but it goes with another: a wish that the trees should grow very quickly. Many of the best ones move slowly and even the Pennsylvanian Snakebark may take fifteen years to reach fifteen feet. If you are in a hurry, you need other types of tree, and here, too, I will begin by commending an Acer.

The Silver Maple, Acer saccharinum, is another variety, familiar in its native New England. I am amazed by it, and although it is brittle in high winds, I cannot imagine why gardeners are negligent of it; usually they simply do not know it. The Silver Maple eventually reaches thirty metres or more, but it has to accelerate to attain this distant goal: after five or six years, you will find you have a light, swaying tree, already a notable feature. Nurserymen sell Silver Maples as standards about nine feet tall; in America, the trees also scatter seed very freely which germinates and grows like sycamores in light shade. These seedlings can be moved and grown on rapidly at no cost: otherwise you can order a full tree from Weston Nurseries who have selected a specially good Silver Queen form. Silver Maples are too tall for your back garden, but they stand well up a driveway or in any adjoining field or smallholding. They are at their best in May when the fresh, pale green leaves show their silvery undersides and flutter enchantingly in a breeze. In a strong wind, however, they tend to snap, especially if planted by walls or buildings which set up their own cross-currents. Speed, as always, leads to a certain fragility: for steadiness, choose slow-growing oaks and hope that you live to be ninety.

If you live on soil which can grow azaleas and is damp or peaty, you should consider a southern cousin of the beech tree called Nothofagus. I have seen this tree planted commercially in Ireland as an experiment in speed, yet English nurseries rarely list it and American mail-firms ignore it: gardeners on the acid soil which it likes show little interest in all it can offer. These southern beeches grow wild in New Zealand and South America, especially Chile, and are a last reminder that the two continents were once joined in their prehistory. Like many plants from the southern hemisphere, the southern beeches grow extremely fast, pacing a Lombardy poplar in gardens which are free of lime and sheltered from wind. Their leaves are small, like a small beech or hornbeam, and their autumn colouring is most remarkable: each leaf changes individually to its own shade of orange, red, brown or plain green, so that the upright shape of the tree looks unusually like a patchwork.

The shape of a southern beech is not particularly attractive, because its fast growth gives it an upright and scrawny appearance. Nor is the Antarctic variety recommended for sites which need a tree, as it divides into several trunks and turns into a shrub with twisting stems; no doubt this habit is a protection against the winds of its exposed home. But a Chilean variety called obliqua is rapid, upright and much to my liking. In twenty years' time, the foresters tell me, it will be at least 70 feet high. Quite a monument, then, to plant, even when you first draw your pension.

As we are on the subject of Antipodean trees, I must give one tip about the eucalyptus. Whole areas of the world, from Ethiopia to California, probably feel that they have nothing to learn about it: the tree grows very fast, is most handsome when young and will tolerate a place as dry as Ethiopia, as its late royal family discovered, importing young plants by the thousand from Australia in order to give themselves street-trees in Addis Ababa. I only want to remind you that eucalyptus grows very easily from seed and that the juvenile leaves of the seedlings are the most beautiful. They are improved by ruthless cutting-back in their third year. By using seed-packets and secateurs, you can have low thickets of shimmering eucalyptus: Thompson and Morgan of London Road, Ipswich still sell seed of fourteen different types, including the Spinning Gum (perriniana) and a 'Frost-resistant Species Mixture', which I recommend to Californians in exile. Otherwise, try the lovely lemon-scented citriodora, which T. and M. list as a 'highly-prized pot plant', because in British winters, it is not hardy: their range is still bigger than Park's Seeds, Burpees and the other American stockists who only list a few varieties.

Results, whichever you choose, are extremely rapid, suited to octogenarians who have felt the Johnsonian impulse rather too late. If they detest Eucalyptus in their mature state, they can always try a Poplar instead. Everybody knows the upright types, but I wish to exhort all planters of alleys, walks and edgings of drives to consider the scented balsam poplar in particular. Balsam poplar seduces by its name alone, and is indeed a delightful tree for an avenue because its young leaves give off a pleasantly tempered scent of the sort of balsam that children are made to sniff under towels when they have bad colds. The sticky leaf-buds are too pungent if you handle them, but alongside a walk to a house or a spinney, they waft their sweetly resinous smell on any warm wind, particularly after the rain.

Only eight years are needed to turn them from saplings into a tall avenue. There are very few difficulties about their life, except that they resent heavy soil and do most of their work underground. They have long and wide-ranging roots, more than 10 yards from their stem, and they are very powerful. I have known a screen of balsams unsettle a surfaced tennis court, while one in a London garden is making a bold assault on a house-wall.

At maturity, an age at which they are seldom seen, they are very tall, three-storied like a high French Gothic cathedral. If you can think big, a balsam every four or five yards will make an avenue of which you can be proud. Be sure to choose the forms known as balsamifera, or tacamahaca, not the less scented candicans. If you know a balsam avenue, simply take long cuttings, 3 or 4 feet high, embed half their length in the ground and you will find that they root with delightful ease at no cost to you or anyone else. For some years, I lived with such a balsam-avenue in the great Oxfordshire garden of Mrs C.G. Lancaster of Haseley Court: she had first known them in her native Virginia and had observed their proper placing and spacing, while storing them for the day that she had a house with a suitable approach. Again, they are not in the mail-order lists in America, but they ought to be available on casual visits to good local garden-centres.

Lucky her, you may feel, but what about the ageing gardener with the same Johnsonian urge and little space in which to act on it? Here, I must add a post-script in favour of planting certain types of tree and pruning them ferociously to keep them as healthy shrubs. The French and the Japanese are masters of this art, which is not confined to indoor varieties. Elsewhere, however, we have simply forgotten the possibilities.

I was reading recently the plans of the great Miss Jekyll, the mistress of Munstead Wood and the modern garden, and I noticed how she advised the hard pruning of plane trees, especially the golden-leaved plane trees, for places at the back of her wide borders. The treatment led to larger and richer leaves and the result would be most unusual: it could be repeated with the catalpa, a favourite tree with town gardeners, the golden catalpa, sea buckthorn, cornel trees, the Stag's Horn sumach (Rhus typhina), the silver poplar, willows (and not only the brilliant red-twigged willows), or the golden-leaved Honey Locust tree called Gleditschia Sunburst. The best of all are two trees which come very easily from seed, again sold by Thompson and Morgan of Ipswich, who will export it willingly. The first is considered hardy only in warmer parts of Britain, but we may be wrong, as Sunset's Western Garden Book claims it will survive in all zones in the U.S.A., flowering in the warmer ones only: Paulownia tomentosa is a big spreading tree, eventually bearing purple-violet flowers like fox-gloves, but it has huge leaves like pale green parasols if you grow it from seed and cut it yearly to within a foot of the ground in spring. Its pair is the admirable Ailanthus, or Tree of Heaven, which revels in this torture and produces wonderfully pinnate leaves if kept down to three or four feet. Like Paulownia, it germinates swiftly from seed: I recommend it, not only as a pensioner's final tree-like fling.

Quick Climbers

Trees, you may feel, are all very well for bigger gardens, but what most of us need are quick-growing climbers, partly to deal with modern architects, partly to deal with the neighbours. As few books or lists are honest about the relative speed of climbing plants I will also set down a few of the fastest for your purpose. Quick growth, of course, depends on site and climate, like most other qualities in the garden. But there are some broad divisions which are true throughout.

The Russian vine (listed as Polygonum baldschuanicum after a Russian, I imagine) is familiar enough and its light sprays of pearl-white flowers are not objectionable. This plant is extremely rampant, only to be used in cases of deep despair or designs by the "architect" Basil Spence. It will jam up the gutters and grow under the tiles of most low roofs where impatient gardeners plant it and regret it within two years. But the Russian vine will also grow from a city basement below the street to the eaves of a three-storied house. It is shy, however, if planted in a tub and left on a hard surface, unless the tub is watered heavily and very frequently. I have always hoped to live where I would not need this climbing knotweed, but many gardeners have to be grateful to it: in America, White Flower Farm present it as Polygonum aubertii and call it, too favourably, the Silver Fleece Vine.

A less common alternative is the Kiwi Fruit or Chinese gooseberry (Actinidia) which is very quick indeed on a west or warmer wall. Where the Russian vine smothers with a curtain, this rapid climber sprawls with long feelers and grows rapidly to a height of 20 feet. It has to be held in position with wires and this need may put you off it, but its bold leaves and hairy stems are far more impressive than a Russian vine's. In August there is a faint but pleasing scent from yellow-white flowers which fade to buff-yellow, like a honeysuckle's, when they are fertilized: in America Wayside Nurseries in South Carolina are more enthusiastic, referring to its "almost indescribably delicious flavour, somewhat suggestive of a tangy banana and strawberry combination". Indescribable, I agree, but there is no accounting for 'delicious' tastes. If you plant both a male and a female (Wayside are the only nursery on either side of the Atlantic to segregate them), you will get fruit: one male, they remark, will provide for six to eight females, which may help you understand the old saying about playing (Chinese) gooseberry. When the leaves first appear, they are reddish and briefly vulnerable to spring frost. Winters can cut back this rampant plant, but if you have a south- or west-facing wall, I think that Wayside are slightly too cautious in talking of "zones nine to ten" and suitability for greenhouses. In Britain, this Actinidia is very much tougher on a warm wall: Scotts of Merriott supply good stock of it.

Neither of these climbers is evergreen: if you share my lack of enthusiasm for ivies, I suggest you try an extremely rapid honeysuckle which is almost always in leaf. Lonicera japonica halliana is not the most handsome in the family, but it is the white-flowered, scented variety which will grow as well in sun or shade, hot or cold, town or country. Only prune it if you must, and please it where you can enjoy its superb scent: in America, Wayside of South Carolina sell it, remarking correctly that its deep roots help to bind the earth onto slopes and banks and make it a good cover when grown on such an incline.

What about the direst emergency, a new garden with a beastly fence or shed or a new intrusion on your landscape? Here, you must turn to half-hardy climbers, grown as annuals from seed sown in early March, planted out in late May from individual pots and allowed to grow rampantly for the next three months. Thompson and Morgan list, sell and export seed of the wonderful Cobaea, a twining plant which thrives in towns and has purple or white bell-shaped flowers; the seeds germinate best, I have learned, if they are sown standing on their edge. They need heat initially, but then they are very easy if you pot them on into single pots and give them long canes up which they can begin to twine. I have known them

131

grow twenty feet in one season: alternatively, in America the purple (but not the rare white) is available from Park's, of Greenwood, S. Carolina.

Tall climbing nasturtiums are invaluable on spaces up to six feet high and really will grow in any reasonable season: they were proven in the heat of India by British Imperial gardeners. Other ideas are the red-flowered Eccremocarpus, a delicate mixture of leaf and flower which fits into most corners, and the rapid variegated Hop, excellent value from seed: again, Thompson and Morgan list both of them conveniently.

The test for perennial quick-growers is whether or not they will look presentable before the middle of their third season after planting. Often the most rampant plants are the slowest to become established. The pink and white forms of Clematis montana, ivies of all kinds, the evergreen garrya and its green winter catkins, the climbing hydrangea which is so lovely when its leaves are turning clear yellow: these familiar 'quick' climbers accelerate, in my experience, only after three years. You have to pick and choose your roses, too. When the third year turns, single roses with wild Oriental blood or rambling varieties like Wedding Day, Albertine, Alberic Barbier and Pauls Scarlet have left behind the more elegant and shapely kinds like Guinee or even Mermaid. Virginia Creeper, usually, makes rapid progress, but I do notice that it likes to be quiet for a year or two before accelerating: the best is not a Virginian, but the Boston Ivy, Parthenocissus tricuspidata, available here or abroad from Hilliers of Winchester, Hampshire and in America from Wayside who have "finally located the original strain", they say, "after a long search". However it cannot compete with my favourite vine, the large-leaved Vitis coignetiae. This wonderful climber likes towns or country villages: it needs only some sunlight to race away up old fire-escapes, eyesores and prefabricated houses. The leaves are big and bold and in autumn they turn a lovely shade of flame-purple: it is a first choice for any wall which needs masking.

Lastly, I return to my fondness for plants from the wild. On lime soils, British hedgerows are alive in late summer or autumn with the wild Clematis vitalba or Travellers' Joy. In autumn, it rounds off its season of pale green flower and leaf with that wonderful show of fluffy seed-heads. I put this climber first for gardeners with no patience, yet they seldom plant it. In the hurry to have a full-grown garden, we do not even stop to look for Travellers' Joy beyond the garden wall: in America, apply to Blackthorne, in Holbrook, Mass., who share my enthusiasm for this generous plant.

132

CLEMATIS VITALBA: *TRAVELLERS JOY*

GERANIUM   MACRORRHIZUM   IN   WILD   GARDEN
SELINUM   TENUIFOLIUM: *GIANT   COW   PARSLEY*

LILIUM AURATUM: *GOLDEN RAYED LILY OF JAPAN*

MUSK ROSES AND CATMINT AT BRILL, OXFORDSHIRE

Travelling Tradescants

As the fluffy seed-heads of Travellers' Joy begin to turn to grey wool and the leaves of my favourite Vitis coignetiae deepen to wine-purple and start to fall, I find myself turning inwards from the garden and withdrawing indoors into the corridors of the mind. It is a time for planning and reflecting and for giving scope to the imagination: a sudden find can take you back to the months of flowers and lush greenery, as I found one November morning on my way to work. Usually, it is the time of day when my thoughts are furthest from the garden. My route lies down a passage lined by classical sculpture. I turn right where the Emperor Augustus casts a provincial glance at his deceptively dainty wife on the opposite wall. I move between cases of Dark Age cutlery and turn left by two large Viking stones engraved with runic script. Until I happened to look behind the doorway, these random relics of the past had always depressed me.

Behind the door stood a gravestone of blue-black granite with a faded but familiar inscription. 'Know, stranger, ere thou pass, beneath this stone, lye JOHN TRADESCANT, grandsire, father, son … '. A chain of happy memories was touched off by these words. In the history of transatlantic gardening, there are few more stirring names than the first two Johns of the Tradescants. I had always believed that their gravestone was still with their bodies, in the cemetery of St. Mary's, Lambeth, in London. But in the 1880s, it seems, it was rescued from ruin and presented to Oxford where the rest of the Tradescant mementoes, their fine family portraits and their museum of knick-knacks had notoriously come to rest.

Gardeners today owe the Tradescants a permanent vote of thanks. Through their travels they enlarged the scope of British gardens, linking them to the flowers and trees of America, Europe and through Constantinople, the East. These avenues were already open to others before they travelled and collected, but the Tradescants pursued them to great effect and gained public esteem for that lasting virtue in imaginative gardeners: a willingness to experiment with the plants and ideas of other cultures. It is hard to be sure exactly which plants they first introduced into Britain, but the list includes a red Maple, an Aquilegia and the glorious scarlet Honeysuckle, Lonicera sempervirens, which were all brought from Virginia by the younger of the two Johns.

The younger John, indeed, enjoyed a sight so often granted to early travellers but lost for ever to their descendants in an arable, industrial world. Like the first Greek settlers in Sicily in the age of Homer, the first English settlers in Virginia were amazed by the dense diversity of trees. "The present wilderness", wrote one such visitor, E.W. Gent, in 1650, "is not without a particular beauty, being all over a natural grove of oaks, pines, cedars, cypress, mulberry, chestnut, laurel, cherry, plum trees and vines, all of so delectable an aspect that the melancholiest eye in the world cannot look upon it without contentment nor content himself without admiration ...". Plants from Virginia had quickly come on sale in early seventeenth-century London: the younger Tradescant exploited the new fashion of his age sailing and collecting in America. His father, the elder John, had already made two notable journeys to Russia and Algeria, both of which had resulted in some worthwhile new plants: collecting was in the family's blood and it seems that the younger John's visit to Virginia in the 1630's was supported by King Charles I himself.

This royal patronage arose from the elder John's remarkable career. He was born about 1570, probably in Suffolk near England's east coast: he was married in Kent in 1607 and died in 1638. Somehow, he came rapidly into contact with the grandest social circles and in 1610, we find him employed at Hatfield House, the most palatial residence of the Cecil family. It was a good time to be working for the family: the great house at Hatfield was being reshaped and the enchanting gardens at their Manor, near Cranborne in Dorset, were being laid out. Both sites, now lavishly replanted, are worth a summer visit: at Cranborne, you can still see the formal mound beyond the croquet lawn which dates back to Tradescant's day. The gardens of these great patrons were more than enough to occupy him and from the family accounts, we have a vivid idea of his materials. His employer encouraged him to travel. In 1611, he was in Flanders and Paris, buying a mass of new plants, especially fruits, including 200 lime trees at half a crown each, 'flowers called anemone', many types of mulberry, medlars, quinces, one pot of gilliflowers (cost: nothing) and a very good brand of redcurrant. He was fast becoming an expert at growing melons; his liking for an avenue of limes was in advance of his age and his fruit was the 'choicest for goodness and size'. The triangular walks, parterres, vines and deer fences at Hatfield passed his time most happily.

Robert Cecil was an excellent patron for the inquisitive gardener, supervising each new plan, sponsoring foreign travels and always extending his flowerbeds further into the park. He was also appreciative. On the grand staircase at Hatfield, he ordered John's picture to be carved, showing him pointing his toe and holding his rake in one hand and a basket of his new fruits in the other. The best memorial is still in the account book: 'to John Tradescant, the poor fellow that goeth to London — 2s. 6d'. Every country gardener can sympathize with that entry, in more senses than one.

From Hatfield, John moved on to Canterbury; from Canterbury he joined an expedition to Russia, keeping a careful diary of sea breezes and scenery as well as a charming section headed 'things by me observed'. His spelling throughout it is frightful but it allows us to work out the plants he encountered, Siberian firs, larches and spruces, cranberries, blueberries, meadow geraniums, Veratrum or helleborine and many others. In 1620, he sailed for seven months in the Mediterranean as part of a convoy against Barbary pirates, using the trip as an excuse to gather more new plants, whether wild double-flowered pomegranates or Spanish onions. Safely back in England, he was taken on by the Duke of Buckingham, planting another lime avenue for his benefit and then sailing off with his troops to the tiny island of Rhé where he found a form of scented Stock and a 'prickly strawberry' and must have noticed the local scarlet corn poppy. John would have preferred the poppy as, on his own admission, he was incapable of detecting niceties of smell — one reason, perhaps, why he revelled in growing fruits and was not satisfied with ordinary aromatic herbs.

In 1630 he received his crowning honour. He was appointed keeper of the Royal Gardens, Vines and Silkworms at Oatlands, serving King Charles I and Henrietta Maria, the 'rose and lily Queen' as his tombstone charmingly puts it. His salary was £100 a year; he had become a man of property, owning a house dubbed The Ark in Lambeth, where he built up a famous collection of curiosities, from Russian vests to Barbary spurs, many of which he had found on his travels. These were later to form the core of Oxford's Ashmolean Museum, home of his fine bearded portrait and, as I found, the famous family tombstone.

It was this career which brought the younger John to the King's notice as a suitable collector for a visit to Virginia: trust was rewarded, not least by the younger Tradescant's introduction of the Tulip Tree to England. The family remains a supreme argument against narrow parochialism in gardening. In the 1630's, a visit to South Lambeth was essential for any serious gardener or herbalist. They had so much which was new to their countrymen: scarlet-flowered runner beans; over fifty varieties of flame-coloured tulip, apart from many other shades; Oriental Planes; five new types of cistus; many types of auricula and then, from Virginia, the Swamp Cypress, Bladder Nut (Staphylea), yellow Virginian Jasmine (Gelsemium) and several starworts and the narrow-leaved Yucca, another Virginian native.

Their name is still commemorated in the Tradescantia, that slightly untidy herbaceous plant with three open petals of violet, white or rose-purple among its rushy leaves. At first, it was believed to be a cure for the bite of poisonous spiders, whence its popular name, Spiderwort: in fact, we know that an earlier Tradescantia had already reached Germany, where it was painted in 1600 with other American and Mexican plants. The younger Tradescant's achievement was to introduce the white-flowered form to Europe, the one which I still prefer in gardens: in America, White Flower Farm, Connecticut are very strong in Trades-cantias and sell a large white Snowcap, not available to English gardeners.

There has never been such a happy cross-fertilization between British and American gardens as these golden decades of the early seventeenth centuries. Perhaps the next fifty years will see a comparable willingness of Englishmen to experiment and import from other tastes. Meanwhile the prettiest memorial to the Tradescants' curiosity lies in the words on the family gravestone:

> Whilst they (as Homer's Iliad in a nut)
> A world of wonders in a closet shut ...
> Transplanted now themselves, sleep here; and when
> Angels shall with their trumpets waken men
> And fire shall purge the world, these three shall rise
> And change this Garden then for Paradise.

Long-Lasting Flowers

Winter is not only a time for reflecting on strange tombstones and collectors from the past: it is also the season when I try to think how to improve the garden. I return again and again to the need for plants with a long season. The smaller the space in a garden the better the use it must make of its time. The mention of a name like Amelanchier canadensis would make most gardeners shy away from it but this ordinary small tree, known as the snowy mespilus (one obscurity after another) is to my mind better value than a cherry, though it has never been popular. Its cloud of small white flowers is followed by fruits in a favourable year, then brilliant autumn colour equal to the brightest Canadian trees. Nowadays we all prefer our pink cherry trees, probably in the mistaken hope that we might one day eat their fruits. But we ought to judge a plant by its season, not only by its old associations.

The timing of flowers varies widely, and it is not a subject on which you can ever trust nurserymen's catalogues. Admittedly, seasons fluctuate from one garden to the next, but there is no way that I would claim the Day Lily flowered from July till September, the hardy Meadow Geranium from May till August or the Evening Primrose from June till October, unless I was trying to sell stock of them. These mis-statements I have chosen at random from English nursery catalogues who ought to know better. They make grotesquely extended claims for clematis, confuse recurrent roses with continual flowers, abuse the word perpetual and jump from a plant's main flush of colour to its minor second post-script as if nothing but full value intervened. In fact, timing is a very subtle matter, varying within families and even within the hours of the day: the Swedish botanist Linnaeus did once plant a garden on the model of a clock so that a different flower would open at each hour of the day but his experiments have never been extended more usefully. Sun roses, evening primrose and that beautiful annual, the Marvel of Peru, were all part of the Swede's clock garden but none of them retains its flowers for more than two days.

There are broad differences which are as well to consider, especially when arranging a group of herbaceous plants. If you needed a true blue flower, 18 inches or 2 feet high, I suspect you would pick that rich dark Veronica called True Blue which belongs with the heaviest and most luxuriant June evening. But in a week the whole of its flower spike has dropped its petals, the lower ones fall before the top ones have had time to open. It leaves a boring clump of plain green for the rest of the season. Not so the bright blue perennial flax, called Linum narbonnense, a slender spidery plant which I associate with spidery sandy gardens. Its lovely flowers keep opening for three successive months and its thin stems sway gracefully in the wind. More value, here, than in the true blue Veronica, and if you enjoy dead-heading, the gardener's best therapy, then the flax will respond to your efforts by lasting even longer.

On the further edges of the blue spectrum, the area I call nurserymen's blue, there are some conspicuous long-lasters, three of which I would not be without. Instead of the common purple border salvia, the gardener who prizes a long season should plant the smaller form called May Night which begins to flower in May, stops in July for dead-heading, then starts again from the axils of the leaves in August. Similar dead-heading gives a second late summer season to phloxes and delphiniums (cut the flower-spikes off both of them) and also to the various carpeting forms of verbena.

For a long season, I strongly recommend the whole penstemon family. Named varieties abound and those which are not reliably hardy can be kept going by cuttings taken in autumn and wintered in an unheated frame. One of the toughest is the red Firebird, not quite so brilliant as its name: I combine it with the late, but long-lasting, Geranium Buxton's Blue, a superb trailing cranesbill for August till late October which enjoys a cool semi-shaded place. I also mix in some of the daisy-flowered Erigerons, one of those splendid plants whose small varieties will flower throughout the summer.

Away from the blues and purples the long service medal must surely go to a free-flowering white viola called cornuta alba which is the answer to almost any gap or doubt. Its mauve form is not so much to my taste, but the white one, even in shade, can be left to trail between clumps of more solid favourites or even trained over a short-lived neighbour, an oriental poppy, for example, which makes such a fuss and bother with its opulent flowers for one week only, then collapses into black fly, shrivelled leaves and unforgivable ugliness. The viola, which begins in May, will still be going strong: it has a second burst in autumn. You can cut it back, haul it up to a height of a foot or leave it flat to seed itself and multiply, though it is not an annual. Grouped near the green-flowered Corsican hellebore whose flowers will often last from January to April, it gives you a point of interest on which you can rely for most of the year. Gypsophila, Everlasting Pea and plain nasturtiums are other admirable plants for training over gaps and a dying June border. All are long-lasting flowers.

There is much more to be said, noticed and practised here, from such elementary advice as the fact that double flowers generally last longer than single flowers to the complicated effects of the weather and latitude on the season of any one flower. It seems to me, for instance, that purple and blue mauve flowers tend to last longer, perhaps because they are visited by bees, above all, for pollination. It also seems that the longest lasting flowers are not always the most beautiful, for a worthy penstemon can never compete with a bright blue and brief-lived Chilean crocus. The distinction must always be borne in mind.

Among shrubs, I must draw attention to the long season of the evergreen Hebes, formerly known as Veronicas. They are admirably suited to life beneath the windows of a house or in one of those narrow beds from which they can spill forwards over a path. They root with remarkable ease from cuttings, taken by the method I have described at any time from June till October. They require sun, a site which is not too exposed and any reasonable soil with or without lime. The one variable is their hardiness. Away from hard frost or snow, many members of this Antipodean family will tolerate remarkably dry conditions: in extreme cases, you should choose the varieties listed as 'whipcords', because they have very small leaves and lose little water to the atmosphere. The rest of us should begin with the evergreen varieties with more solid leaves, of which the blue, mauve and violet forms are the most reliable. Names vary, but I grow two called Margery Fish and Autumn Glory, the latter of which is an astonishing plant: its flowers will appear right through the year, most freely in late summer, but also in early spring and even winter if the weather is mild. A brief pruning in July encourages this winter flowering. Like a polyanthus, which shows colour in autumn, hebes bear flowers outside their main season. They do respond to dead-heading, a slow but rewarding job as each of their seed-heads has to be picked out of the joint of the leaves and there are very many of them.

The hebes' only rival in summer and autumn is the shrubby Potentilla with clear yellow flowers. Breeders and plant-spotters have been busy in this family, but the best is still the same clear yellow, arbuscula or, in common terms, Elizabeth. Orange-flowered forms, tangerine sports and the misnamed 'Red Ace' are all to be avoided: the flowers are smaller and more variable and the season is much too short. Potentilla arbuscula (Elizabeth) makes a broad bush about two feet high and can even be turned into a charming low hedge beside a path. It is ridiculously easy to grow and from July to October it is covered in single flowers which look like those of some large strawberry plant. Its disadvantage is its dead and twiggy appearance in winter, too lifeless for me to want it near the house where it is usually planted; if you break a branch in winter, do not be misled by its brown and apparently lifeless pith. It is quite normal, though it would be a sign of death in most other plants. Potentilla Elizabeth is extremely hardy in any aspect: in America, it is available from Weston Nurseries, but ask for Arbuscula, so as not to confuse them.

Lastly, my favourite long-lasting cover, perhaps the plant which I would least like to lose. Other hardy geraniums flower for two weeks and are gone, but the one enduring winner is the form called Endressii: in England, it is common, but I recommend Scotts of Somerset; in America, Weston Nurseries have it. Its leaves remain light and fresh: its stems trail across several feet and exclude weeds without ever becoming invasive: after a season, one plant can be split into fifty or more. The small flowers are a particular shade of strawberry-pink, like icing on a sugary cake: they appear from June till late September and remain my prize companion for shrubs, old roses, bare spaces, wild corners and even the yellow-flowered Potentilla Elizabeth. By choosing the right variety, you can have months of interest and colour, not one concentrated fling and fifty weeks of dullness.

December Roses

You may be wondering how roses fit into this scheme. 'God gave us memories that we might have roses in December': the first conclusion to draw from that remark is that J.M. Barrie had never grown China roses in his garden. You do not need an all-embracing memory or a quiet half-hour in which to think back over the high garden moments of summer in order to enjoy a China rose in the depths of winter. This branch line of the family continues flowering into early winter, making you wonder how breeders ever lost this quality in so many of their new varieties.

China roses are not only the most persistent: they are also among the oldest garden types of rose. We know from Chinese works of art that recognizably similar roses were being grown in China by 1000 AD; western travellers from c. 1550 onwards allude to the charm and interest of these roses and it is possible that a rose in a portrait by the Florentine artist, Bronzino, is a China variety, somehow known in Renaissance Italy. The China roses' public career certainly took wing in 1781 when the pink form, still on sale as 'Old Blush', arrived in Holland. Soon afterwards, a red form was shipped from Calcutta to England by a captain of the East India Company and before long, this type of rose was heading west across the Atlantic. People were quick to notice the length of the flowers' season: swamped by new varieties, we have forgotten them ever since. In America nurseries do not feature any wide range of China roses, so once again I recommend you to import from Peter Beales.

The most persistent variety is the 'changeable rose', Rosa mutabilis which will show its flowers in most months of the year. In some ways, I wish it would stop, as its colouring is a confused mixture of flame, pink, apricot and orange, changing with age. It is not very bright and I would not bother with it. The variety which I particularly urge you to try is rather more conventional. Its name is Natalie Nypels, not a lady, I feel, whom I would have unduly wished to meet. But its merits more than compensate. Its shape is not very inspiring, for it makes a typical twiggy rose bush about two feet high. If it was used as a mass bedding plant, it would certainly become rather boring, but its semi-double pink flowers refuse to give up, whatever the weather.

Its first burst comes in early June and even in late July, that awkward moment when all old roses are hanging fire, its small shape is alive with shell-pink clusters of its 2-inch wide flowers. At home, we planted half a dozen in the light shade of a walnut tree and half a dozen in a sunny new bed, and between them they kept the summer alive and were still in bud in the first week of December. The sunny ones flowered first, the shady ones a week later and this carefully planned show continued unabated. Mixed with silver cotton lavender or casually scattered amongst a bed of hostas with a backing of grey-leaved buddleia and some plants of dark-leaved fennel for contrast, they would give a perpetual touch of interest and would bring the various shades of their neighbours' leaves to life.

Natalie Nypels is not totally a China, but she has one China parent and is hardier than several Chinese, even in savage winters which cut her growth to the base. Among the true Chinas, I believe the best to be Hermosa, a small rose-pink flower which stands prettily among grey-green leaves and appears throughout the season. Hermosa is only two feet high and can be tucked into the front of any border even in a restricted town garden: she is becoming better known, deservedly, and I hope she brings greater fame to this old class of flower.

What about Cécile Brunner, the tiny pink button-hole rose which is the best known of the Chinas? Frankly, avoid the bush variety: it is not very hardy and even when it survives the winter, it tends to be rather ungainly. The better buy is the Climbing Cécile Brunner, a rose which flourishes to considerable heights in shade. It is cut back by very cold winters, but always sprouts new wood: there are, however, two problems. The flowers are so small that they cannot be appreciated at any height off a wall: I overcome this by allowing my Climbing Cécile to fall forwards off the wall and grow into a wide, informal bush at eye level. The other problem, oddly, is that this climbing form only flowers once in profusion. On shaded walls it is useful, then, but lacks the China's main point; the recently-found Sophies Perpetual is a longer-lasting substitute.

Instead, you can explore the conventional Chinas: Old Blush, the original monthly rose, Perle D'Or with its hint of apricot and the small white-flowered Irene Watts, a favourite of mine and of Peter Beales, the main grower and exporter of these China roses from his Norfolk nurseries. In 1982, Peter Beales received seeds and cuttings from an alert visitor to China who saw the possibilities of these neglected China varieties. The seed has yet to germinate, but the cuttings have already revealed a form with sulphur yellow flowers, flushed with pink. In Chinese, its name means 'The Tipsy Imperial Concubine': watch carefully for new intoxications from this branch of the rose's family.

Easy Indoor Orchids

If you have no space for China roses, you will usually find a few wet, belated flowers on those vigorous floribundas, the white Iceberg and the pink-flowered Queen Elizabeth. The less you prune them, the more freely they grow: as soon as you see the colour showing on the buds of any rose late in the year, you should pick them and bring them indoors where the heating will help them to open safely.

Inevitably, we have withdrawn indoors as the year comes to a close. Even here, there is more to attempt and enjoy, whether or not you have a garden: three ideas appeal to me particularly, some orchids, some alpines and some big flowering bulbs between these dark months and the ending of a winter's drip.

The orchids are not the awkward exotics, the expensive Phalanopsis or the hot-house Cattleyas. They are a type which rock-gardeners know and which almost everybody else ignores: the near-hardy pleiones. They require no heating and for part of the year they require no watering. Best of all, they need very little earth or complex compost, so they are ideally suited to life in a sky-scraper, apartment or urban home. I assure you that they are extremely easy to grow well and are fit, indeed, for children. They win prizes at alpine garden shows, yet they are seldom seen in gardening homes. They do have an exotic appearance, though they are only 6 inches high when they bear their 4-inch-wide flowers of white or mauve-pink. These flowers resemble a flatter and broader daffodil whose central trumpet is flushed deeply or flecked with brown.

Pleiones flower generously in March and April. Their single leaf of pale ribbed green does not get in the way of their buds. They can be crammed six to a 5-inch pot of peat. Their pseudo-bulbs should not be buried when you plant them, preferably in December. They do not want heat, though they do not object to it. Gardeners in mild zones can even grow them outside beneath a pane of glass to protect their flowers from mud and wind. I prefer them in a cool room where I can inspect them without a pane of glass to detract from them.

After flowering you gradually reduce their water until the leaf dies down. You are left with a blank pot of earth and often twice as many pleiones as when you began. Their merit is that they are happy in a shallow pan and do not need an ugly big pot. Unlike, say, an amaryllis they do not follow their flowers with sheafs of unmanageable leaves. Formosana is the easiest and cheapest mauve-pink variety: limprichtii is darker, costlier and very lovely, while Polar Sun is particularly well named if you have ever seen the mauve-white effect of early morning sun over the Arctic ice-packs.

Indoor Rock-Gardens

Having noted the pleiones, or pink-mauve orchids, you should now be ready for the practice which surprises me more than any other in gardening. I mean the growing of plants in rock without any earth at all.

Mountain climbers will at once see how natural this is. Between the cliffs of the Dolomites or Engadine the fussiest alpine plants will often be found living on a diet of broken rubble and dust and forming tighter and smaller cushions because of their lack of food; this contentment, a lesson for us all, can be brought inside your house with the help of a stone called tufa. Tufa is a soft and porous sort of limestone which does not have to be chiselled; you simply saw it into small pieces like a gorgonzola cheese and then use a screwdriver or the like to bore holes in its surface for your alpine plants.

There are tufa outcrops all over the world; in England there is one in Derbyshire near Matlock and another near Wells in Somerset; tufa is also to be found in the crypt of Rochester Cathedral; otherwise, for despairing gardeners whose builders' merchants cannot help them out, it is in the catalogues of the alpine nurseries whom I list at the end of this book, along with pleione-fanciers: in America, Stonecrop Nurseries, New York and in England, Clwyd Concrete, Bodfari, Nr Denbigh, Clwyd have stocks and the latter actually have a franchise on the stuff and supply any amount of it, anywhere. It is a very light rock indeed and a hundredweight of it will go a long way, so do not be deterred by the price of a load. Mostly, you are paying for the transport: a few pieces will give you enough fun.

In the raw, tufa is an unpleasant plaster-white which you will certainly want to soften to a natural honey-yellow: paint it over with sour milk and you will hasten the growth of mosses and a weathered coating of old age, but you must be careful not to block the entire stone with moss-greenery, for its surface is also to be your flower-bed. Tufa contains small pockets of air which will drain away water and give a cool run to the long roots of alpine plants; it is riddled with lime and with traces of useful chemicals such as magnesium. It needs no other food at all to grow the finest alpine campanulas you have ever considered possible. Indeed, the most remarkable collection of rare alpine plants in this country is housed in an artificial cliff of tufa with a glass-paned roof overhead like an old conservatory; it is sited within a mile of Birmingham's city centre and grows the hairiest and fluffiest alpine androsaces and verbascums because it can offer them such perfect drainage, even in an area that is far from smokeless.

A small weathered piece of tufa is extremely pretty in its own right: you could, I imagine, find a cheap but presentable plate on which to stand it and by writing or visiting one of the alpine nurseries I list, you can find a whole range of lime-loving plants to bore into a tufa hole. Ideally you want manageable seedlings, whose roots are not too long and whose attached earth can be accommodated in the rock; indoors, for a cool room which does not get much above 55°F, I would enjoy a chunk of tufa filled with the reliable rosettes of a spring saxifrage, preferably the lime-loving aizoon sort (sprays of yellow or white flowers in April) or the furry red-stemmed grisebachii, especially in its Wisley variety which has a decidedly shocking look to it.

144

Bolder gardeners will experiment with Phyteuma comosum, a flower which I cannot really describe for you except to say that it could be called flask-shaped, purple-flushed and black-tipped and that it is known as one of the glorious curiosities of an alpine mountain; the timid will turn to a tight mat of Sempervivums or houseleeks, which the Romans grew on the arid roofs of their houses, thinking them to be lightning-conductors, or the stonecrops (Sedums) which have white-coated stems and succulent leaves of purple, green or yellow according to choice. Big chunks of tufa could hold Verbascum dumulosum, a furry-leaved beauty with mustard-yellow flowers to a height of 9 inches, the white or blue Campanula isophylla, the well-known harebell of hanging baskets, or a clump of any of the small wild pinks.

Smaller lumps could make do very prettily with smaller campanulas, such as raineri, zoysii, aucheri or pusilla, the related forms of edraianthus, the unfailing scarlet spikes of the easy erinus, the solid small pads of Gypsophila aretioides or the small carpet of Androsace sempervivoides. Their tufa home should be watered over its surface every few days, preferably without wetting any plants with hairy leaves: it does not matter if you go away for a week and leave it dry, as the centre of tufa is porous enough to keep roots happy on the water.

Choosing plants for your tufa is a matter of hunting around in your local alpine nursery-lists, but there is one particular family I suggest you try, because it is so excellently suited to life in a limestone rock. I mean the Lewisia. In Britain, the leading specialists are now Ashwood Nurseries, Greensforge, Kingswinford, West Midlands, who offer an intriguing seed-list of the family and sell flowering plants of their superb Ashwood strain to visitors: their exemplary garden centre is just outside Kidderminster, but it does not run a postal business. Particular expertise is available from American growers, as the Lewisia is a North American family, mostly found in the wild in the western United States; the Siskiyou Rare Plant Nursery, Medford, Oregon is a happy hunting-ground for all alpine gardeners, and its seed-lists include varieties of Lewisia found near the nursery in the Rogue River Valley. The seedlist of the American Rock Garden Society is also very strong in Lewisias: you can join by contacting the Secretary, at SR66 Box 114, Norfolk Road., Sundisfield, Mass. 01255, a valuable contact for keen alpine gardeners in any country.

In cultivation, all but the very brave grow evergreen Lewisias, most of which are variations on Lewisia Cotyledon. The others are a marvellous sight in the wild and one of them, indeed, gave its name to the family when discovered in Oregon by Mr Lewis in the early 1800's. For gardeners, they are almost always too difficult, and so we must content ourselves with the fleshy rosettes of leaves and the striped rose, red, pink and white flowers on their close relations. These evergreens run to leaf, not flowers, if they are kept on too rich a diet: in Siskiyou's proven opinion, they can be allowed to go dormant after their flowering in late spring. They also like to grow in tufa or pumice-stone if they are fed with liquid fertilizer. Together, these two tastes suit the indoor gardener admirably; I have had the greatest pleasure from evergreen Lewisias in the sitting-room. I have also had no mess.

Some years ago, I ordered the wine-red George Henley, the orange and rose-red Sunset Strain (which was bred in Scotland), the rose-red Trevosia and the Birch Hybrids from Ingwersens of East Grinstead, Sussex (who have stopped supplying small orders by mail). Then, I loosened them from their pots, shook the soil off their roots and fitted them into the large holes which I had chiselled into a thick lump of tufa. It is fun to cut holes into tufa: you can take revenge for the tribulations of your teeth by drilling this soft rock and practising dentistry on it by filling its holes with plants.

In their first year, these young lewisias flowered quite well. I was pleased with the results, but I had not tried the wide range of colours in Ashwood's strain, grown to flowering size before sale. As small house-plants in under-heated rooms, these Lewisias are magnificent. They will flower up to three times in their first season and if you continue to repot them, they will grow to the size of a big evergreen lettuce: at Ashwood, the chief propagator, Philip Baulk, shows huge Lewisias, eight years old. In a pot, they like sharp drainage and only the minimum of soil: a plain potting compost suits them well, mixed with leaf-mould. In tufa, I often forgot to water them for days on end: they curled up, but lived nonetheless. Siskiyou assure us that the cotyledon hybrids can be left dry for their flowering in May until autumn, when water revives them: in the British climate, Ashwood doubt this treatment, but they have not tried it. It bodes well for those of us who take long summer holidays. Lewisias need no heat, but they do prefer to be shaded in the sunny months. If possible, stand them in a cold frame or unheated house and only bring them indoors to admire their flowers. They have one vice: their lower leaves sometimes turn yellow for a while during flowering. This habit does not reflect on your care for them, and breeders are trying to remove the tendency.

Visitors think that growing a Lewisia is a sign of extraordinary talent. In fact, these evergreen forms almost grow themselves. The one difficulty is their response to water: when you do give them a drink, you must see that no water settles on the rosette of leaves, as it tends to rot them. Outdoors, Lewisias are not easy to please, because the climate is against them, unless they are wedged at an angle between rocks. Indoors, the difficulty vanishes: either you can grow them in pots surfaced with grit and water them from below, or you can plant them at a sharp angle in drilled tufa so that the water runs into the stone, not the crown of the plant. If any water stays where it should not, shake the tufa after watering and free it.

In flats, small houses or cities, people cut themselves off from gardening and make for the nearest rubber-plant and bowl of cut-flowers. They are missing a chance. The Lewisia's stems are slender and only six inches high, but their small, open flowers are wonderfully bright, showing reds, pinks and oranges or striped variations of all three colours in great profusion. In Western America, the Indians used to value the roots of Lewisia for their taste of bitter rice. If you cannot eat them, do please grow them. They are lovely refutations of the view that gardening ends at the escalator or the countryman's back door.

Bulbs Without Soil

Even if you would rather be seen dead than have tufa-rock in the sitting-room, please do not write gardening books off as irrelevancies because you live in an apartment on the fifth floor. You do not need rocks, either. In autumn, any windowledge or shelf indoors can have a row of flowering colchicums, or autumn crocus, resting on a saucer, one to each bulb, with or without water. Colchicums arrive with sufficient impetus from previous years to allow them to flower without leaves or earth: after flowering naked on a saucer, they should be transplanted into the garden so that their leaves can develop for the following spring.

The flowers resemble huge, cupped crocuses, but personally, I do not like a colchicum as much as an autumn crocus; indeed, I believe that the common blue Crocus speciosus would also produce its clear blue flowers quite happily without any soil on a saucer. I have had it in flower in paper bags, having bought it and failed to plant it in time. The yellow lily of the Biblical field, Sternbergia lutea, will also flower on a bare ledge. After one year, however, it is finished.

As far as colchicums go, and their glossy green leaves do go a long way in springtime, the white-flowered kind called album has always seemed to me to be the prettiest. Stand it on your windowsill indoors in September and it will flower within three weeks on last season's impetus. No earth is needed for it, and if you give it water after flowering, add a little liquid manure from time to time and tolerate its spring greenery, it will build up strength for a repeat performance next year. The mauves, 'blues' and violets are also very impressive: howevern, avoid a highly praised variety called Waterlily which has such heavy double mauve flowers that it collapses at the neck and leaves you with a tattered confusion of shapeless petals. It reminds me of an emergent moth with muscle failure.

After the autumn crocus and before the pleiones and the spring flowers in tufa, you can take two easy routes. The first leads you to glasses of water, in which you can grow handsome hyacinths at no risk to your carpet or coffee-table. People still do not realize that these bulbs, too, will flower without any earth: stores sell convenient glasses in which a fat hyacinth bulb can rest in the top half while its roots descend through the glass's wasp waist into the water in the bottom half. The water should include a piece of charcoal to keep it sweet and for the first two months, the glass should stand in a dark cool place, such as a clothes-cupboard. Then, the roots have formed and the leaves begin to show. When they are two inches high, bring the glass into the light and warmth and rapidly, the bulb will flower.

Over the years my results have varied. The stringy white roots of the hyacinth look very elegant through the glass as they coil down into the water, but the flowers sometimes fail to grow a stalk; they are stunted at the top of the bulb, even though I have kept them in darkness to let them form roots. At other times, they shoot up and look top heavy. A hyacinth cannot be tied upright when it is balanced in a water glass and so I have tried to stand mine on top of a piano and pretend that they look like flowering candles at a jaunty angle. They never do, really, but the sight of their roots in water is pleasing for a while, magnified through the glass's surface.

Sporting With Amaryllis

Indoors, the most spectacular results come from the forms of Amaryllis.

KOELREUTERIA PANICULATA: *GOLDEN RAIN TREE*

RHUBARB AND SPURGE AT DOWER HOUSE, BOUGHTON

Whether you have a garden or not, you really ought to make the simple experiment with them: they are almost fool-proof and have established themselves in the past two decades as the one house-plant which we can all buy with confidence from a chain-store. When they flower for the first time, they are as weird and wonderful as magic aliens, suddenly appearing in your apartment.

My first bulbs came from Father Christmas. Actually, I think I asked for Hippeastrum, but the old boy knew what I meant, even though the best book on the family, by Hamilton P. Traub, their American enthusiast (in 1958) declared Hippeastrum to be an incorrect name, devoted a six-page appendix to proving the point and entitled itself 'Amaryllis', defiantly. The plant sounds more romantic by this name: 'sporting with Amaryllis in the shade', a position, incidentally, which Mr Traub observes it to prefer during the summer when the leaves are still green.

Amaryllis are not a prominent part of the 'Englishman's garden': their various forms are native to South America, the Caribbean and so forth and their great growers are Dutch or American. The American Amaryllis Society is a primary authority; the great breeders, Howard and Smith, Olaf Nelson and Hermon Brown, worked in California; Pierre du Pont achieved some subtle shadings by crosses on his family estate of Longwood in Pennsylvania; in Florida, the first doubles were bred and Theodore Mead developed hybrids which could be grown in open fields; in the south west of Florida, Amaryllis belladonna, a West Indian, has run wild. The last World War was a serious time for the Amaryllis: in 1940, the Ludwigs had to sell their famous Dutch business; the last of the U.S. Department of Agriculture exhibitions, supervised by the Byrnes family, was held in 1939, exhibiting an amazing 1260 flowering bulbs to nearly 40,000 visitors in Washington. England has never kept up with this international circuit: only now are we aware what easy variety the plants can offer, and even so, we import them.

Even at the top of a skyscraper, the Amaryllis is a fine performer. The bulbs are bigger than tennis balls with such prominent necks that you do not risk the cyclamen-problem of planting them upside down. The professional wisdom is that you should only bury two thirds of the bulb in a pot, surfacing the last layer of soil with grit or sharp silver sand, to give a neat apparance. The sides of the bulb should be only an inch from the sides of the pot and the pot itself need not be very deep, as it is a good idea if the

Amaryllis's long roots can knot themselves inside the ball of earth and become pot-bound. If you buy an Amaryllis Gift Set from a store, you will find that it comes with a bag of compost and a smallish plastic pot. You are not being short-changed, but you will face a problem when the Amaryllis flowers. Its stems shoot up like spears and bear heavy flowers at their tops: the weight causes a plastic pot to overbalance suddenly and crash onto the carpet. Hide it in a bigger container, or ornamental cache-pot if you have one, or hold it in position between heavy books when you see the buds emerging.

In late autumn, even in December, you begin with a dormant bulb, pot it up and begin to water it in your centrally-heated sitting-room. Suddenly, the flower-stems thrust out of the centre of the bulb, two or even three if you are lucky and have bought reputable stock. You must stop them bending one way towards the window-light: turn the pot round every other day, and the stems will remain more or less straight. Wedge the pot, as I have warned, because the leading green spear will then break at a height of about two and a half feet and reveal a clustered head of buds, perhaps three to each stem. Keep on watering and the buds will open into wide five-petalled flowers of white, pink, red or a striping of these colours: the sexual parts will be so prominent that you can teach your children the facts of plant-life from any nearby armchair. An amaryllis can bear up to nine flowers from one bulb, an astonishing feat of packaging and production, as they all have to develop in a bulb slightly bigger than a tennis-ball. Non-gardeners, wishful-thinkers, interior designers: anyone, I promise, can coax this extraordinary display of trumpet-shaped flowers, like giant lilies, in any frost-proof room during the winter months. Probably, your bulbs will have been forced and timed to flower in the dark months by the growers who shipped them to the chain-stores. There is a neat art in calculating the times and seasons of an amaryllis, depending on the degrees of light and temperature: if you wish to try, I recommend Mr Traub's manual for the necessary procedure.

Meanwhile, your amaryllis flowers; your friends think you are enviably green-fingered; personally, you feel that it is perhaps a little too prolific and vulgar, and stirred, maybe, by finer feelings, you creep back to what I have just written about Pleiones and decide to try them too: next year, it might even be tufa. After flowering, however, the amaryllis tests your skill. Quite simply, you must continue to water the pot for the next five or six months while the green leaves appear and lengthen. Add any of the liquid manures sold locally for house-plants and give the bulb a feed on it once a week. Then, the leaves will start to look tired and perhaps even go yellow: stop watering, and they will die away, leaving you with a bare bulb which you can activate in late autumn or early winter by starting the water again. While you have been feeding the leaves, the bulb has been building up strength and developing the tightly-packed stems for next season's flowers, buried deep inside its inner onion-layers of skin. You may also find that it develops a second baby bulb at its side: cut this free, without qualms, and pot it up on its own roots, growing it on for two years like its parent. Then, it will be a prolific amaryllis on its own unsteady perch, at least if you have fed it carefully.

I confess that I find there is no more to its culture than that. The life-cycle is a miracle and we indoor-gardeners can enjoy it yearly: major growers can be found through the thriving American Amaryllis Research Institute, Box 92, Westfield, IN. 46074, unrivalled by anything in Britain. I do rather like the self-explanatory Candy Stripe, a pink and white variety with a slightly green throat; the pure pinks, I think, are the least interesting. Amaryllis, in short, are for everyone, for wild gardeners in Florida and Louisiana, hungry gardeners in the West Indies (people used to eat the bulbs) and experts who kept alive the Amaryllis Society magazine, Herbertia, through the 1930's, the peak of the family's fortunes. The professionals do like to make it more mysterious: H.P. Traub suggests a compost of "one part *dry, pulverized* clay loam treated with the soil conditioner Krillium *before* the clay loam is mixed up: one part black acid carex peat (New Jersey origin). To correct for any sourness, add one handful of crushed oystershell to each six-inch pot". Perhaps exhibitors should go to such trouble, but I doubt if they greatly improve on you and me, growing the bulb in a straightforward compost from a well-known store.

Travels On The Tundra

At this point, a gardening book arranged by seasons would normally sign off with a reminder to water and repot the over-forced azaleas which you have given each other for Christmas. It might add a hopeful prospect about flowers on the loose-leaved winter irises, which are about to show buds beneath dry south-facing walls. My conclusion turns in a different direction, because of my memories of the coldest floral experience of my life.

For years, I had devoted time, money and energy to an ambition which was not really very ambitious. I wanted to see masses of garden-worthy wild flowers growing in nature; I do, however, stress the garden-worthy, as field botanists lose their hearts to sandworts or rare sedge grasses which may be thrilling as lost links in the earth's evolution but which, to a gardener's eye, are as appealing as a field of groundsel. Myself, I wanted lilies, narcissus, roses and at least two million gentians: I tried Switzerland, but arrived when the cows had already cropped the lower pasture, and it emerged that I had headaches at great heights. I tried Bavaria, on expeditions to see the Lady's Slipper orchid: after two days' walk with ladies in lederhosen, we did indeed find it, but it was only in seed and I was sitting on the plants by mistake. I then tried Greece but was diverted, necessarily, by the ruins. Matters were made worse by belonging to a society whose quarterly bulletin was filled with other members' happy holidays. There were maps of where to walk for cyclamen in Yugoslavia; there were arguments about whether the Secretary had found Iris histrioides or histrioides major growing by the thousand in the Balkans. I alone had missed out.

Then, one spring, I agreed to an expedition in the Arctic Ocean, projected from Nome, Alaska through the Bering Strait and eastwards, along the ice-pack, to the sea-channels into Greenland. Our transport was to be a canoe, made on the Eskimo principle of stitched skins of walrus hide: the crew were partly Eskimoes and my role, in theory, was to see to the supplies. Eventually, we almost starved, except for occasional pot-shots at seagulls, but my ambition, at least, had been realized. Not even I could fail to coincide with the Arctic's flowers by the thousand, unvisited and growing wild.

I had not expected this happy result. When I packed the luggage, my mind was on warm trousers and pills for the necessary vitamins to bring us through four months: only as an afterthought did I include my trowel and a collection of polythene bags. What, after all, could possibly grow in a summer of two months and a winter of −50°F? The answer, apart from a billion mosquitoes, was almost everything I could have wished to see. If the life of the sea multiplies the nearer man goes to the North Pole, the same could be said of the life of the mountains. Space seems infinite, as the ice-pack stretches away to the sea's horizon, but time is frantically quickened, as the snow melts in a week, the willows and tundra appear beneath it and a host of plants must flower, fade and set seed in the course of a summer of six weeks. Within three months, I had seen the full cycle of the flowers' season, touching perilously on the sudden approach of winter, which caught us far from our journey's beginning, as the snow began to fall near the Coppermine River in Canada. In early July, I had admired the pink and white bramble-flowers of the salmonberries and other relations of the rubus family whose stems I admire at home. By mid August they were bearing berries and within another week, their leaves were turning to red and shades of purple. Viewing and recording had to be done quickly. When I first saw a hillside of arctic poppies I thought I would return and photograph them a week later; when I came back, they were already setting seed, knowing they must hurry through the few days which served as summer. At last, not even I could miss. Spring, summer and autumn were happening everywhere at once, and the abundance startled me after so many failed visits to find it.

The richest flora lies inside the Brooks range of mountains or on the edge of the Arctic Circle, along the western coast of Alaska, where the conditions of marsh, moor, seashore and mountain cliff-face can often be seen in succession in a walk of only an hour. It was the coastal flora I came to know best, up the line of the northernmost Eskimo whaling-camps and along the tip of America to the Canadian border. Time and again, we would moor the boat on the edge of the ice-pack and walk inland onto ground which had probably never been trodden by man. In one afternoon I moved from a coastline of blue marsh irises and bog myrtle to a scrub of Arctic willow, then up to carpets of the oak-leaved dryas, a white flowered native of northern Scotland, mixed with dodecatheon, or shooting stars, five different kinds of poppy, pink silene or campion, a beautiful crucifer called Parrya after the British admiral, three potentillas and so much Anemone sylvestris that I trampled on it without any scruples. Arctic forget-me-not grew with three different colours of the lousewort which is so much more beautiful than its name. After half an hour's walk, I was within sight of the sea-shore and standing among fourteen types of wild plant which Eskimoes use as occasional vegetables. A few minutes more and I was at the foot of a mountain-face whose upper scree was covered, to my amazement, with white brothers of the androsaces which climbers risk their necks to see in the Alps, grey-white gentians, brilliant scarlet anemone, violet harebells, two cushion-saxifrages and the cousin of the

153

King of the Alps itself, the legendary eritrichium, here in its rare aretioides form, 2 inches high and 3 inches wide, but so blue that few cameras ever capture it and so fussy and hairy that no gardener has grown it properly despite a thousand attempts at collection. Rewarded at last, in the least likely landscape, I sat down among delphiniums, a fumitory and the glacial buttercups and tried to beat away the mosquitoes which I had not learnt to leave alone.

Further up the mountain, there were traces of the snow which lies like a blanket above the frost: snow, in fact, is quite scarce in the Arctic for most of the year and technically, the frozen North ranks as a desert. In this sparser and more alpine setting, four of the Arctic's many saxifrages grew in tightest hummocks, none the worse for a soil only 2 inches deep and winter frosts which snows only lessen, but do not keep off. I am extremely fond of the rock jasmines, or androsaces, which range from the coarse and leafy to the hairiest and fussiest small tussocks: here, there were clumps of a small pink variety called ochetensis, again unknown elsewhere, which had hidden themselves in a mass of flowers, like mop-headed chrysanthemums.

Growers of alpine, or 'rock', plants and gardens are advised to see mountain flowers in the wild in order to appreciate what is needed. Very sharp drainage through chipped stone and desert-dry peat, plenty of water from melting snow, intense and clear light; these are the conditions which an Arctic mountain can offer, and it is no wonder that alpine gardeners sometimes have difficulty at lower altitudes. Often, the difference between a bare desert and an Arctic wild garden relies on the presence of water or manure. Where a trickle of melted snow runs down the hillsides, the rare Bering Strait primrose, Primula beringensis, grows in abundance, showing a mass of the small rose-coloured flowers which know no other home in the world. In similar rockfaces 20 yards away there is no trickling water, and so no primroses. Manure, too, makes all the difference. On the shore of the Alaskan whaling villages, the dog-teams of huskies are chained for the summer season, relying on scraps to survive. At each change in the wind, they howl expectantly, hoping for the colder weather which will bring their release. Meanwhile they manure the ground around them and on it grow the most richly-coloured clumps of the Arctic's ubiquitous yellow poppy (Papaver radicatum) and mats of dark blue forget-me-nots (Myosotis alpestris). They are never quite so vividly coloured elsewhere.

But it was the tundra that intrigued me most. While travelling along the north of America to the Northwest Passage, I came to know its peculiarities, like some old and exotic friend. There were days when we would ride the sea's swell all night and turn at last to the shore to dry out our skins, both our own and the boat's, because its walrus-skin, too, grew softer and began to sag with constant use. We would climb some unnamed ridge and jump and stamp to restore the circulation after hours on a chilling sea: as we spread out to collect driftwood, the Arctic's ever-present rubbish, we would walk on white cotton-grass and clear yellow poppy, half a dozen of the Arctic's fifty saxifrages, buttercups wedged between blocks of lichen and mosses whose links lay with those of New Zealand and thus were a possible echo of the ecology of twenty million years ago. They grew on the tundra (the word means 'without trees'), a damp, dark and spongy substance which resembles elemental peat. It goes no deeper than two feet before it rests on the 'permafrost', or perpetually-frozen subsoil. It never, therefore, drains, and is covered in pools of melted ice, which show up as blue as a kingfisher under the twenty-four hours of sunlight that make up most summer days. As if by some primeval conspiracy, every tundra pond lies on the same axis, facing northeast and southwest, perhaps because of winter's prevailing wind.

To see poppies, willows and primulas, take a trip to the tundra: you cannot fail to coincide with the summer season of an often-forgotten flora. My ambition had been realized when I least expected, but my aims had also changed in the process. On my first trip to America, there would be early mornings when the boat tossed and crashed through incipient breakers and the sun lit up the sedge-brown and moss-greens of uninhabited islands. Through the spray, we would see the first of the poppies, the Arctic buttercups and clinging willows. Was it not, in its own way, an untrodden garden, whereas now, there are pavements in every English village; my neighbours come to their house only for weekends: there is talk of street-signs and street-lighting to bring the village up to date? I have seen garden-flowers growing wild by the thousand, and yet by seeing the wild I have changed my views of what gardens can offer and how nature, that man-made concept, can be brought within the garden-fence. It is on this wild note that I wish to round off my sequence of a garden's seasons.

WILD GARDENING

Double crimson Peonies in grass at Crowsley Park,
from William Robinson, The Wild Garden (1870)

Wild Gardening

Wild gardening sounds as attractive nowadays as a wild woman or a wild party. Those patient hours of seed-raising, hoeing and spraying can be abandoned in a wild garden. Nature, so the theory goes, will do the work in a wood or orchard which would otherwise prove too much for its owner. We are all tempted by the wilderness, believing that its ground can be covered with one of those ground-covering creepers and that the weeds can then be left to do their worst on a mere three days' work a month.

As an idea a wild garden sounds lazy and romantic. Like all romances, it is better explored before you take it too far. Wild gardening is difficult, its beauty elusive and never achieved without planned effort. For the gardener who wants a reliable show in a wild piece of field or former garden adjoining his own I can recommend nothing more strongly than bulbs. This may sound dull because we all know that bulbs can be naturalized, yet they are the only form of lazy wild gardening which is always satisfactory. The most frequent error is an excessive keenness to tidy them up.

Ideally, the long grass in which bulbs are planted should not be cut before late June so that the bulbs can seed themselves and die down with fully ripened leaves. The cutting is not easy, and unless you are happy to use a scythe, you need something stronger than the ordinary rotary lawnmower. Arm yourself with a stronger machine if you live in a thick grass-growing area: I find that if I tip my Mountfield rotary mower upwards, so that it rests on its back wheels, it can cope quite easily with thick long grass. Tilting improves the stamina of quite ordinary rotary mowers on wheels.

If bulbs sound ordinary, ask yourself whether you have tried to naturalize wild anemones, Stars of Bethlehem, Snakeshead fritillaries, Lent lilies, ornamental onion or autumn crocus. I would guess that you have not. Of these, the forms of Anemone blanda are beyond reproach. They are cheap, especially in their mixture of rose, white and pale violet which is the prettiest combination. They spread rapidly, especially in light soil. They flower abundantly, and even if they only open their flowers to their full width of an inch and a half in bright light, they flower in March and April when sunny periods are likely. They are 3 inches high and matched with a sea-green leaf, cut into a delicate shape.

Their red relations, called Anemone pavonina, the peacock anemone, are possibly even more lovely, but they are happier in an open and sunny bed where they do not compete with turf. I cannot imagine why these anemones are not popular. I promise those of you who are as bored with the florists' St Brigid anemones as I am that the blanda varieties are wild wind-flowers, graceful, simple and wise enough not to flower the whole year round for every florist's shop.

Wild windflowers, then, for a wild bulb-garden, and perhaps some wild narcissi, too, beside the conventional varieties like Fortune, Carlton, Ice Follies and the trumpet daffodils in yellow or white: I find that white daffodils are less persistent when planted in turf.

The finest little daffodil for wild gardening, to my eye, is the smallest, our own wild Lent lily (Narcissus pseudonarcissus) which is pale lemon and primrose and only 6 inches high. This, an English wild flower, is more natural than a drift of golden-yellow giant trumpets. If you want a bright small yellow try the Tenby daffodil (Narcissus obvallaris) another English native and only 9 inches high. Spring bulbs in a wild garden should look like the foreground of a Botticelli painting where flowers stud the ground in single pinks and whites. They should not be too tall if they are to flower early in the foreground or beside its mown paths. Reserve the taller varieties for the inner areas of the wilderness: the cheapest source of these bulbs in bulk is Peter Nyssen, Station Road, Urmston, Manchester who will also ship by sea, if you order from abroad in good time. They handle bigger orders only but wild gardens have to be generously colonized.

Most Tulips (except the wild yellow sylvestris) are unreliable for this purpose and so, of course, are the little wild cyclamen which put up their leaves when you want to be mowing. A much better bet is the bluebell, both the English bluebell and the false, or Spanish, variety. Gardeners near bluebell woods need look no further for their wild garden's bulbs. The white varieties of the false bluebell, Scilla campanulata, also match those drifts of blue most pleasingly. Those who are denied the charm of bluebells locally, perhaps because their garden is too open and sunny, can content themselves with the samll white and green flowered Star of Bethlehem (Ornithogalum umbellatum) and any of the rampant white garlics called Allium: Allium ursinum and triquetrum are two vigorous possibilities.

What happens after late May when the grass is growing as furiously as the weeds and the sun is heating everything? In England, you must avoid almost every lily: none of them likes to compete with grass, although I have made one variety do so, the fabulous Lily Enchantment (from Nyssens or in the U.S., Brecks and Blackthorne). It is the one which produces open flower-heads of a very strong vermilion orange in June or early July and tolerates lime and a reasonable degree of drought. The autumn-flowering Lily Henryi with its long stems and reflexed orange flowers is another possible competitor but its shoots are at their most fragile when you want to mow the grass in July and I really cannot advise it. In Britain, the place for lilies is a specially-cleared bed. In America, there is more scope, because more lilies are wild competitors in native meadows: I like the look of Blackthorne's selection of Ecological Lilies, including the obliging red Turks Cap Lilies. Even so, avoid planting them in special little beds, because they then interfere with the design and purpose of a wild setting.

Whether or not you can grow these tough lilies, I suggest you pester suppliers for the wild Mediterranean gladiolus called byzantinus: in London, Amand's list it and will ship bigger quantities at a very reasonable price. You may know this mid-summer bulb from your holidays if you go to Spain or southern France in June, not August. In Andalusia, on the southern hills of Spain, I marked down this vivid flower as a bulb for my next orchard. Its spikes of magenta-purple flowers are slender and elegant, quite unlike the florists' autumn gladioli. It grows in cornfields and likes a sunny home. It is not expensive and competes victoriously with other plants.

After this spattering of wild gladioli, the grass has to be cut and any leaves of naturalized summer bulbs would be hopelessly spoiled. In special clearings, the Summer Hyacinth, or Galtonia candicans, is the best value, but its floppy leaves will not compete with grass and you have to make some attempt at weeding if you are to enjoy the tall stems and hanging white hyacinth-flowers.

Instead of lilies and summer hyacinths, the autumn crocus are an obvious successor to the second grass-cut in the wild garden's year. It is possible to cut down an orchard for the second time in late August without ruining the snouts of a late crocus like zonatus which is just showing through the ground. The common speciosus is a prettier shade of pale violet, but it begins to grow earlier and is likely to be damaged during this late summer mowing. Other autumn crocuses are lovely and often sweetly scented, but I prefer them in pots or in a raised bed, perhaps on top of a small wall, where they can be admired more closely.

So much, then, for the laziest wilderness, the field naturalized with bulbs: I am assuming, of course, that you begin the year with the little bulbs we discussed elsewhere, the tough snowdrops, aconites and the various forms of Crocus tommasinianus which are such excellent seeders and spreaders. Planting the stock can be a bother, especially if the ground is hard in a dry autumn and the daffodils, which like an early start, are already wasting in their 25 kilogram bags, the cheapest way of buying them. Here, you need a bulb-planter: the best range in the U.K. is on offer in the catalogue of Joseph Bentley, Chemical Works, Barrow on Humber, South Humberside, DN199AZ. If not, use a spade and cut round three sides of a piece of turf, folding it back on the fourth side, as if on a hinge. There is only one trick in good planting: never dig a V-shaped hole and drop your bulb into it, wedging it half way down with a deadly air-pocket under the roots. Always be sure that the base of the bulb is resting flat on soil, not air. Incidentally, the "planting depths" suggested by suppliers and bulb-books are only approximate, but in their authors' minds they run from the upper tip of the bulb to the surface of the soil.

A point, too, about arrangement: do not plant your bulbs in straight lines nor, I think, in regular circles. I learned from Miss Jekyll's books that there is much to be said for drifts, longer than they are wide. These wedge-shaped plantings "have a more pictorial effect", she believed, "and their thin long shape does not leave an unsightly empty space when the flowers are done and the leaves have perhaps died down ...". When planting crocuses, she attacked 'patches' and concentric circles round trees: "drifts, a little wider in the middle and narrowing into nothing at the ends, may be of any length, according to the space that has to be planted; they had better be more or less parallel to the path or more usual point of view ...". She felt that the purples and whites should be in the slightly shadier places, while the yellows should drift into the open. "The three colours should not be in view at the same time ...". While accepting her point about drifts, I am not sure I agree about the vices of the three-colour combination: I like it and I find that quite small drifts of crocus, enlivened with a few whites, are a better use of resources than one long wedge, using up all the bulbs you have bought.

Does this idea sound too arduous? If so, I would remind you of the obliging grape-hyacinth, or muscari. We line out these bulbs along the edgings of beds and then complain that they seed too freely. The king of wild gardening is still the Irishman, William Robinson, author of the classic Wild Garden, first published in 1870. Subsequent editions tempered parts of its enthusiasm and broadened its ideas, but his views on grape hyacinths were unchanging. He thought they were superb bulbs in turf where they multiplied very freely. He did not even dig them in: he "used to throw the bulbs in little hollows in grassy places and then fill up with a couple of inches of soil, thus saving the trouble of lifting the turf to plant". He "had some very pretty effects, the only trouble being that these bulbs could not be got by the million". Next autumn, toss your grape hyacinths into dips and hollows, a happy activity which we have quite forgotten nowadays.

The Upper Layer

Bulbs in a wilderness are the easiest form of wild gardening because they can precede or compete with the great rush of competitive growth from spring onwards. As soon as you plant anything which is to last above ground, you must face up to problems in the wilderness you have inherited.

At this point, it helps to think of your planting in layers: bulbs on the underplanting, then flowers in the meadow, then shrubs, trees and a final layer of creepers and climbers through the branches. Your first move, I think, should be upwards, to the tree-branches and the climbers they can accommodate. You can then wonder if you want to go any further, and if not, you can rest contented with an upper canopy and a lower under-planting.

161

The art of growing climbing plants through trees is to place them at a distance of a few yards from the trunk and allow them a space in which to breathe, gain momentum and then hurl themselves up into the branches. The 'Englishman's garden' thinks only of white roses, the rampant Rose Kiftsgate which is really too vigorous and not always willing to flower, Alberic Barbier, which I prefer to Kiftsgate for most purposes, Bobbie James, multicoloured Wedding Day, the lighter Rose The Garland and in milder areas, Rambling Rector. I also recommend the tiny button flowers of Felicité et Perpetué, a primrose-scented rose which commemorates two early Christian martyrs, now made doubly famous by feminist history.

Why, though, stop at white roses? Clematis montana, flammula and vitalba will run readily up and over trees; so will the Russian Vine (Polygonum) or the Dutchman's Pipe (Aristolochia), Virginia Creeper and robust honeysuckles. The most vigorous roses will eventually smother most of the leaves on a modest tree, but they are unlikely to kill it entirely: the clematis kills nothing, and although the honeysuckle takes a throttling grip on branches, it distorts and constricts then, but does not destroy them. Englishmen like to grow roses up old apple trees, a habit which certainly puts paid to their yearly crop: in fact, roses do not need a support at all. The great gardeners of the late nineteenth century were much more relaxed about this placing than we are. They realized that roses sprawl, but do not 'climb' naturally, and so they allowed them to arch and spray in all directions into large free-standing tangles. For this use, you need roses with rambler blood in them: Albertine and Bobbie James are excellent.

This informal use of climbers was not the original discovery of Miss Jekyll, let alone Vita Sackville-West or some named female heroine of "Englishwoman's" gardening. Already, in the 1870's, William Robinson quoted letters from forgotten gardeners who had huge fountains of roses which were grown in this style. He himself recommended Hops as a draping for trees: only three or four shoots should be retained as climbing stems, he discovered, while the rest should be cut away each spring. He also planted "many wistarias" against tall pines and other trees in plantations; I know a splendid one, growing through a pink-flowered Malus. He recommended Virginia Creeper to grow in Weeping Willows and finally, he quoted an intriguing letter from Mr Hovey of Boston, Massachusetts: before 1870, this forgotten gardener had lined out Virginia Creeper, the brightly-fruited Celastrus (still on sale from Wayside) and

Moonseed (Menispermum) through his walks of hawthorn, malus and philadelphus. The results were superb, an American example which Robinson particularly cited. Indeed, one of the boldest uses of climbers I know nowadays is in the garden of Mr MacIlhenny, an American patron of the American Lanning Roper, in northern Ireland. There, great trailers of Clematis montana drip from the branches of tall pine trees, like white garlands, an idea as yet uncopied by English wildernesses with their pale-flowered roses in plum trees.

Covering and Colonizing

With this underplanting of bulbs and overplanting of climbers, you may well be content. You have flowers, romance and the illusion that you have made a garden in more ground that you can control. It is when you come down to the intervening levels that the problems begin, especially if you do not live on tundra above permafrost.

The first problem is one of style, inherited from the past. The wild garden, nowadays, lives in the shadow of late Victorian gardeners who bought rhododendrons like bedding plants and dropped lilies wherever their bank accounts permitted. Their wild flowers were exotic flowers, newly found in China and the Far East. They were massed in glades and in areas called clearings. They gave the impression that they had always lived in peace, without the attention of an army of labourers who had kept off the rabbits and bracken in their early years. Azaleas were stored behind post and rail fences like animals in private zoos. They were to be visited down mown paths and tracks which were weed-killed and surfaced with grit. On an open plan, their banks could sweep down closely-mown vistas, about as wild a setting as St. James's Park on a July afternoon.

As the heirs to these great gardens, modern authorities on the wild garden cannot conceal for long that they expect you to begin by making beds. They dress them up with other names, drifts or clumps or ambiguous terms, like ground cover. They urge you on with pictures of mature plantings, where huge banks of day lilies have run into each other and blocked out rival weeds. "Ground cover" is a drab definition of wild gardening, as if the aim was simply to cover ground which the grass or natural "weeds" would cover anyway. Densely practised, it can look exhausting, as if nature has suddenly sprouted great island-beds of interlocking conifers and carpeting mats of heather. It is trouble-free gardening by another name.

Sometimes, it is not even trouble-free. At the herbaceous level, gardeners are tempted into trying ineffective plants as cover, things which die out, like trilliums, or need dividing, like asters, or which make loose top-growth, like catmint, not thick clumps of weed-proof roots, like day lilies or hostas. You have to cut back the straggling growth of these plants in late summer and do something about their hundreds of rotting dead flowers. It is not easy to combine several cover-plants successfully: one of them always gets the upper hand and reduces the expanse to a single main season of flower.

If you think I am being unfair, I suggest you make two experiments. First, try reading that bold and optimistic set-text, *Plants for Ground Cover* by Graham Thomas, published by Dent in the U.K. in 1970, when the Gardens Advisor to the great stately gardens of the National Trust was covering ground by the acre. It sums up the hopes and successes of modern wild gardens, but its choice of plants for cover is often too rarified for hard-pressed gardeners. Throughout, the aim is to cover the ground so thickly that it becomes an alternative garden, packed like a flower bed in which nothing wild and weedy can compete.

Secondly, I suggest you visit one of these ground-covered gardens and ask yourself if you find it restful and convincing. The National Trust's gardens at Hidcote Manor, Gloucestershire are a good example: the design of their "quiet American" owner, Lawrence Johnston, was ground-covered busily in the 1960's. After a while, I long for some peace and a few clumps of buttercup and meadow-grass. The leaves of its early flowering plants become very drab by mid-summer and I begin to wonder why these alternative "weeds" were ever thought to be worth such an effort.

Much prettier effects come from colonization, not cover: here, you introduce plants into your existing flora, woodland, prairie or meadow and leave them to compete with your neighbours. To level up the competition, I suggest you begin by clearing and weed-killing the ground before you introduce your new colony. Here, the business has been revolutionized by the new herbicides which are based on glyphosate. They kill through the leaf only and do not poison the soil: I have planted ground quite happily less than six hours after spraying its weeds. In England, buy Roundup from a farm chemical supplier, as it is a bulk version of the Tumbleweed which is sold in more expensive form for gardeners: Monsanto make it, and Murphy's market Tumbleweed. I find that you know within seven days if the poison has worked: the plants begin to droop. The instructions tell you to wait three weeks, but this delay usually pitches you into the middle of the growing season. Apply a second dose after a week if you are in doubt. The job should be done in spring weather which is not too wet or dry, a difficult requirement but essential to success. Roundup kills grass, many broad-leaved weeds, bindweed, ground-elder and so forth: it disposes of nettles, but if in doubt here, I follow up with a 2-4T compound, available in England as SBK Brushwood killer. Two doses of glyphosate and one of this stuff disposes of almost anything: except to very woody plants, they are best applied in April when the leaves on weeds are bursting into growth.

The soil, I would emphasize, is not damaged by either of these compounds. It is, of course, difficult to be specific about clearing a wilderness when natural "weeds" vary from meadow-grass to heather or fireweed: glyphosate is simply the best killer in a conventional English tangle of long grass. The principle, however, is the same everywhere. Spend one season clearing out your colony and only plant it after a year's preliminaries.

At this point, the dream of broadcasting wildflowers surfaces again, as it did for the man by the bomb-crater on Box Hill, Surrey. Gardens of loose grass and ox-eye daisies now turn up at Chelsea Flower Show: seed-mixtures are sold as "Farmers' Nightmare"; people write as if we are on the brink of a new era of informal gardening by scattering seeds of wild flowers all over the lawn. In fact, sowing wild flowers is no new idea. It was praised by Vita Sackville-West in the 1940's, practised in big country gardens in the 1920's and 1930's, and recommended by Edwardian planters: in the eighteenth century, Capability Brown was deliberately sowing huge weights of clover-seed to add colour to his grass-parks. In America, the idea is common currency. Whereas British seed-lists have just begun to advertise cornflowers and poppies in special "wild mixtures", American seedsmen like Park's and Burpees offer several pages of choice, graded into separate zones and provinces. Park's mixtures are particularly rich in perennials which will persist if they germinate: they even have a special blend for Texas.

This difference of emphasis connects with the difference in the floras of the two regions. America's wild flowers are much more spectacular in many areas than the wretched Cow Parsley and nettles of an English summer. Until recently, few English gardeners were nostalgic about ox-eye daisies and cowslips, because they grew quite freely in grass pastures and there was no need to allow them into the hallowed ground of a smooth, emerald-green lawn. Spraying, mechanical cutting and ruthless farming have now made England's flora an object of regret. The cult of the wild flower has been helped by agricultural savagery and British prairie-farming, financed by the European Community.

It has also been helped by misguided British illusions. We all know the legends and pictures of scarlet poppy-fields, staining the corn-crops of a hot summer's day. Could we not have poppies in our own long grass? In fact, the poppy is an annual and only shows for a year in the place where people sow it. Its reappearance thereafter is a matter of luck, although it will sometimes sprout after lying dormant for years: Thompson and Morgan now sell the true Flanders Poppy (red with a black spot) as a separate annual for bedding, but I use it as a garden plant and mix it in with my borders. Most of the 'wildflower mixtures' have a similar result. In the first year, you have a wonderful display of white ox-eye daisies, cornflowers, pink campion and poppies. Next year, you have daisies and poppies. Next year, you have daisies and meadow-grass; then you have grass. I cannot generalize for every climate zone, but in a grassy area of Britain wild gardening by seed-growing is not cheap and not very reliable. You will do best with cowslips on most soils and you are quite likely to establish harebells: remember that harebell-seed is very light and fine, so you need much less by bulk and should not shy away from a heavyweight load's high price. Otherwise, you are best advised to colonize by buying individual plants, setting them in ground you have Rounded-up and leaving it to them if they wish to seed and multiply in competition with other "weeds". This method is vastly cheaper.

Here, again, you run up against divergent views of the plants' stamina. I am not thinking of colonies of Lenten Roses, bog primulas or willow gentians, although there are nurseries which offer all these plants as "suitable for wild gardening". These descriptions confuse a woodland garden, carefully mulched, maintained and weeded, with a wild garden whose plants must compete with "weeds", grass and late summer mowing. In America, the confusion also seems to be rife. Wayside, for instance, sell the lovely Trillium, or Wake Robin, as a "wild flower" for naturalizing with the rare Ladies Slipper Orchid and white Canadian

Blood-root. These flowers are woodland flowers, best in special beds kept clear of weeds and heavy with mulches of leaf mould. In a wilderness, the only hellebore I would attempt is the green-flowered Foetidus which prospers on English limestone and seeds itself well. You need primroses, not primulas, celandines, not trillium: even in a colony, choose the plants with the greatest vigour.

Individual plants of cowslip, harebell or meadow cranesbill are now on the market, and here I ask myself a simpler question: if we are colonizing anyway, why should we restrict ourselves to native flowers, when our own native flora is relatively dull? By all means, colonize ground with native plants which still have floral or architectural style: the primrose, the foxglove, the celandine, the wood anemone, the evening primrose, the hellebore, the cranesbill, the fumitory, sweet woodruff, comfrey, wild iris and the shrubby rubuses, relations of our wild bramble. I can imagine a plausible wild garden planted partly with forms of these wild flowers, partly with bulbs.

The hellebore would be the green-flowered foetidus, whose thin and glossy leaves are well able to cope with a surrounding carpet of ground cover. The cranesbill would weave a carpet with selected forms of its meadow-varieties (Geranium pratense) which seed freely. The fumitories are more delicate and would have to be placed in carefully cleared patches on the edge of the rampant tangle. All forms of fumitory are worth collecting, especially the pale-cream-flowered Corydalis ochroleuca, and they soon start seeding themselves. Sweet woodruff (Asperula odorata) is small and lowly but will also smother a shaded clearing, especially if the earth is damp, a taste shared by the fumitories which match it neatly. Its white flowers smell of mown hay. Tiny though they are, they are too delicious to neglect.

The comfrey is coarser but an admirable blue: it will compete with dry shade and weeds and is not upset by a scything or mowing which removes its ragged summer leaves: Symphytum grandiflorum is as good as any, growing about two feet tall. Foxgloves are good companions, both the white forms and the crushed raspberry-red of Digitalis mertonensis which can be raised from a seed packet by the thousand. The coarse-leaved Evening Primrose, Oenothera lamarckiana, is a superb, tall competitor among grass or thick weeds, well able to show its clear yellow flowers above them in July and early August.

Why insist only on our own wild flora? Here, I return to the inspiration of William Robinson whose Wild Garden developed from a narrower "native" edition in 1870. It contained a wider range of wild plants by the 1890's, after reports and suggestions from gardeners whom we have all forgotten. Their concern was not "ground cover" nor the haphazard broadcasting of seeds. They had understood the capacity of good garden plants for colonization from individual rootstocks and for self-seeding in competition with the wild. They were very slow to mow and unwilling to regulate their plants in special serpentine beds. Behind them stretched the older legacy of the "flowery mead", enjoyed in the Middle Ages when there were no mechanical lawn-mowers and the grass grew long round moated houses and gravelled parterres. In these flowery meads, medieval couples did not only lie and admire the daisies: they read and sported, conversed and made love. The neatly-mown sward has been the ally of traditional morals. Once upon a time, a tapestry of flowers in long grass was the aim of any garden designed for pleasure.

If you put Robinson's Wild Garden beside Graham Thomas's modern plea for Ground Cover, you begin to see what we have forgotten. Robinson's book called for coexistence and competition, not "cover" to exclude all weeds. To illustrate the idea, he cited many gardens, two of which are in my own Oxfordshire, one at Crowsley, the other at Tew Park. Both have returned to nature long ago, although Tew has traces of its former colonists. They were almost natural in his day, for he presents them as gardens in which "not to mow is almost a necessity". Perennials were grown everywhere among the meadow grass without any beds.

More than 2,000 species, Robinson remarked, could compete very well with meadow grasses, just as they do in nature all over the Alpine meadows. In these gardens, there were no beds, no sweeps of cover. Instead, irises and aquilegias grew up through the unknown grasses. We cosset hybrid aquilegias in cool places, but wild aquilegias delighted Robinson in their random groups, showing their heads of flower among the waving plumes of grass. They were not segregated, nor were they protected in any way. Like daisies they were introduced and left to take their chance. Foxgloves kept them company by the hundred, spread into the meadow from their own seed. Hardy geraniums ran through the turf wherever they could and were set off by clumps of herbaceous peonies in double red and purple forms. These peonies were dug into a clear space at first, but as soon as the grass encroached, nobody came to the rescue. To prove the point, they are shown in a wood-cut, competing in full flower with long sprays of wild grass and cow parsley.

The style, Robinson rightly insisted, is cheap and very simple. Lupins, sweet williams, and oriental poppies were painted as individual colonists and left to fend for themselves, like crocus and daffodils. They were followed by tall evening primrose, whose tap roots combat any sort of turf. Fennel and climbing roses were grown loosely without support and continued to brighten the long grass in later summer. Perennial campanulas were scattered like dandelions. Almost every flower, after all, is wild somewhere on the map: in New England, you would find wild asters, in North Carolina, the red Lobelia and everywhere, the indestructible Golden Rod. To us in England, these are border plants for isolation, just as our Stinking Hellebore is a special rarity in several American lists. It is you and I who define the idea of a garden: a "wild" garden should be no more limited to native flowers than anywhere else in our plan. Gardens and wildernesses, "wild" flowers and garden-plants should run across boundaries, merging into each other, like drifts of blue anemones running into the cowslips of early spring. By colonizing, not sowing, you can recapture the style we have lost.

List of Suppliers

(E = willing exporter of orders over £60 value)

General Nurseries

Britain:
John Scott, The Royal Nurseries, Merriott, Somerset.
Sherrards, Wantage Road, Donnington, Newbury.
Notcutts, Woodbridge, Suffolk.
Sandwich Nurseries, Dover Road, Sandwich, Kent. (E)
Bressingham Nurseries, Diss, Norfolk: herbaceous plants especially. (E)
Slocock and Knaphill, Barrs Lane, Lower Knaphill, Woking, Surrey:
   especially azaleas and rhododendrons.
Burncoose and Southdown, Gwennap, Redruth, Cornwall.

America:
Wayside Gardens, Hodges, South Carolina, 29695.
Weston Nurseries, East Main Street, Route 135, Hopkinton, Mass.
   01748.
Woodlanders, 1128 Colleton Avenue, Aiken, SC 29801.
Gossler Farms Nursery, 1200 Weaver Road, Springfield, Oregon 97478.
   Magnolias, witch hazels and corylopsis a speciality.
White Flower Farm, Litchfield, Connecticut 06759-0050.
Blackthorne Gardens, 48 Quincy Street, Holbrook, Mass. 02343.
Roger Reynolds Nursery, 133 Encinal Ave., Menlo Park, California
   94025. Trees and shrubs; excellent, qualified advice.
Verba Buena Nursery, 19500 Skyline Blud., Woodside, California 94025.
   Trees and shrubs and good perennials, especially Californian native
   plants.
Holbrook Farm, Route 2, Box 2238, 2004 Fletcher, N.C. 28732.
Lamb Nurseries, E. 101 Sharp Avenue, Spokane, WA 99202. Good range
   of hardy perennials and rock plants.

Bovees Nursery, 1737 S.W. Colonado, Portland, Oregon 97219.
  Exceptional range of Rhododendrons, Azaleas, hardy in the
  north-east. Ask for Lucie Sorenson.
Dutch Garden, P.O. Box 400, Montvale, New Jersey 07645. Best for
  bulbs, Hostas, Hemerocallis, Alliums.
Sonoma Horticultural, 3970 Azalea Avenue, Sebastopol, Calif. 95472.
  Excellent Azaleas, including Exbury varieties.

Roses

Peter Beales, London Road, Attleborough, Norfolk. (E)
  Lists over 1000 old-fashioned bush and climbing roses: experienced
  exporter, but requires import permit from customer and adds 10%
  surcharge to cover the necessary root-washing. Export orders must
  exceed £60 (about 15 roses, at 1986 prices).
David Austin, Bowling Green Lane, Albrighton, Wolverhampton.
  Major list of old-fashioned varieties and the excellent English Roses
  bred at the nursery in the past twenty years.
R. Harkness, The Rose Garden, Hitchin, Herts.
  Excellent stock of modern bush, shrub and climbing roses, carefully
  selected from a wide range.
Roses of Yesterday and Today, 802 Brown's Valley Road, Watsonville,
  California 95076.
  The major U.S. list of old roses, but not recommended for gardeners
  in the north east, as the stock is grown on the West coast and does not
  adapt easily between zones.
All-American Rose Society, 513 West Sheridan Avenue, Shenendoah,
  Iowa, 51601.
  Advises on local merit and availability of all varieties tested in the
  Society's trials and 132 publicly-accredited gardens in 43 states. The
  American Rose Society's annual Handbook for Selecting Roses
  contains the yearly survey of the Proof of the Pudding Committee,
  which grades varieties by merit-marks; the monthly American Rose
  magazine lists local suppliers and handles members' queries and
  difficulties.

Clematis

Treasures, Tenbury Wells, Shropshire.
Fisks, Westleton, Saxmundham, Suffolk.
Blackthorne Gardens, 48 Quincy Street, Holbrook, Mass. 02343.

Fruit trees

John Scott, The Royal Nurseries, Merriott, Somerset.
Highfield Nurseries, Whitminster, Gloucester, GL27PL.
Henry Lewthardt Nurseries, Box 666, East Moriches, N.Y. 11940.
    Excellent espalier fruit trees of all sizes.
Living Tree Centre, P.O. Box 797, Bolinas, California, 94924.
    Fruit trees, especially apples.
Kelly Brothers, Dansville, N.Y. 14437. Fruit, especially figs.
J.E. Miller, Canandaigua, N.Y. 14424.
North American Fruit Exporters, c/o R. Kurle, 105.55 Madison Street,
    Hinsdale, Illinois 60521.
    Excellent advice on sources of non-standard apples, strawberries and
    other fruits.

Bulbs

Potterton and Martin, The Cottage Nursery, Moortown Road, Nettleton,
    Nr Caistor, North Lincolnshire, LN76HX. (E)
    A notable specialist in all the alpines, rare bulbs and cyclamen which I
    mention. Willing and experienced exporters to U.S.A.
De Jaeger, The Nurseries, Marden, Kent.
Jacques Amand, 17 Beethoven St., London, W.10. (E)
    Very full list, including Amaryllis, Fritillaries, Nerines and wide range
    of autumn crocus, and lilies.
Butterfields Nursery, Harvest Hill, Bourne End, Bucks.
    Orchids, especially many types of plcione.
Peter Nyssen, Station Road, Urmston, Manchester. (E)
    Naturalizing bulbs for larger orders.
Brecks, 6523 North Glena Road, Peoria, Illinois 61632.
    Recommended.

Van Bourgondian Bros., P.O. Box A, 245 Farmingdale Road, Route 109, Babylon, Lond Island, New York 11702.
  Good basic range of flower-bulbs.
Blackthorne Gardens, 48 Quincy Street, Holbrook, Mass. 02343.
  Lilies, cyclamen and much else.
Dutch Gardens, P.O. Box 400, Montvale, New Jersey 07645.
  Alliums particularly good.
Nerine Nurseries, Welland, Worcestershire, WR13 6LN. (E)
  Huge list of named forms of Nerine. Supplies to U.S.A.
Avon Bulbs, Bathford, Bath, BA1 8ED. (E)
  Very good range of everything I mention: crocus, fritillary, pleione and species tulips. Cyclamen a particular strength. Very keen exporters, anywhere.
B. and D. Lilies, 330 P Street, Port Townsend, Washington 98368.
  Excellent lilies, including species.

Alpines and small hardy plants

Jack Drake, Inshriach, Aviemore, Scotland.
Elizabeth Strangman, Washfield Nursery, Hawkhurst, Kent.
S.W. Bond, Thuya Alpine Nurseries, Glebelands, Hartpury, Glos.
J. and A. Watson, Mill Farmhouse, Mill Lane, Whatlington, Battle, E. Sussex.
Hopleys Plants, High Street, Much Hadham, Hertforshire.
Alpine Garden Society, Lye End Link, St. John's, Woking, Surrey.
  Lists many suppliers: superb annual seed-list to members worldwide.
American Rock Garden Society, Norman Singer (Secretary), Norfolk Road, South Sandisfield, Mass. 01225.
  Excellent source of advice and nurseries.
Siskiyou Rare Plants, Dept. 52, 2825 Cummings Road, Medford, Oregon 97501.
  Excellent range, and lewisias a speciality.
Stonecrop, Cold Spring, N.Y. 10516.
  Cash and carry only, but a superb range and worth a long detour. Sells tufa.
Nature's Garden, Route 1, Box 488, Beaverton, Or. 97007.
  Ramondas, Lewisias, Gentians, Primulas and much else.

Far North Gardens, 15621 A.R. Auburndale, Livonia, Michigan 48154.
   Famous for Barnhaven and Silver Dollar primroses; auriculas; very
   good range of seeds.
E. Parker-Jervis, Marten's Hall Farm, Longworth, Nr Oxford, Oxon.
   Superb colchicums, snowdrops and many special selections. Supplies
   visitors only; will prepack orders for collection and work on larger
   orders for export, provided they are picked up and do not require
   postage.

Miscellaneous

Ramparts Nurseries, Bakes Lane, Colchester, Essex.
   Excellent for silver leaves; also old and new pinks.
Three Counties Nurseries, Marshwood, Bridport, Dorset.
   Excellent pinks, including new prize-winning varieties.
Careby Manor Gardens, Careby, Stamford, Lincs.
   Perennials, violets, foliage plants.
Richard Cawthorne, Lower Daltons Nursery, Swanley Village, Swanley,
   Kent.
   Violas and violettas.
Hollington Nurseries, Woolton Hill, Newbury, Berks.
   Herbs.
Thorps Nurseries, 257 Finchampstead Road, Wokingham, Berks.
   Pelargoniums, including Lord Bute and many of the best American
   varieties.
John Chambers, 15 Westleigh Road, Barton Seagrave, Kettering,
   Northants.
   Wild flower seeds and plants for new colonies.
Barnhaven Nursery, Brigsteer, Kendal, Cumbria.
   Fine primroses and polyanthus.
Norfolk Lavender, Caley Mill, Heacham, King's Lynn, Norfolk. PE31 7JE.
   Dazzling displays of lavender, Britain's biggest: lavender-seed and
   plants.
Logie's Greenhouses, 55 North Street, Danielson, Connecticut 06239.
   Exceptional source of half-hardy plants, but also geraniums and herbs.
Kartuz Greenhouses, 1408 Sunrise Drive, Vista, California 92083.
Far North Gardens, 15621 A.R. Auburndale, Livonia, Michigan 48154.
   Barnhaven strain of primroses and polyanthus.

Seeds

Thompson and Morgan, London Road, Ipswich.
Thompson and Morgan, P.O. Box 100, Farmingdale, New Jersey 07727.
S. Dobies, Upper Dee Mills, Llangollen, Clwyd.
Thomas Butcher, Shirley, Croydon, Surrey.
Chiltern Seeds, Bortree Stile, Ulverston, Cumbria. LA12 7PB (E)
    Biggest list of all: over 2500 varieties.
Suffolk Herbs, Sawyers Farm, Little Cornard, Sudbury, Suffolk.
    Wild range of herbs, vegetables and wild flowers from seed.
Park Seed Co., Highway 254N, Greenwood, South Carolina 29647.
Burpee Seeds, Warminster, Pennsylvania 18974.
Joseph Harris, Moreton Farm, Rochester, N.Y. 14626.
Moon Mountain, Box 34, Morro Bay, California 93442.
    Seed-list and reference catalogue of U.S. wildflowers "from Alaska to
    Texas and California to Maine".
Nichols Garden Nursery, 1190 WC Pacific, Albany, Oregon 97321.
    Rare herbs and vegetable seeds.
Herbertia, Box 150, La Jolla, California 92038.
    $10 subscription to the famous quarterly journal and participation in
    the excellent seed-distribution scheme.

Index

The figures in brackets after botanical names refer to the zones of the plant's hardiness in the U.S.A. They are approximate guides only and conform to the chart of the Arnold Arboretum (zone 3, minus 20°F to minus 35°F; zone 4, minus 10°F to minus 20°F; average annual minimums only).